THE CHINESE HEROIN TRADE

The Chinese Heroin Trade

Cross-Border Drug Trafficking in Southeast Asia and Beyond

Ko-lin Chin and Sheldon X. Zhang

NEW YORK UNIVERSITY PRESS
New York and London

NEW YORK UNIVERSITY PRESS
New York and London
www.nyupress.org

ISBN: 978-1-4798-9540-3

For Library of Congress Cataloging-in-Publication data, please contact the Library of Congress.

New York University Press books are printed on acid-free paper, and their binding materials are chosen for strength and durability. We strive to use environmentally responsible suppliers and materials to the greatest extent possible in publishing our books.

Manufactured in the United States of America

10 9 8 7 6 5 4 3 2 1

Also available as an ebook

This project was supported by Grant No. 2004-IJ-CX-0023 awarded by the National Institute of Justice, Office of Justice Programs, U.S. Department of Justice. Points of views in this book are solely those of the authors and do not necessarily represent the official position or policy of the U.S. Department of Justice.

To our wives, Catherine and Susan

CONTENTS

PREFACE

Along with its red-hot economy and behind the glitzy urban high rises, China is facing growing social problems that have plagued developed countries for decades, one of which is the abuse of illicit drugs. After losing two wars and subsequently seceding territories to Western powers over opium a century ago, the issue of drug addiction still hits a nerve in the Chinese psyche. The Chinese government has for decades applied extreme measures in an attempt to curtail the spread of illicit drugs, executing hundreds if not thousands for drug crimes and sending drug abusers to compulsory treatment facilities en masse, only to find that the problem has become worse. With heroin still accounting for the largest share of the consumption, China's addict population has now developed an appetite for an even more diverse marketplace, including crystal meth, ecstasy, and ketamine.

Burma is considered the major producer of illicit drugs and conduit for entry drugs into China. Political strife between the Burmese government and remote warlord-controlled regions creates complex geopolitical situations that gave rise to a thriving irregular commerce. Since the collapse of the Communist Party of Burma (CPB) in 1989, there have been two significant changes in Southeast Asia's drug trade. One, more heroin from the Golden Triangle began to leave Burma via China instead of Thailand; and two, there has been a shift from the production of heroin to methamphetamine. This study focuses only on the first issue.

In this book, we attempt to examine how heroin produced in Burma is transported into China and also to understand the changing patterns of heroin trafficking between Burma and China over the past 20 years. We focus on four groups of people in the drug trade: the producers, the traffickers, the wholesalers, and the retail dealers. We explore who they are, how they enter the drug business, how they conduct their business, and how they respond to market and law enforcement constraints to maximize their profits and minimize their risks. In the process, we pay particular attention to the question of how an illicit drug market in an authoritarian, communist state like China differs from drug markets in other parts of the world where there is a developed democratic state or an underdeveloped weak state. Moreover, we discuss the role of women in the drug trade in the Golden Triangle and seek to explore the underlying causes for the feminization of transnational crime. We also take a look at how China is coping with drug addiction and what is unique about its coping mechanism. Finally, we examine what various countries in Southeast Asia, and particularly China, are doing to stop drug trafficking and the problems and prospects of international cooperation.

In chapter 2, we examine the history and recent development of the heroin trade in Burma and China. We focus on how the drug business inside Burma changed after the Burmese junta signed cease-fire agreements with various armed groups along the border areas in 1989, especially in the areas of Shan State, Rangoon, and Mandalay. We detail the trafficking of heroin into China as that nation began to engage in economic reform and encouraged legal cross-border trade in the late 1980s, focusing on several major checkpoints along the border on both the Burmese and Chinese sides. We conclude the chapter with an analysis of the characteristics of the Burmese drug market.

We discuss the characteristics of the wholesale heroin market in chapter 3 by examining some of the major drug trafficking cases between Burma and China since the mid-1980s. We also take an in-depth look at the rise and fall of a heroin kingpin and a mid-level heroin trafficker. The role of southern China in wholesale drug trafficking, especially Guangdong and its vicinity, is examined in this chapter. We conclude with a discussion of the general characteristics of upper-level heroin traffickers, including the extent of their engagement in violence and corruption.

After discussing upper-level drug traffickers in chapter 3, we move on to focus on mostly low-level drug traffickers in chapter 4. Using a survey of 578 convicted drug traffickers inside a Chinese prison and in-depth interviews with a small number of drug inmates, we examine the individual and group characteristics of these convicted drug traffickers. We also explore what they were convicted for, what were their sentences, and how they entered the drug business in the first place. In this chapter, we also analyze one particular method of drug trafficking between

Burma and China, the "ants-moving-house" method. In response to law enforcement crackdowns on large-scale heroin trafficking activities and to take advantage of the strong supply of willing risk takers, many traffickers in China move only small quantities of heroin by mule. We discuss what the routes are, where and how mules are recruited, and the social organization of this particular method of heroin trafficking.

We discuss the rise of entrepreneurial traffickers (both upper- and lower-level) in the Chinese drug market in chapter 5. First, we examine the relationship between organized crime groups and drug trafficking and distribution, and then move on to the social organization of the drug trade by exploring issues such as fragmented trafficking process, hierarchy and division of labor, mobility within the drug trade, and self-preservation measures.

After examining the individual and group characteristics of upper- and lower-level drug traffickers, we examine the social organization of street-level heroin distribution in Kunming, the capital of Yunnan Province. As will be discussed later in the book, traffickers, regardless of whether they are upper- or low-level, are very different from street-level retailers. As a result, they are discussed separately. Based on in-depth interviews with 39 heroin retailers in Kunming, we explore the individual characteristics of street-level heroin dealers, the reasons for their engagement in heroin retail, and the modus operandi of street-level heroin distribution in Kunming. We also discuss *maima* (literally "selling horses" or snitching)—the most prevalent method used by drug enforcers to go after heroin retailers, and what these retailers usually do to protect themselves from being arrested by the authorities.

Women's engagement in the drug trade is the focus of chapter 7. We examine why there are so many women in the drug trade, and how women take advantage of their gender role in the facilitation of the movement of heroin across the border and also in the interior of China. We also analyze the role of women in organized criminality, the gendered differences among incarcerated drug traffickers in China, and the gendered pathway into the drug trade. We conclude by utilizing a gendered market perspective to explain the role of women in the Chinese drug market.

We examine the issues of drug addiction and rehabilitation in China in chapter 8. We explore some of the factors contributing to the rise of addiction in China, discuss how drug users in China are normally treated in compulsory or voluntary drug treatment centers, and explain how repeat drug abusers are often sent to labor education camps for one to three years. We also evaluate the effectiveness of these three treatment regimes and examine some of the new treatment models made available to drug users in China.

In chapter 9, we discuss how authorities in China are combating the drug trade. We focus on measures adopted by the Chinese authorities, especially community mobilization, harsh punishment, and the professionalization of the drug enforcement police force. We also examine how Chinese officials are working together with authorities from the United States, Burma, and Hong Kong to stem the flow of drugs across international borders.

In the concluding chapter, we discuss the rise of consumption of amphetamine-type stimulants in Southeast Asia and examine policy implications of our research findings. We close the chapter with a call for more comparative study on drug markets.

ACKNOWLEDGMENTS

A project of this scale requires the assistance of many. Had it not been for all of the individuals who helped us, with or without compensation, we never would have been able to amass such a large volume of data that provides an unprecedented look into a secretive world that purportedly sustains an enormous illicit market in the most populous country in the world. The data collection activities were prolonged and the scheduling daunting and politically sensitive. We were able to do it because of our networks of contacts in the communities, government agencies, and academic institutions in China, Burma, Thailand, and Hong Kong.

There is a long list of individuals to whom we would like to express our gratitude. First, we want to thank all the subjects who entrusted us with the most sensitive information about their involvement in the drug trade and about their struggles with addiction and social ostracism. Without these individuals, whose identities we cannot divulge, this study would have been mostly about official viewpoints and news media reports, something both authors were familiar with and yet determined to balance.

We express our heartfelt gratitude to Ko-lin's uncle in Kunming. He and his family not only helped Ko-lin with his research by referring potential subjects, but also provided a variety of much needed assistance while he was living and working in Kunming. We are also extremely grateful to Feng Yu, the coordinator of Rainbow Community Care Center in Kunming, for referring so many people in Kunming's drug scene to us.

In Rangoon, another of Ko-lin's uncles was instrumental in helping him to re-familiarize himself with a city he had left so many years ago. His aunt in Mandalay offered invaluable help during his visit there. Ko-lin is especially thankful to a high school classmate in Taipei for introducing his brother-in-law in Rangoon. The brother-in-law played a key role in locating subjects for Ko-lin in Rangoon and Mandalay to interview.

Ni Na, a college student in Kunming, was hired to help us with data management in China. We thank Miss Ni for her contribution to our research project. Huan Gao, then a PhD student at Rutgers University–Newark, was our research assistant in the United States. To her, we express our sincere gratitude.

A cadre of Chinese academics and researchers provided invaluable assistance and connections that allowed us to expand our field activities. In particular, we are grateful to Professor Wang Yong of Fujian Police Academy for accompanying us to many other parts of the country, such as Guiyang, Guangzhou, Shenzhen, Chengdu, and Chongqing, where we were introduced to their networks of drug enforcement officers. These conversations with Chinese drug enforcement officials provided us nuanced understanding of the challenges confronting the country's narcotics control.

Moreover, the information, advice, and generous assistance of law enforcement officials made our work a satisfying and enriching experience. We wish to make a special note of the efforts of many drug enforcement officials in Beijing, Kunming, the border area between Burma and China (especially Muse and Ruili), Taipei, Hong Kong, and Rangoon.

Ilene Kalish, our editor at New York University Press, was enthusiastic from the start about our book proposal, and nurtured this project from the beginning. We greatly appreciate her advice and editorial suggestions. Thanks to Judy Mellecker and Karen Verde for editing the manuscript. We want to thank the two reviewers who provided thoughtful suggestions and comments, of which we strove to attend to most, if not all, in the subsequent revisions. In particular, we are grateful to their excitement and enthusiasm in support of this manuscript. Still, we are solely responsible for any errors and omissions in this final product.

Finally, and most important, Ko-lin is very grateful to Catherine for her patience and support throughout this study. Sheldon wants to thank Susan for her unwavering support and understanding during the many months of fieldwork, and for pulling double duty in taking care of our children. This book is dedicated to Catherine and Susan. Sheldon is also grateful to his in-laws, Ken and Iva, for providing childcare on numerous occasions while he was away from home.

Major financial support for this study was provided by a grant (2004-IJ-CX-0023) from the National Institute of Justice (NIJ), Office of Justice Programs of the U.S. Department of Justice. Sandra Woerle, our grant manager at NIJ, provided administrative oversight for this study. The Yunnan Police Officer Academy provided essential infrastructure that facilitated our fieldwork in Yunnan Province. We are especially grateful to Professor Liang Jinyun at the academy for making all the necessary arrangements for us to conduct our research. He also traveled with us to many townships along the Yunnan-Burma border, where we got to meet frontline drug enforcement officers, as well as drug dealers and addicts.

Opinions expressed in this book are solely ours and do not necessarily represent the views or policies of the U.S. government or any other individuals and institutions that have helped us. Parts of this study have been presented previously at conferences and published in journals.

1

The Chinese Connection

One of the world's major opium-cultivation and heroin-producing areas is the Golden Triangle, a 150,000-square-mile, mountainous area located where the borders of Burma (or Myanmar),[1] Laos, and Thailand meet.[2] Although there is a geographical region promoted by the tourism industry as the Golden Triangle where the Mekong River flows through the three countries, when it comes to drug production and trafficking activities, the territory refers to a much larger area, including most border regions between Thailand and Burma and between China and Burma.[3]

For decades and up until the late 1990s, the Golden Triangle had a notorious reputation as the "breadbasket" of the world's heroin trade.[4] By the end of the decade, Burma was producing more than 50 percent of the world's raw opium and refining as much as 75 percent of the world's heroin.[5] Recently, Burma has also become a main source of amphetamine-type stimulants (ATS) in Asia, producing hundreds of millions of methamphetamine tablets annually.[6]

The Golden Triangle has long fascinated researchers and anti-narcotics agencies around the world, and much of the fascination centers on Burma because of its colonial past with the West and its political isolation. Burma's major opium-growing and heroin-producing area is located in the Shan State, which is occupied by various ethnic armed groups and was the base of the Communist Party of Burma (CPB) before it collapsed in 1989.[7] According to Burmese authorities, the CPB was bankrolled by China as well as supported by various non-Burmese ethnic groups and was considered the major threat to their regime.[8] After the disintegration of the CPB, the Burmese regime arranged cease-fire agreements with various former CPB groups in the Shan State.[9] The ethnic groups promised not to fight against the Burmese government and, in return, the Burmese authorities allowed these ethnic groups to keep their armed forces and to continue their opium trade.[10] The areas associated with the three armed groups believed to be most actively involved in the drug trade are the Kokang Area or the No. 1 Special Zone, the Wa Area or the No. 2 Special Zone, and the Mengla Area or the No. 4 Special Zone (see map 1.1).[11] Consequently, U.S. sources estimated that Burma's opium production virtually doubled from 1,250 metric tons in 1988 to 2,450 metric tons the following year and continued to increase thereafter, to 2,600 metric tons in 1997.[12] As the relationship improved between the Burmese authorities and the ethnic groups in the Shan State, more and more money from the drug trade poured into legitimate businesses and fueled the expansion of the Burmese economy.[13]

Although international anti-narcotic efforts have affected the scale of raw opium production, the scale of opium poppy cultivation is still considerable. Since most opium poppy cultivation is located in northern Burma, bordering China's Yunnan Province, the Chinese authorities for years have attempted to intervene and reduce the production of raw opium and heroin because much of the drug has been exported either through China or directly for China's consumption. Since the late 1990s, Chinese authorities have been tracking and estimating the size of opium cultivation acreage via informants on the ground and satellite imaging. The estimates are reported, although not consistently, in the Annual Report on Drug Control in China. According to the reports, the total opium cultivation was on an overall decline to a low of 279,000 mu (or 18,600 hectares) in three decades.[14] In the past few years, however, the total opium poppy cultivation in northern Burma started an upward trend and the magnitude of increase alarmed the Chinese authorities. Figure 1.1 depicts the data assembled from the annual reports issued between 2001 and 2012.

Before the mid-1980s, heroin produced in the Golden Triangle was mostly smuggled into Thailand over land and then to Hong Kong on Thai fishing trawlers before being transported to the United States, Europe, and Australia.[15] Hong Kong was, and probably still is, the organizational and financial center for the region's heroin trade.[16] However, in the late 1970s, rapid expansion in commerce and population migration inside China led to the opening up of cross-border drug trade between Burma and China.[17] On April 12, 1986, 22 kilograms of heroin were seized by the authorities in Yunnan Province, in the southwest

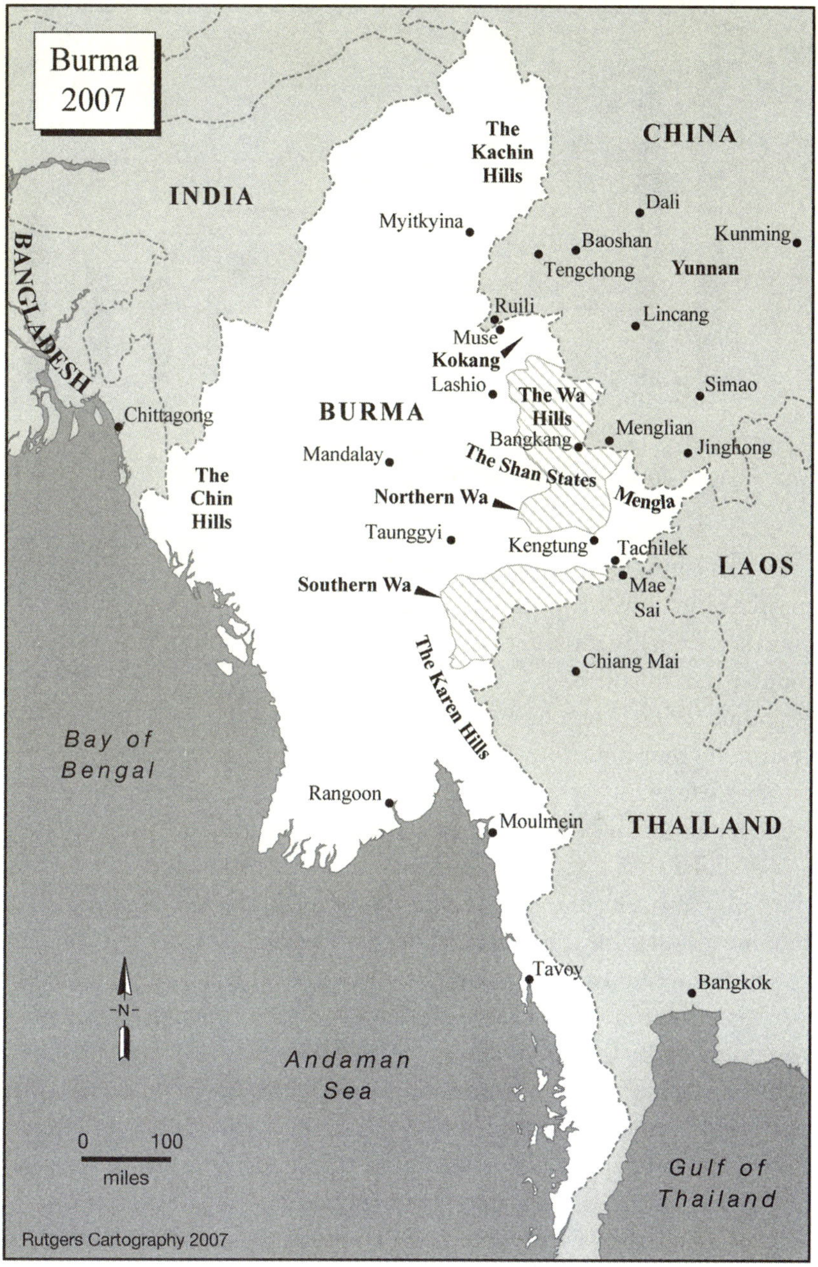
Burma
2007
The
Kachin
Hills
CHINA
INDIA
Dali
Myitkyina
Baoshan
Kunming
Tengchong
Yunnan
BANGLADESH
Ruili
Lincang
Muse
Kokang
Lashio
The Wa
Hills
Simao
Chittagong
BURMA
Menglian
Bangkang
Jinghong
Mandalay
The Shan States
The
Chin
Hills
Northern Wa
Mengla
Taunggyi
Kengtung
Tachilek
LAOS
Southern Wa
Mae
Sai
The Karen Hills
Chiang Mai
Bay of
Bengal
Rangoon
Moulmein
THAILAND
Tavoy
Bangkok
N
Andaman
Sea
0
100
miles
Gulf of
Thailand
Rutgers Cartography 2007

Map 1.1. Burma.

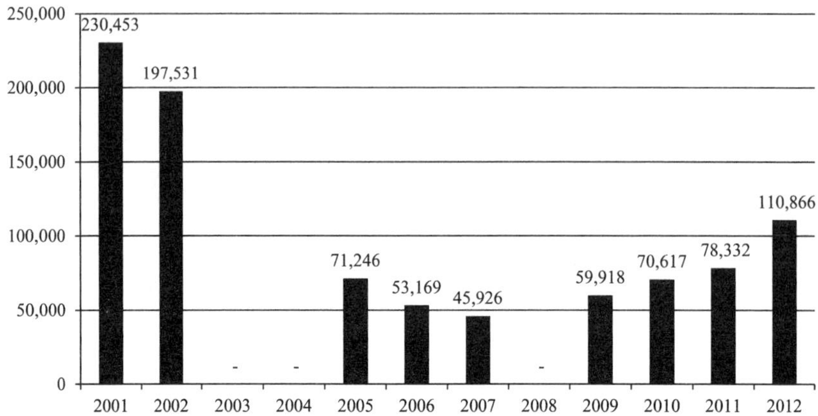

Fig. 1.1. Opium poppy cultivation area in Burma (in acres).
Note: Opium cultivation acreage was not reported for three years (2003, 2004, 2008).

corner of China that borders Burma, Laos, and Vietnam. The drug case, masterminded by drug traffickers from Thailand and Hong Kong, was considered the first major case of its kind since China came under communist control in 1949.[18] The authorities at the time simply had not encountered any such heavy loads. In May 1994, the police in Yunnan caught another notorious drug lord named Yang Maoxian (the brother of Yang Maoliang, who was then the leader of the Kokang area) and sentenced him to death.[19] A year later, Lee Guoting, another Kokang leader and a well-known heroin kingpin, was arrested and executed by the Chinese authorities. It was clear by then that the Chinese route had become popular for transnational drug traffickers.

The booming drug trafficking business in China can be attributed to two main factors. First, a sizeable domestic drug consumption market has emerged. By the mid-1980s, drug addiction was no longer confined to the border areas. The Chinese government now openly acknowledges that every province and all major urban areas have drug problems. China is no longer just a transit country favored by transnational criminal organizations; it, too, has a sizeable addict population of its own.[20] According to official statistics, there were 148,000 officially registered drug addicts in China in 1991. A decade later, the number had jumped to more than 900,000. The latest official count of drug addicts in China exceeded 1.5 million.[21] Heroin remains the predominant drug of choice for addicts; however, users of synthetic drugs are also increasing rapidly, particularly among urban youths.

Second, drug traffickers developed alternative routes through China (mostly along China's southern provinces—Yunnan, Guizhou, Guangxi, and Guangdong) in response to changes in the regional drug trade (see figure 1.2 and map 1.2). In 1989, after the Burmese authorities signed peace agreements with the various armed groups located in northeastern Burma, they turned their attention to Khun Sa, also known as the King of Heroin, who had long dominated the heroin business along the Thai-Burma border. After the Burmese assaults intensified, and as more and more Wa soldiers joined forces in the campaign against Khun Sa, the drug lord abruptly surrendered to the Burmese authorities in 1996.[22] With the collapse of Khun Sa's Mong Tai Army (MTA), the southern, or Thai, trafficking route was disrupted. As a result, the China route became all the more important for drug traffickers in Burma, especially when, in the late 1990s, their investments and savings in Thailand and Burma were diminished by the depreciation of the Thai baht and Burmese kyat. Drug traffickers came to realize that the Chinese yuan was more desirable than either the Thai baht or Burmese kyat.[23]

Moreover, for drug traffickers in the Golden Triangle who are predominantly ethnic Chinese, the China route is far better than the Thai route because of geographical proximity, better road conditions, and cultural and linguistic familiarities. However, armed group leaders in the region have traditionally been reluctant to take full advantage of this route, fearing that if China shuts down its border, the area will be

BEFORE

Burma → Thailand → Hong Kong → International Market

PRESENT

Burma → Yunnan → Guizhou → Guangxi → Guangdong → Hong Kong → International Market

Fig. 1.2. The changing patterns of heroin trafficking in the Golden Triangle.

Map 1.2. China.

completely isolated. Ironically, when a major confrontation erupted in 2001 between the Burmese and Thai border forces, and the Burmese authorities shut down all the border crossings in retaliation, the Thai-Burma border trade all but came to a complete halt. This incident prompted drug traffickers to earnestly cultivate a passage through China.[24] Despite China's efforts to combat drug imports along its southwestern borders, Burma remains its largest source of illicit drugs. After analyzing all the drug cases between 2006 and 2007 for six jurisdictions in southern China, Huang Kaicheng and his colleagues at China's Southwest University of Political Science and Law found that "more than two thirds (68.9%) of the cases with drugs destined for the mainland were coming from Myanmar."[25] Seizures of heroin and synthetic drugs from Yunnan Province alone account for more than half of the national total.[26]

Even though tens of thousands of kilograms of heroin are being smuggled every year from Burma into China, a country with probably the world's largest heroin consumption market, there is little systematic research on the heroin trade in China. We do not know much about the people behind the transnational smuggling of heroin, the social organization of the traffickers between Burma and China, and the characteristics of heroin trade compared to those in other parts of the world. In this study, we attempt to answer some of these questions based on an empirical research project we have conducted in Burma and China. In fact, as suggested by British criminologists Geoffrey Pearson and Dick Hobbs, high-level drug trafficking is not a well-developed research field, even in drug markets in other parts of the world such as the United States and Europe.[27] Thus, it is imperative to examine the social organization of a major drug market that is located in China, a country with the world's largest population and the second largest economy.

Theoretical Guidance

A more detailed description of our conceptual framework of the social organization of the drug trade in China is presented in chapter 5. Our main theoretical interest in this project was geared mostly toward understanding how individuals find one another in their social networks to gain entry into the drug trade, manage law enforcement risks and logistical obstacles inherent in the business, and collectively and individually move toward the common goal of making money. To consider drug trafficking as an organized crime, there must be structural arrangements and patterns that transcend individual behaviors. Throughout our data collection and field activities, we were keen on examining the market conditions or transactional requisites that appeared to restrict and mitigate how individual risk takers enter the illicit marketplace, interact with one another or delegate tasks, and develop strategies and patterns of behavior to manage risks.

Broadly speaking, there are two main theoretical approaches in understanding any criminal organizations[28]—the corporate model and the enterprise model, which for the past two decades has been used to explain the many variations of criminal groups engaged in illicit economic crimes.[29] The corporate model compares organized crime to the structure and organizational mandates of legitimate corporations.[30] Organized crime, such as the Italian Mafia and the Colombian drug cartels, essentially model their organizational arrangement and business conduct after legitimate businesses, with clear hierarchies and divisions of labor. Like their legal counterparts, these crime groups seek to dominate criminal enterprises by expanding in size and forming large cartels of national and international scope. They operate gambling casinos, prostitution rings, drug trafficking schemes, and offshore banks.[31] In some cases, such as in Italy and in the republics of the former USSR, crime syndicates have developed a symbiotic relationship with the government to the point where they gradually assume political and administrative functions.[32]

Much of the traditional discourse on Chinese criminal organizations follows the corporate model, in which "godfathers" at the top of an organization direct local and overseas branches.[33] Although contemporary triad societies are said to be far more fragmented than their predecessors, they still possess well-defined organizational structures with at least three levels of hierarchy and clearly assigned roles and responsibilities at each level.[34] Within the context of drug trade in the Golden Triangle, criminal organizations are also believed to possess a clear division of labor and chain of command: tasks and responsibilities are assigned according to members' skills and abilities; rules and regulations govern members' activities; and membership is restricted.[35]

The enterprise model, on the other hand, suggests flexible and adaptive networks that expand and contract to deal with the uncertainties of the criminal enterprise.[36] Enterprising agents are organized only to the extent that they can effectively carry out illicit activities, which, as economists have argued, is rather utilitarian or rational behavior.[37] A number of studies have focused on the entrepreneurial nature of organized crime and have described the transitory alliances of bold risk takers who seize opportunities to make large profits on investments such as human smuggling,[38] heroin trafficking,[39] and gambling.[40] Apart from a relatively small core group, most are brought in as needed to provide special services.

Scholars have for some time moved toward a more continuum-oriented perspective to describe criminal organizations as adopting various forms in response to the demands of the illicit market conditions.[41] In our study of transnational human smuggling, we found a unique mixture of organizational patterns and operational characteristics that resemble parts of both theoretical models.[42] Human smugglers form loosely connected groups with little vertical differentiation (i.e., smugglers essentially treating one another as independent contractors). They nonetheless have highly differentiated roles and responsibilities. Human smugglers within a smuggling organization typically engage in one-on-one transactions. They each may in turn maintain additional circles of contacts to procure or sell smuggling services. We subsequently named this hybrid organization a *dyadic cartwheel network* to describe these complex yet fluid organizational realities in transnational human smuggling. Human smugglers maintain singular connections with one another and engage in one-on-one transactions. Each smuggler may maintain additional circles of such one-on-one connections with resources necessary for smuggling operations. Such an organizational structure, containing members of one's close social network and oriented toward specific tasks, appears to be highly effective in coping with uncertain market environments.

Small social networks of entrepreneurs engaging in illicit enterprises have attracted much research interest in recent years. Instead of concerning themselves with command structures, the network perspective examines specific roles and functions of individual players inside a criminal enterprise and how they move between the local and the global, where both sophisticated specialists and opportunists seem to find their useful positions. For instance, Dutch criminologists Gerben Bruinsma and Wim Bernasco used social network theory to describe three types of transnational criminal activities: drug trafficking, trafficking in women, and trading in stolen cars.[43] University of Montreal professors Carlo Morselli and Julie Roy, in their study of automobile theft and exportation businesses, focused on the brokers inside criminal networks whose functions seemed responsible for smoothing otherwise disjointed facets of an illicit enterprise—from stealing and pawning stolen vehicles to arranging for their exportation.[44] In a competitive market environment, brokers are functionally imperative in connecting otherwise disjointed partners for business transactions.[45] The nodal positions occupied by the brokers also control access to the desired services or goods; therefore, as long as the asymmetries of information and access remain, the broker will benefit from this competitive edge.[46] By analyzing both the crime process and social networks, Morselli and Roy found that the removal of a few brokers would cause major disruptions to the automobile theft operations and significantly reduce the options for others involved in the enterprise.[47] In other words, the criminal network would simply fall apart without the hinges provided by these brokers. The flexibility often found in illicit enterprises therefore mostly results from such brokerage functions.

Network analysis has attracted much attention in recent years from the organized crime research community.[48] This approach enables researchers to analyze criminal networks by measuring "players" for their centrality and their betweenness within the multitude of relationships. Often wiretap transcripts are used to code for such connections. The analysis finds the players and brokers, and also examines the types of skills or knowledge that these people bring into a criminal enterprise. Different scenarios then can be played out by observing how the removal of certain individuals may disrupt the criminal network, hence their importance or centrality to the eventual goal. Furthermore, network analysis using wiretap transcripts can also describe the command structure of a criminal enterprise through frequency and direction of captured communication.

In addition to these common theoretical perspectives, there are other theories of organized crime, such as the alliance theory and rational choice theory.[49] These theories have shed much light on the functions of different organizational structures and operational arrangements.

In this study we continued this conceptual orientation to apply key concepts of both corporate and enterprise (including the network perspective) approaches in our examination of patterned organizational behaviors among the drug traffickers along the Burma-China border and within China. Using this hybrid model, we explored the basic organizational requisites such as hierarchical arrangement, division of labor, conspiracy, risk management strategies, and roles and functions of different individuals in the drug trafficking business. We focused on the social organization of trafficking groups, irrespective of the illicit substances these individuals were transporting.

Because drug trafficking is a serious crime in the region, one that often invites the death penalty, we paid particular attention to the interplay between the punitive legal environment (or effective illegality) and the drug market characteristics. According to criminologists Letizia Paoli, Victoria Greenfeld, and Peter Reuter, countries can be described as following three methods of enforcement—strict, lax, and non-enforcement.[50] They define strict enforcement of prohibition as regularly imposing significant risks of incarceration and asset seizure: drug production and trafficking are not only formally but also effectively criminalized. Drug markets in Western Europe, the United States, Canada, and Australia are viewed as operating under strict enforcement.

Lax enforcement involves countries with governments that are weak or unwilling to enforce prohibition due to extensive corruption. Paoli et al. presented two second-tier drug-producing countries (India and Mexico) and five key transit countries (Albania, Kosovo, Pakistan, Tajikistan, and Turkey) as examples of lax enforcement countries.

Non-enforcement is either the stated or unstated official policy; the government itself tolerates or promotes the production and trade in opiates and opiates become de facto legal commodities. The two largest illicit opium producers—Afghanistan and Burma—are prominent examples of non-enforcement.

According to Paoli et al., in countries with strict enforcement, the size and organization of the opiate market can be characterized as (1) nonhierarchical; (2) small; (3) not vertically integrated (wholesale dealers do not also sell retail); (4) dependent on preexisting social relationships (such as family ties or bonds of friendship or locality); (5) limited in the number of customers and employees to reduce vulnerability; and (6) poorly organized due to fragmented, decentralized, and short-term partnerships. The operating methods of the opiate markets in strict enforcement countries are characterized as having (1) modest inventories, (2) less open violence, (3) incorruptible state officials, and (4) no monopolies or oligopolies and the traffickers are price takers. Moreover, according to Paoli et al., the heroin markets in strict enforcement countries exist on the margins of society; few people are willing to risk their reputation, freedom, and physical safety to be associated with the heroin trade. As a result, the drug market is not a major component of the economy as a whole in these countries.

In countries with lax enforcement, opiate entrepreneurs can operate without the constant threat of incarceration or asset seizure, even though the opiate market may be, in theory, illegal. The size and the stability of illegal businesses operating under lax enforcement far exceed those of enterprises operating under strict enforcement, as many of the former groups are extended families, clans, tribes, or quasi-military organizations. According to Paoli et al.: "Large quantities of opiates are processed into heroin and possibly held as inventories in the countries with lax enforcement," and "well-connected criminal entrepreneurs can lead very comfortable lives, publicly enjoying their wealth and circulating in high society in the company of high level politicians."[51] Drug-related violence is quite common in lax enforcement countries, and illegal enterprises may be able to secure an oligopolistic position in the local market. Lax enforcement also fosters the legitimacy of opiate-related economic activities.

In non-enforcement countries, opiate entrepreneurs do not have to operate against the state. Large-scale hierarchical enterprises become more likely, and can take advantage of economy of scale and scope of operation when a strong, quasi-state authority directly plans and controls key phases of the illegal opiate industry. Opiate entrepreneurs in non-enforcement countries "are free to carry out visible and bulky activities, such as cultivating the formally legal opium poppy, processing its derivatives, and holding large stocks, without concern for the costs that would accompany those risks in the cases of strict or lax enforcement."[52] Drug entrepreneurs in these countries also "have no need to hide themselves or their criminal revenues and are free to reinvest the latter in their enterprises or in the legitimate economy."[53] Finally, the state or quasi-state authority's tolerance or support of opiate production and trade inevitably enhances the legitimacy of these activities.

Paoli and colleagues summarized the impacts of effective illegality on the opiate market as follows:

> The degree of effective illegality affects not only the distribution of opium production across countries, but also the size, organization, and operating methods of emerging enterprises. For example, when enforcement is lax or absent, larger enterprises are more likely to emerge and consolidate; moreover, they may assume modern bureaucratic (for example, military) organizational forms and exercise government-like functions. In addition, the strictness of enforcement may influence the levels of inventories that entrepreneurs choose to hold, the ways in which they interact with other illicit entrepreneurs and the nature of their relationships with government officials. Lastly, it may also affect illicit entrepreneurs' use of violence, although such violence occasionally has expressive and thus non-strategic roots.[54]

Although China was one of the primary target countries in the Paoli et al. study, the authors did not discuss at any length the Chinese heroin market, nor were they explicit about how strict drug enforcement was in China. In this book, one of our major aims is to explore, under the theoretical framework proposed by Paoli et al., the characteristics of the Chinese heroin market. We will pay particular attention to how heroin traffickers (or importers), wholesalers, and retail-level distributors react to the enormously strict enforcement regime in an authoritarian state such as China. We will use the concept of "ants-moving-house" to characterize how traffickers and distributors develop various self-preservation strategies to deal with market uncertainties caused by strict enforcement and harsh punishment.

The concept or strategy of ants-moving-house is not only applicable to the trafficking of heroin from Burma into China, but is also relevant to wholesale and retail distribution within China. Under this strategy, the Chinese heroin market is saturated with large numbers of "ants," or small, family-based, independent groups. Major traffickers, distributors, or retailers who can dominate the market at their respective levels are relatively rare in China, as is the presence of drug cartels. It is especially true after Chinese authorities dismantled the Tan Xiaolin heroin trafficking organization in 2001 and the Liu Zhaohua amphetamine manufacturing organization in 2005.[55]

China is an authoritarian state controlled by one very powerful political party—the Communist Party of China (CPC)—for more than 60 years. There are no other organizations in China, either political or non-political, that can remotely challenge the supremacy of the CPC. It is a country where the authorities can still exert enormous control over the lives of its citizens, as is evident in the implementation of the one-child policy and the security and logistic measures adopted during the 2008 Olympics in Beijing and the 2010 Asian Olympics in Guangzhou.

China is not only under the grip of one political party staffed by non-elected officials; its criminal justice system is considered to be one of the harshest in the world. There is no jury system in China; if a person is arrested and prosecuted, the chance of conviction is very high. In China, punishment is also relatively harsh; more than 60 crimes can draw the death penalty, including tax evasion, embezzlement, and drug trafficking. In 2008, Chinese authorities sentenced 7,003 to death and carried out 1,718 executions.[56] Cross-border traffickers and wholesale distributors are particularly vulnerable to punishments meted out by state authorities. Street-level drug dealers who are drug addicts, female, a minority, or from neighboring countries are generally treated much more leniently. As will be discussed later, a person in possession of as little as 50 grams of heroin can be sentenced to death, and tens of thousands of drug traffickers with less than a kilogram of heroin in their possession are sentenced to long prison terms (mostly life sentences) every year. Execution of drug traffickers is also a yearly ritual in many parts of China; the authorities in every major city will execute scores of drug traffickers around June 26 (the international drug prohibition day), often attracting wide media coverage. As a result, drug offenders in China often call their participation in the heroin market as *ti naodai zou* (walking about with your head in your hands) or refer to the drug business as *shatou shengyi* (head-chopping business).

Although the stakes are high in this business, there seems no shortage of risk takers. We believe several factors combine to create a market environment that proves difficult to resist for many entrepreneurs. First, China's geographical proximity to a major drug-producing country like Burma is a major reason for China to become a transit country, and later a consumption country, once China began to promote cross-border economic activities with Burma in the late 1980s. According to Paoli et al., "proximity to major producing and consuming countries, and strong commercial and demographic connections usually override all other factors in determining which countries become principal transit countries. State weakness, complicity, and the non-enforcement of the global prohibition regime encourage trafficking, much as they do cultivation, but our analysis demonstrates that geographic proximity and strong commercial and demographic ties are even more important."[57] Second, the rapid development of a sizeable heroin market within China created a very strong demand for heroin and thus transformed the heroin trade into an extremely lucrative business. As the Chinese like to say: "No one wants to get involved in a money-losing venture, but if it is a money-making business, many people are willing to be engaged in it even if it is a head-chopping business."

Research Methods

In this study we applied a variety of research methods. We conducted a self-administered survey, many formal and informal interviews, and several ethnographic field trips. Our interviews were with a variety of human subjects, including traffickers, dealers, users, enforcers, and other key informants. We also conducted our research activities in as many sites as possible by traveling to several countries and dozens of cities and towns.

Research Sites

This study was conducted primarily in Yunnan Province in southwest China, the major gateway to the Golden Triangle and one of the poorest provinces in China (see map 1.3).[58] Yunnan completely covers the Chinese border with Burma. Furthermore, Yunnan also borders Laos and Vietnam. According to Chinese government sources, the amount of drugs seized in Yunnan Province in the late 1990s represented 80 percent of all heroin and 70 percent of all opium confiscated in China.[59] Data collection activities were carried out in Kunming (the capital city of Yunnan) and remote towns along the China-Burma border. Additional

Map 1.3. Yunnan Province.

field activities took place in the urban centers of Southeast Asia where major international drug distribution centers are located (i.e., Rangoon or Yangon, Mandalay, Bangkok, Hong Kong, and Taipei).

During the data collection stage of this study, Ko-lin spent almost a year in China as a visiting scholar. He was hosted by the Yunnan Police Officer Academy in Kunming. With the help of a professor from the academy, we were able to gain access not only to Chinese drug enforcers but also to local compulsory rehabilitation centers.

Primary Data Sources and Samples

We collected data from six groups of subjects: incarcerated drug traffickers ($N = 578$), drug enforcement authorities ($N = 89$), street-level drug dealers ($N=39$), drug users ($N=25$), armed group leaders ($N=12$), and our own community contacts ($N=51$).

First, we managed to gain access to a prison facility in southwest China where the vast majority of the inmates were convicted on drug charges. It currently holds more than 5,000 inmates. Prison officials told us that more than 70 percent of the inmates, men and women alike, were convicted of drug offenses.[60] Altogether, 578 prison subjects (281 male and 297 female) participated in the survey.

For the prison survey, we developed a questionnaire in English and then translated it into Chinese. We tested the questionnaire with a small number of inmates and then revised it to make it easier for the subjects to fill out. We went to five prison buildings and recruited about a hundred or so subjects from each building to participate in the survey. Our sampling was not probability-based. Whenever we arrived at a prison building, we requested that prison officials bring inmates who were available at the time to a big classroom to fill out the questionnaire. The project staff explained to the participants the purposes of the study, how to fill out the questionnaire, and asked for their cooperation. It was repeatedly emphasized during the instruction phase that the study had nothing to do with any government agency, that no identifying information would be collected, and that no one would be singled out from any of the questionnaires. We also emphasized that it was up to the respondents to decide what questions to answer and how they would answer them. We then collected the questionnaires and left the prison.

We also conducted in-depth interviews with ten inmates during our visits to the prison facilities. The interviews were conducted face-to-face in a small room, without the presence of a third party. The interviews were conducted informally by the authors. No standardized questionnaire was used nor was the interview tape-recorded. This was intentional, to put our subjects more at ease as they told us about themselves and their involvement in drug trafficking.

Second, we interviewed 89 law enforcement officials in China and Southeast Asia. Because the focus of this study is on the trafficking of drugs from the Golden Triangle into China, we interviewed a disproportionately large number of drug enforcement officials in China. We interviewed several law enforcement representatives in Kunming, where the provincial public security headquarters are located. Several drug enforcement officials in the Chinese Ministry of Public Security were interviewed in Beijing to gain insight into the central government's anti-drug policy. The remaining law enforcement subjects were recruited from the townships located along the border areas of southwest China. These towns are considered by Chinese government officials and drug experts to be "drug disaster areas" because of rampant drug trafficking and drug use over the past two decades.[61] We interviewed one or two officials in each of these towns. In addition to the interviews on the China side, we also interviewed 21 law enforcement officials in Rangoon, Bangkok, and Hong Kong. Some of the interviews with law enforcement in the border towns were conducted with a standardized questionnaire.[62] Interviews with authorities in Kunming, Beijing, and certain Southeast Asian cities were conducted informally and without the aid of a standardized questionnaire. The authors conducted most of the interviews with government officials; a researcher from Beijing with strong ties to local governments in the border areas was hired to conduct the interviews with Chinese drug enforcers there.

Third, 39 street-level drug dealers were interviewed. We recruited these subjects with the help of the staff from a community-based drug rehabilitation program located in Kunming. Workers in the program were ex-drug users/sellers, and they recruited 25 active drug vendors to participate in our study. The interviews were conducted face-to-face by trained interviewers with a standardized questionnaire. To augment these standardized questionnaires, the authors also interviewed 14 active drug dealers in greater detail with open-ended questions.

Fourth, we interviewed 25 heroin users in Kunming. We recruited these subjects from another two community-based drug rehabilitation centers in the city. Both programs were operated and funded by foreign-based organizations. The interviews were conducted one-on-one inside the offices of the community-based centers, where former and current drug users congregate during office hours. The centers provide individual and group counseling, and a place for former and current drug addicts to socialize. The interviews were conducted by the authors using a standardized questionnaire.

Fifth, we interviewed 12 armed group leaders or the so-called drug lords in the Wa area or Special Zone No. 2. Both authors visited the

Table 1.1. In-Depth Interviews by Locations ($N=227$)

Types of subjects	China	Burma	Thailand	Hong Kong	Total
Law enforcers	68	5	8	8	89
Incarcerated drug traffickers	10	1	0	0	11
Drug lords	0	12	0	0	12
Street-level drug dealers	39	0	0	0	39
Drug users	25	0	0	0	25
Community contacts	10	19	19	3	51
Total	152	37	27	11	227

Wa area and conducted these interviews personally. Plans to interview subjects in two other special zones inside Burma, Special Zone No. 1 (the Kokang area) and Special Zone No. 4 (the Mengla area), were postponed, and later abandoned, because of the difficulties and potential risks in traveling to these two areas.

Finally, while we were making the field trips, we also talked extensively with our community contacts. Some of these contacts were our personal friends, while others were referred through the snowball technique. These were individuals who were longtime residents in the communities where our field activities took place and were familiar with local cultures and political events.

In sum, 227 subjects were interviewed and 578 convicted drug traffickers participated in a prison survey. See table 1.1 for a list of the subjects who were interviewed for this study.

Secondary Data

We also collected as much secondary data as possible during our stay in China. Because official statistics or reports on drug-related crimes are not easily available in China, we asked a locally recruited research assistant to systematically collect drug-related articles in local newspapers, weekly magazines, and police and scholarly journals. Books written in Chinese by local practitioners or scholars were also collected.

Fieldwork

We conducted fieldwork in the border areas of Yunnan, met and talked to people from diverse backgrounds, including ordinary citizens, drug users, drug enforcement authorities, businesspeople, and local government officials. We also visited correctional facilities, drug treatment centers, and drug enforcement units. Our ethnographic fieldwork focused on three townships that are considered by the Chinese authorities to be "drug disaster areas." The first is Pingyuan, a Muslim town in the Weishan Prefecture near the Vietnam-China border where drug trafficking was once so rampant that the Chinese government had to call in the military in 1992 to crack down on armed drug traffickers.[63] The large number of local Muslims involved in drug trafficking and other cross-border illegal trade and their past history of armed resistance to law enforcement measures prompted us to explore their relationships with outside Islamic entities and their participation in politically oriented activities. The second town is Lancang, located in the Simao Prefecture near the Wa State (Burma) headquarters in Bangkang. This town has a historical reputation for being a major transit hub for drug smuggling where traffickers from both sides of the border congregate. The third town is Ruili, located in the Dehong Prefecture near the China-Burma border known for its proximity to the town of Muse, a major drug-producing center in northeastern Burma.

We also made field trips to the Wa State along the Burma-China border, a warlord-controlled region where purportedly most of Burma's heroin and ATS were produced and stored.[64] Additional trips were made into Thailand along the Burma-Thai border, Hong Kong, Rangoon, and Mandalay, where the authors conducted ethnographic observations and interviewed community contacts, in addition to meeting with law enforcement officials.

Limitations of the Study

The resourcefulness of our contacts in China helped us tremendously in gaining rare glimpses into a hidden world. Still, this study has several limitations which may affect the interpretation and generalization of the findings. An obvious problem with this study was our heavy reliance on our own personal contacts in the community, as well as their extended social contacts. Such a field approach has its inherent limitations. Most notably, our exposure to this extremely secretive world was influenced by the access afforded to us. In other words, the type of contacts we developed in the communities in Southeast Asia determined the type of information we would gather. Since our contacts and their social networks introduced us to mostly loosely connected entrepreneurs, our findings have thus been tainted with perspectives gathered from these individuals. For instance, the fact that we did not find any traditional organized crime syndicates (i.e., the China-based mafia-like gangs, the Hong Kong–based triads such as the 14K and the Sun Yee On, the Taiwan-based organized gangs such as the Bamboo United and the Four Seas) in drug trafficking ventures in the Golden Triangle does not mean that their involvement did not exist. We just did not find any evidence to make such a claim.

Furthermore, although we strove to include different types of drug dealers and users to expand our knowledge, the selection of the subjects was for the most part limited to the initial contacts, and therefore could very well be systematically biased. For instance, most of our referrals to active street-level drug dealers and users came from two community-based drug treatment organizations. Although these rehabilitation centers were well-known in the addict and street dealer community in the city, their outreach effort was limited to only a few urban ghetto areas, thus excluding all other prospective subjects who did not have access to, or use, the centers' services (i.e. non-users, non-Han minority).

Another limitation of this study was that our understanding of the drug trafficking activities in and around the Golden Triangle was built upon information pieced together from multiple sources. Only a few subjects provided complete descriptions of their trafficking operations. Most stories we gathered pertained to only limited or specific segments of the trafficking enterprise, which engendered our primary belief that drug trafficking was mostly fragmented and controlled by many players at different stages. It is possible that some well-organized trafficking groups were able to coordinate long-distance operations and to transport drugs from the source to street vendors. Characteristics derived from the "fragmented" stories and interpreted in this book were therefore inferred from data provided by individuals who were unrelated to one another in their trafficking activities. For obvious ethical and safety reasons, we did not attempt to follow a trafficking operation from start to finish. Therefore, we pieced together the fragmented descriptions to construct our understanding of the "trafficking organization."

Finally, regardless of what strategies we employed to gain the confidence of our subjects or how successful we had been in convincing the subjects of our sincere intent to protect their identity, the extent to which these drug dealers and users gave honest answers was difficult to gauge. As researchers of sensitive topics must do, we relied on multiple sources of information and our intuitive understanding from field observations and direct interactions with these people. Much more research is needed to substantiate the findings in this study and to improve our understanding of these versatile groups of entrepreneurs.

Generalizability of the Study Findings

Our access to criminals, informants, and police officials in the Golden Triangle region gave us unprecedented access to a world few had ever before peered into. However limited our entry point may have been, our conclusions and findings were all based on firsthand data gathered along the routes and regions frequented by drug traffickers. Furthermore, we employed several strategies to increase the validity and reliability of the data we gathered. First, we relied on our personal contacts, people living in the communities who knew us for many years and had no reasons to deceive us. Relying on their referrals, we were able to reach other informants. Such reliance on one's own social networks had worked well in our other studies of sensitive topics, such as street gangs,[65] political corruption and organized crime,[66] human smuggling,[67] and sex trafficking.[68] Second, we relied on multiple sources and cross-checked the data obtained from interviews, social conversations, and our field observations. We were able to construct questions with sufficient prior knowledge of the region and tailored our questions to specific subject populations. In other words, we were not navigating in an entirely foreign territory. Third, we compared our findings about the operation and structure of drug trafficking in Burma and China with known cases that have been made by Burmese and Chinese law enforcement and that were reported in official reports or the news media. We found that our interview findings matched relatively well to trafficking cases that were prosecuted. Finally, most of our interviews were conducted in confidential environments or settings that our subjects deemed comfortable. We let our subjects decide what questions they would answer and how much they would answer them. Our years of field research experience rewarded us richly in terms of building trust and confidence with prospective subjects. The fact that responses from our subjects became repetitive and patterned gave us some degree of confidence that the data were reliable.

To increase the representativeness of our subjects, we strove to: (1) reach traffickers of different types (e.g., mules, concealment specialists, coordinators, and street vendors); (2) gather information at multiple sites (i.e., many cities in China, border regions between Burma and China, Burma, Thailand, and Hong Kong); (3) interview active and retired traffickers, at large and incarcerated. In short, there were few, if any, alternatives to gathering firsthand data on drug trafficking other than the ones we have attempted here.

Despite the many limitations discussed, we are confident that the findings and conclusions presented here are at least accurate to the extent of the trafficker population with whom we were able to interact. However, it is prudent to assume that the traffickers we were able to reach represent only incomplete aspects of the drug trafficking business in the Golden Triangle region. Since such empirical studies are rare, we take pride in the fact that we were able to contribute substantively to the knowledge of this secretive underground economy that sustains a large addict population in the most populous country in the world.

2

The Drug Market in Burma

In this chapter we will take a look at the history, development, and patterns of drug production and trafficking in Burma and its border. First, we briefly discuss some of the major political and economic developments in Burma and China over the past two decades and explain how these developments might have affected the drug trade in these two countries, as well as Southeast Asia and other parts of the world. We will then move on to the drug trade in Burma, focusing on the three areas that are the centers of the drug business there: Shan State, Mandalay City, and Rangoon City. We set aside a section on Shan State, which borders Thailand in the south and China in the north. Shan State commands special attention when it comes to the drug trade in the Golden Triangle because of its unique geopolitical location. For Mandalay and Rangoon, we focus on the recent movement of Yunnanese (Chinese from Yunnan Province) from the border areas to these cities and how the influx of Yunnanese has brought Mandalay and Rangoon closer to drug producers and traffickers along the border areas.

Most of the drugs from Burma, especially heroin, are trafficked into China via the Burma-China border. Several towns along the border are home to some of the most active drug traffickers, and their cross-border drug trafficking activities occur in these towns. In particular, we focus on the three special regions located in northern Shan State where drug cultivation and production are most active: Special Region 1 (Kokang), Special Region 2 (Wa), and Special Region 4 (Mengla).

Burma and China: A Tale of Two Countries

In 1988, after many years of pent-up frustrations with the ruling military junta, college students in Burma took to the streets and made demands for political reform and democracy.[1] A year later, college students in China occupied Tiananmen Square in Beijing to express their dissatisfaction with official corruption and ask for more freedom and governmental transparency.[2] On both occasions, the governments sent in the troops and quelled the protests by shooting and killing scores of students. Since then, the two countries have taken very different paths economically, though both countries remain authoritarian states with little tolerance for democratic reform. Burma, however, surprised the world in 2010 by releasing Aung San Suu Kyi, a key opposition political figure who had been under house arrest for more than a decade, and establishing a civilian government the following year. In this section we examine the developments in Burma and China and the evolving relationship between the two nations since those violent crackdowns occurred more than two decades ago.

Burma

Burma is bordered on the north and northeast by China, on the east and southeast by Laos and Thailand, and on the west by Bangladesh and India (see map 1.1). Its total area is 2.6 million square miles (6.77 million square kilometers), with a population of about 60 million. The main ethnic groups are Burman (about 70 percent), Shan, Kachin, Karen, Kayah, Chin, Mon, and Rakhine.[3] Almost 90 percent of the population is Buddhist.[4] The political and economic center of Burma was in the city of Rangoon (or Yangon) for centuries before the authorities moved the capital in 2005 to Naypyidaw, an up-country site near the town of Pyinmana in Mandalay State.

Burma was colonized by the British and became annexed to India in 1886, and it was briefly occupied by the Japanese during World War II.[5] Following the war, the British administration was reestablished in Burma. On February 1947, Aung San, a charismatic Burman leader (the father of Aung San Suu Kyi), concluded the Panglong Agreement with Shan, Kachin, and Chin leaders that laid the foundation for the establishment of a union of equal states in Burma.[6] Unfortunately, in July 1947, Aung San and several other prominent leaders were assassinated as they assembled for a meeting in Rangoon. After gaining independence from the British the following year, the country began to disintegrate as many ethnic groups became disillusioned with a central government that was dominated by the Burman.[7]

Only three months after independence, the first battle between the Communist Party of Burma (CPB) and government forces broke out and fighting soon spread throughout central and upper Burma.[8] In the meantime, many insurgencies sprang up around the country as various ethnic groups also began to fight the Rangoon government.[9]

On March 1, 1962, Prime Minister U Nu was ousted after a coup masterminded by a group of army officers led by General Ne Win, a career soldier who played a key role in the anti-Japanese resistance movement during World War II and in the suppression of insurgent ethnic groups after independence.[10] After the coup, the Revolutionary Council was formed to implement many new policies to change Burma from a relatively liberal state into a uniquely Burmese socialist state. The Revolutionary Council formed the Burma Socialist Programme Party (BSPP) in 1962 and announced its philosophy in "The Correlation of Man and His Environment" in the following year, which provides philosophical underpinnings for the "Burmese Way to Socialism," an "inward-looking development strategy with emphasis on self-reliance, isolation and strict neutrality in foreign policy. Foreign direct investment was barred."[11]

Mixing European socialist policies with Chinese communist strategies, the Revolutionary Council began to implement dramatic policies that would eventually drive out of Burma the Indians and the Chinese, the two ethnic groups that dominated the Burmese economy. First, in February 1963, the Revolutionary Council nationalized many economic enterprises.[12] Second, the regime devalued 50- and 100-kyat banknotes without compensation; the intention was to remove wealth from foreign hands. After the departure of Indian and Chinese businesspeople, Burma's economy faltered. The establishment of communist-style cooperatives also depressed the economy and helped to develop a vast black market where the rich still bought what they wanted by paying much more than what was paid in the state-controlled stores.[13]

From the time of the coup in 1962 till 1988, Burma was wracked by armed conflicts between the Rangoon government and militant ethnic groups. On several occasions, the rebel groups were poised to take over Rangoon. The Rangoon government also clashed frequently with students who participated in street protests against the government. In 1988, a brawl in a teashop in Rangoon between students and local youths turned into massive, anti-government street demonstrations led by college students.[14] The Rangoon government reacted violently: many students were gunned down and thousands were arrested, and all universities, colleges, and schools were closed. However, large-scale street demonstrations continued to spread to other cities and towns, and soon the entire country was shaken by daily demonstrations.

Ne Win resigned as BSPP chairman, and in September 1988, the State Law and Order Restoration Council (SLORC) was formed to shore up the regime. The pro-democracy movement established the National League for Democracy (NLD) and Aung San Suu Kyi was named as general secretary.[15]

Under pressure from the international community, the SLORC conducted a multiparty general election in 1990. The NLD won a landslide victory and captured about 60 percent of the vote and 392 of the parliamentary seats, including all 59 seats in the Rangoon Division. The military-backed National Unity Party won only ten seats. However, not only did the SLORC refuse to turn over power to the NLD, but it also begin to round up NLD leaders. By then the SLORC had already put Aung San Suu Kyi under house arrest in 1989. People in Burma were again deeply disappointed with their government, and their hopes for reform were crushed.[16]

In November 1997 the SLORC renamed itself the State Peace and Development Council (SPDC), presumably to project a softer image. However, things have remained the same in Burma since the military coup in 1962. On October 20, 2004, General Khin Nyunt, 65 years old, was forced to resign his dual posts as prime minister and chief of military intelligence. After Khin Nyunt was ousted, Chairman Senior General Than Shwe and Vice Chairman and General Maung Aye appointed Lt.-Gen. Soe Win, SPDC secretary No. 1, as the new prime minister.

Three years later, in September 2007, thousands of Buddhist monks in Burma launched major protests against the military junta. Again, as in the previous protests, the demonstrators were violently quashed by riot police and soldiers. The Burmese authorities shot and killed more than ten protestors (at least that is what the government has admitted to), including a Japanese reporter; raided monasteries; and beat or arrested hundreds of monks who led the demonstrations.[17] The United Nations sent an envoy to Burma to urge the Burmese junta to take steps toward political reconciliation, but this advice fell on deaf ears as Burma's lonely ally in the region, China, continued to be reluctant to take a tough stand against the military regime.[18]

The authors visited Burma several times between 1996 and 2006, and every time we were there, we witnessed that life was getting worse and worse for most Burmese people. During our latest visit, we met a second-year college student working as a waiter in a luxury hotel who told us that he was making $15 a month working six days a week from five in the morning to one in the afternoon. He said he was actually spending more than he was making.[19] When we visited a small, state-owned candy factory, we were shocked to learn that the young women who were sorting, weighing, and packing candies were all college graduates and that they were making $11 a month working long hours five days a week in a hot, humid room. But in Burma, people who were working were the lucky ones; many other people we met were simply trying to get by without a job.

Ordinary people in Burma suffer in silence.[20] Ko-lin was born and raised in Burma; one of his former neighbors recently retired from a government unit after working there her whole life since graduating from college. She told us she was paid about $15 a month after retirement, when she reached the mandatory retirement age of 60. A Muslim born in Burma whose parents were from India, she also described how Chinese and Indians were systematically excluded from government employment. The same is true with religion; only Buddhists are likely to be hired and promoted. On the other hand, low-level government employees try their best to survive. While we were conducting fieldwork in Rangoon, our car was often stopped by police in the middle of the road who would then ask us politely for tea money. Once, our driver gave them 200 kyats (15 cents). They waved goodbye with a big smile.

While many countries in Asia and Africa that were once brutalized by dictators had finally gotten rid of their victimizers after many years of struggle, the grip on Burma by the military junta appeared to be getting tighter until very recently. Isolated from the world community and always fearful of being overthrown by their own people (students and monks led by Aung San Suu Kyi), as well as non-Burman people living in the division and border areas, and Westerners, the military junta developed a siege mentality that people in and out of Burma were constantly conspiring to topple the regime and throw the nation into chaos. Consequently, the junta was determined to hold onto power at all costs, believing that only they were in a position to hold the country together.[21] During that time, all over Burma, women and elderly people went to the pagoda regularly to share their thoughts with the gods, and young people congregated in curbside tea shops every day to vent their feelings against the regime. They were waiting, hoping that one day the military regime would collapse.

To achieve the junta's idea of "disciplined democracy," a well-orchestrated general election was held in Burma in 2010, during which many generals retired from their army posts and ran for public office as civilians, and won. The main opposition party National League for Democracy (NLD), led by Aung San Suu Kyi, boycotted the election. After the election, however, Aung San Suu Kyi was released from house arrest, but her every move was carefully monitored by the regime. On March 2011, Thein Sein, a retired military officer, was sworn in as president of a civilian government and replaced the military junta that had been headed by Senior General Than Shwe for the past two decades.

In April 1, 2011, by-elections were held to fill 46 vacant parliamentary seats. The NLD participated in the elections, and won 43 out of the 44 seats they contested. Aung San Suu Kyi ran in the seat of Kawmu and won. On September 30, 2011, the Burmese government ordered the suspension of a controversial hydroelectric project, the Myitsone Dam project, that was financed and led by a state-owned Chinese company and had become a showcase project for the previous military government.[22] Dissidents in Burma welcomed the halt in construction of the dam due to its environmental impact, and government officials in the West were encouraged by the sign that the new civilian government was trying to distance itself from decades of army rule and Chinese influence in Burma.

Shortly thereafter, U.S. President Barack Obama commented that "after years of darkness we've seen flickers of progress in these last several weeks" and ordered Secretary of State Hillary Rodham Clinton to visit Burma, the first visit by a U.S. secretary of state to the country in more than 50 years. After Clinton's visit in December 2011, many high-ranking government officials from Europe and Asia also showed up in Burma, followed by a variety of international organizations eager to offer help. The Obama administration also upgraded the relations with Burma by sending the first ambassador there in 22 years. Two weeks after being reelected in November 2012, President Obama visited Burma. Even though he stayed there for only six hours, no sitting American president had ever before visited Burma. Mr. Obama's visit was part of a larger effort to reorient American foreign policy more toward Asia, mainly to contain the rise of China.

After more than half a century of conflict and military-dominated government, Burma is at a critical juncture, as commented by a report by the Transnational Institute, a Netherlands-based research and policy advocacy organization:

> Since the 211 accession to power by the government of President Thein Sein, a new energy and openness have occurred in many aspects of national life. This reform potential had been welcomed by Western governments and international institutions that have begun to lift or suspend different sanctions. At the same time, renewed conflict in the Kachin and Shan states and the continued domination of government by Tatmadaw (armed forces) veterans suggest that there is a long way to go before a democratic and representative system of government is truly in place.[23]

China

With a population of more than 1.35 billion, the People's Republic of China (PRC) is the most populous country in the world. It is bordered by 14 different countries, including Russia, India, Kazakhstan, Afghanistan, Pakistan, Burma, Vietnam, and North Korea. It has 22 provinces, five autonomous regions, four direct-controlled municipalities (Beijing, Tianjin, Shanghai, and Chongqing), and two special administrative regions (Hong Kong and Macau).

After thousands of years of control by the various dynasties, Sun Yat-sen and his followers overthrew the Manchu Qing Dynasty and established the Republic of China (ROC) in 1911.[24] Prior to its collapse, the dynasty was humiliated by foreign powers and weakened by a series of social unrests. However, not long after the republic was born, China was in turmoil again as many warlords were at war with one another and the central government was weak. Soon, Chiang Kai-shek's Kuomintang Party (KMT) and Mao Zedong's Communist Party of China (CPC) became the two dominant forces after the two parties consolidated themselves with other forces. The two sides then began to engage in a struggle to rule China.[25]

Japan invaded China in 1937 and by the time the Japanese attacked Pearl Harbor in 1941, a large part of China was under their control. After the Japanese surrendered to the Allied Forces in 1945 and World War II ended, the KMT and the CPC promptly resumed fighting. After the KMT fled to Taiwan in 1949, the CPC established the People's Republic of China (PRC) in the mainland.[26]

The CPC then embarked on a series of social and economic reforms, including the ban on vice activities such as gambling, opium smoking, and prostitution. The Communists also launched the Great Leap Forward from 1958 to 1961, an ambitious social and economic campaign led by Mao Zedong to transform China from an agrarian economy into a communist society through industrialization and collectivization. The campaign was one of the biggest disasters in human history; it resulted in the Great Chinese Famine that cost more than 40 million lives.[27]

The CPC also commenced the Anti-Rightists Movement between 1957 and 1959, during which a series of campaigns were launched to purge alleged "rightists" within the party who were pro-capitalism and against collectivization. More than half a million people, mostly intellectuals, were uprooted and sent to the countryside for re-education.

As if the Great Leap Forward and the Anti-Rightists Movement were not devastating enough, Mao Zedong started the Great Proletariat Cultural Revolution (commonly known as the Cultural Revolution) in 1966 to get rid of capitalists and revisionists (bourgeoisie elements who wanted to restore capitalism in China) from Chinese society and to maintain a strictly communist spirit within the CPC. Mao believed revisionists should be eliminated through violent class struggle. The Cultural Revolution touched every corner of the country and resulted in widespread violent factional conflicts. Millions of ordinary people and government officials were persecuted as "revisionists," "capitalists," or simply "bad elements"; many were killed or forced to commit suicide.

The brutal social movement ended in 1976 with the death of Mao and the arrest of the Gang of Four, led by Mao's wife Jiang Qing.[28]

When the Chinese woke up from the nightmare of the Cultural Revolution, they began to make a concerted effort to reestablish ties with the West and adopted its open door policy.[29] China also began to move from a central-command economy to a market-oriented economy. Government-owned enterprises crumbled quickly in the face of thriving private ventures.[30] Foreign investors were lured to China to open factories in the many newly established special economic zones in the coastal areas.[31]China suddenly began to embark on a reform movement with impressive economic achievements. In the late 1980s, even though Chinese people were living much better than before, they were disappointed with official corruption, social inequality, and the lack of freedom. The students took the initiative to express their displeasure with the Chinese government during a memorial of their beloved leader, Hu Yaobang, at Tiananmen Square in Beijing in 1989. Soon, the protests spread to all walks of life and it became a major embarrassment to the Chinese regime. After the students occupied the square for a few weeks, Chinese leaders decided to send in the military. Scores of protestors in the square were killed, and the world community was stunned to see how the event had ended in such a bloody episode.[32]

Contrary to what many had predicted following the Tiananmen Incident in 1989, China's leaders continued to engage in economic reform. When Deng Xiaoping, the paramount leader who single-handedly led China toward a market economy, stepped down in the early 1990s, Jiang Zemin, an engineer, emerged to replace him.[33] Under Jiang's leadership, the economy continued to grow significantly and consistently for a prolonged period of time. In 1997, China reclaimed Hong Kong from Britain; two years later, Portugal returned Macau to China. China also continued to maintain a good relationship with the United States and the rest of the world during that period.[34]

In 2002, Jiang stepped down to make way for a "fourth generation" of leadership, led by Hu Jintao. Hu continued to stress economic development, but remained highly conservative in political reforms. During Hu's tenure, the Communist Party of China tightened its control of the masses but became more active in international affairs;[35] China's influence in many developing countries was increasing.[36] The relationship between China and Taiwan also dramatically improved after Taiwan once again came under the control of the Kuomintang Party (KMT) in 2008.

Following almost three decades of mind-boggling economic growth, China is now the world's second largest economy after the United States. Although most people in China still remain relatively impoverished, the size of the middle class is expanding rapidly, with a few becoming extremely wealthy. Even though China is still a communist state controlled by a single political party, it is hard for anyone walking down the main streets of a Chinese city to think of it as such. Organized crime, corruption, gambling, prostitution, and drug use are all making a comeback with a vengeance, very much like the good old days of the Kuomintang era known as the "Old Society."[37] It is no wonder, then, that when Xi Jinping became the top leader of China in 2012, one of his top priorities was to crack down on official corruption.

China-Burma Relations

The relationship between China and Burma is an ever evolving love-hate affair between two nations and their peoples.[38] China invaded Burma in the Yuan and Qing dynasties, and these invasions historically caused the Burmese to feel insecure when dealing with the Chinese.[39] However, the Burmese and the Chinese are very close; the Burmese calling the Chinese Pauk-Phaw (kins) and the Chinese viewing the Burmese as one of the "few loyal friends." The history of China-Burma relations is replete with ups and downs and unexpected turns.

When China was at war with Japan during World War II, China relied heavily on the Burma Road for supplies from the Allied Forces because the Japanese had occupied much of the coastal areas of China to the east. In 1949, soldiers from the defeated Kuomintang (KMT) entered Burma from China's Yunnan Province to seek shelter and staging grounds for future counterattacks.[40] The arrival of KMT armed groups had a crucial, long-lasting effect on the region's drug trade, as some of the troops became key players in the business.[41]

When the PRC was established in 1949, Burma was the first noncommunist country to recognize the PRC.[42] Between 1950 and 1967, the two sides maintained a cordial relationship. China was careful not to intervene in the war between the Rangoon government and the Communist Party of Burma insurgent groups active in the border areas. In return, Burma was willing to serve as a buffer state between China and the West and a bridge between China and those countries that were friendly to the Chinese.[43] Chinese descendants living in Burma also maintained a good relationship with the Burmese and other minority groups and were treated with respect.[44]

The China-Burma relationship took a dramatic downturn when an anti-Chinese riot broke out in Burma in 1967, a result of Burmese reaction to the Chinese Red Guard activities in Rangoon and other cities during the initial years of the Cultural Revolution. After many Chinese in Burma were killed or assaulted and the Chinese Embassy in Rangoon ransacked, China abruptly changed its policy of non-interference in Burma's internal affairs and began to openly support the Burmese communist groups. China also terminated almost all diplomatic and economic ties with Burma.[45]

This hostile relationship between China and Burma continued for 11 years, until 1988, when the Burmese government violently cracked down on a pro-democracy movement carried out by college students.[46] The West, led by the United States, responded by cutting off all diplomatic and economic relations with the Burmese military junta. As Burma became more isolated from the world community because of U.S. sanctions, the country moved closer to China, because China was willing to protect Burma from international criticisms for its own geopolitical reasons.[47] Consequently, Burma was not only allied with the Chinese in the political arena, but in the economic sphere as well.

For the next 24 years (1988–2012), the relationship between China and Burma grew stronger and stronger. According to Thai scholar Pavin Chachavalpongpun: "While under the strict military regime in the pre-2010 election period, the main source of legitimacy for Burma had been China. China provided political support for the junta, defended the government at international gatherings (with China serving as one of the permanent members of the Security Council of the United Nations), and helped sustain the regime, financially, through large-scale investments."[48] China became Burma's biggest investor and second largest trading partner (after Thailand).[49]

According to Chinese scholar Sun Yun, "Beijing's fundamental interests in Myanmar include three basic factors: border stability, economic cooperation, and an energy transportation route."[50] As a result, argued Sun, "This importance is manifested through four initiatives China has taken since the inauguration of the Thein Sein government: the establishment of a comprehensive strategic cooperative partnership; China's seeking of Myanmar's support in regional diplomacy; the potential enhancement of military cooperation; and Yunnan's bridgehead strategy."[51]

Indian scholar Raviprasa Narayanan suggested that several variables influence Beijing's behavior: "Myanmar's strategic location as a land-bridge to the Indian Ocean is a feature that policy makers in Beijing find very attractive for several reasons; Myanmar's role as a 'southwest' corridor into China is an aspect that has triggered several sub-regional initiatives in the region linking up with China's landlocked southwest regions; and the abundant natural resources of Myanmar."[52]

In private, however, most Burmese told us that they would prefer to do business with advanced countries such as the United States and certain Western European countries; however, they had no choice but to work with the Chinese for political reasons. Local Chinese entrepreneurs in Burma, working closely with entrepreneurs arriving from China, began to dominate economic activities in Burma, and of course with the blessing of the generals and the participation of the generals' offspring and in-laws. According to a Chinese businessman in Rangoon we talked to in 2006: "This is how you do business in Burma; you must have a good relationship with the generals. Besides the sons, the daughters, and the in-laws of the generals, the Chinese are also very active in the Burmese business sector. They maintain a close relationship with the Burmese leaders to obtain all sorts of business opportunities." According to Min Zin, an exiled Burmese journalist and scholar, "since at least the mid 1980s, there has been an observable negative attitude among the people of Burma against the Chinese."[53]

To take advantage of the cozy relationship with the military junta, Chinese in Burma would not, and do not, support Aung San Suu Kyi; they want Burma to remain close to China. The Chinese in Burma think Suu Kyi is pro-West, and if she gains power, that means she would weaken the ties between Burma and China.[54] However, after President Thein Sein suspended the Myitsone Dam project on September 30, 2011, and subsequently improved relations with the United States, China also began to reconsider its strategies toward Burma.[55] Sun Yun summarized how these recent developments in the region affected the relationships between China and Burma:

> Economically, Chinese investments have come under increasing scrutiny, criticism, and even oppositions, threatening the viability of strategic projects such as the oil and gas pipelines. Politically, the initial success of the democratic reform in Myanmar raises questions about Beijing's continuous resistance to reform. Strategically, the changes in Myanmar undercut China's original blueprint about the strategic utilities of Myanmar for China at ASEAN [Association of Southeast Asian Nations], in the Indian Ocean and more broadly in the region.[56]

Sun further suggested that "China has responded to the changes inside Myanmar in several important fronts. These include a major reduction of Chinese direct investments, the cooling off of the political relationship, the establishment of relations with the democratic forces and major public relations campaigns."[57]

From the preceding discussions, it is clear that China-Burma relations, as pointed out by Narayanan, "are motivated by geo-strategic and geo-economic consideration. There is no client dependency in this bilateral relationship."[58] With the rise of China and India, together with the reengagement of the United States in the region and Burma's ASEAN chairmanship in 2014, geopolitical alignments and considerations are going to have a major impact on the drug trade in the region and official responses to it.

Burma and China are neighbors; there is a long history of codependence between these two countries.[59] At one point, the two countries were moving in the same direction and both experienced economic hardships, but now they are heading in different directions and their economic conditions could not be more different. In this book, however, we are most interested in how heroin has emerged as an important commodity within the political economy of the border area, and how it later penetrated into the political economy of the inland areas of China.

The Opiate Market inside Burma

Even though this section focuses on the Shan State and Burma's two major urban centers—Mandalay and Rangoon—it is important to point out that the drug business thrives in other areas too. According to a Burmese police officer we interviewed, there are many other places in the country where the drug trade is flourishing; it is just that most people do not have access to these areas and outsiders know very little about these places. Regardless, it is also probably true that the levels of opium cultivation and heroin production outside the Shan State are nowhere near those found inside the Shan State.

Shan State

Shan State is home to the Shan people, the largest ethnic minority in Burma. Many other ethnic groups live in the state as well. The Shan State is also the most important area in Burma when it comes to drug production and trafficking, mainly because there are three special regions in the state that are occupied by armed groups that include former members of the Communist Party of Burma. These three regions are the Special Region 1 (Kokang), Special Region 2 (Wa), and Special Region 4 (Mengla).

The major opium-growing area in Burma is in the Shan State.[60] The Wa area was responsible for 60 percent of the opium produced there in the late 1990s.[61] However, the significance of the Wa area for opium cultivation has declined gradually since then, and by 2005, according to the United Nations' Opium Survey in Burma, "94 percent of total opium poppy cultivation in Myanmar took place in the Shan State and 40 percent of national cultivation (or 42% of Shan State cultivation) in the Wa Special Region."[62]

Within the Shan State, many other armed groups also are engaged in opium cultivation. According to a leader of one these groups, there are major differences between armed groups situated to the west of the Salween River and those groups that are located east of the river:

> Unlike the Kokang and the Wa, our group has never been involved in antigovernment activities. Our people did grow opium, like many other

small armed groups west of the Salween River, but the conversion of opium into heroin was primarily conducted east of the Salween. Many opium traders from Kokang came to buy our opium.

Tachilek, a town in the Shan State, is located across from Mae Sai, Thailand; the two towns are separated by the Mae Sai River. A large number of street vendors in Tachilek go to Mae Sai every day to sell their goods in the streets, and many businesspeople in Mae Sai cross the border into Tachilek to deliver their merchandise or work on large-scale construction projects. Tachilek is Burma's major trading post because most consumer goods from abroad are transported into Burma via Tachilek. For the Thai government, the border trade between Mae Sai and Tachilek is important for the well-being of the Thai economy; this was especially true after the country was hit hard by the financial crisis of Southeast Asia in 1998.

As legitimate business activities between Tachilek and Mae Sai began to flourish in the 1990s, a cross-border methamphetamine trade also began to develop. According to the 2002 report of the Office of Narcotics Control Board of Thailand, the Mae Sai area became the region's largest smuggling point for methamphetamine.[63] Meth tablets produced in Muse, Kokang, Wa, and other parts of the Shan State were transported to Tachilek to be smuggled into Thailand. Moreover, meth factories were established near Tachilek to avoid transporting the tablets through Burmese-controlled territories. One subject told us that there are about nine *yaba* [methamphetamine] factories in Tachilek: five belong to the Wa and four, non-Wa. According to this subject, Thai authorities know where the factories are located, but without the cooperation of the Burmese authorities, Thai law enforcers cannot do anything about these factories.

Mandalay

Mandalay is the last royal capital of Burma.[64] It is now the capital of Mandalay Division in Upper Burma and the second largest city after Rangoon. According to various sources, Mandalay has gone through major changes over the past 20 years, essentially transforming itself into a "Chinese City" after many people from Kokang and Wa moved there, thus significantly enhancing the city's economic ties to China.[65] Most people we talked to believe that the main catalyst for the movement of Kokang and Wa people to Mandalay was Khin Nyunt, former head of Burma's military intelligence who, in 1988, ordered the immigration department to allow anyone with a Kokang or Wa identification card to move to any part of Burma, no questions asked. Kokang and Wa people took advantage of the unprecedented opportunity to move their families to Mandalay and Rangoon. Many Yunnanese and Sichuanese from China also moved to Mandalay after they obtained a Kokang or a Wa ID. It is now believed that the Chinese make up 30–40 percent of the city's population of one million.

With the arrival of large numbers of genuine Kokang and Wa people and alsoYunnanese posing as Kokang and Wa people, the economy of Mandalay was revitalized as the newly arrived Chinese transformed the city's center into a major commercial hub dotted with shopping malls, hotels, and office buildings. However, law and order in Mandalay also deteriorated. According to a Chinese businessman we interviewed in Mandalay:

> Kokang and the Wa people began to arrive in Mandalay in 1988, and ever since then, they have been coming steadily. Once they got here, they built their houses or rented the houses of high-ranking government officials and then used the places as gambling dens and drug transaction places. Because of Khin Nyunt, the police did not dare do anything about these Kokang and Wa offices because the police did not want to offend Khin Nyunt's military intelligence apparatus. The whole thing was quite blatant. People go in, gamble, use all kinds of drugs, and negotiate a drug deal. Besides the Wa and Kokang, there were also offices of the Yang clan, the Peng clan, and many other armed groups. As these offices became a refuge for drug and crime, many branch offices were established by people affiliated with the armed group leaders; these people in turn also used the branch offices to make money through illegal means.

According to the people we interviewed in Mandalay, many drug producers and dealers from the border areas might build a house in Mandalay and move their families there. Then, they can run their drug business in the border area, controlling it remotely in essence. It follows that Mandalay is now the main distribution center for Burma's own drug market. All sorts of drugs from the special regions are delivered here first and then distributed to Burmese cities such as Rangoon, Lashio, Mitkyina, and Bagan. However, because the drug market in Burma is relatively small, the quantity of drugs being distributed from Mandalay is limited.

Many Chinese in Mandalay are also involved in the lucrative jade and gem business. But local people that we met commonly believed that most of the riches in Mandalay were made from selling drugs. Locals also assumed that any Chinese person who moved to Mandalay from Mitkyina, Lashio, or Chinese cities such as Tengchong or Longlin was likely a drug dealer. For a Chinese to get into the drug business, all he or she needs is to know a few other Chinese. While such folklores are difficult to verify empirically, we believe some Chinese people who get rich from the drug trade may eventually leave the drug trade since Mandalay offers greater commercial opportunities, but most will likely remain involved until they are arrested.

Rangoon

Rangoon (or Yangon) is still the political, economic, and cultural center of Burma, even though the military junta had moved the central government to Naypyidaw in 2005. The relocation was viewed with dismay by ordinary Burmese people and foreigners because the new capital is located in an isolated area 200 miles north of Rangoon.

Chinese in Mandalay may also move to Rangoon after they have established their beachheads in Mandalay. For example, we interviewed a methamphetamine trader who is ethnic Chinese and had recently moved from Mandalay so that, according to him, his children would be able to get a better education at an English school in Rangoon. The drug trader bought a new house in Rangoon and continued to engage in the drug business. He has many relatives living there and most of them are linked in some way to either the heroin or methamphetamine trade and have close ties to drug dealers in all the border areas.

Before the 1967 anti-Chinese movement, most of the wealthy Chinese businesspeople in Burma were Cantonese, Fujianese, and Hakka. However, a Chinese businessman we interviewed in Mandalay said:

> After the anti-Chinese movement, many Cantonese, Fujianese, and Hakka moved to China or Taiwan. The Yunnanese pretty much stayed put in Burma. Moreover, as the Burmese economy began to disintegrate due to the massive out-migration of Chinese and Indian entrepreneurs, trafficking of goods from Thailand into Burma became very prevalent. The Yunnanese began to play a key role in the Burmese informal economy, and when Sino-Burma border trade took off in the late 1980s, the Yunnanese naturally became the main force behind the trade. Now, their economic power far surpasses that of the Cantonese, the Fujianese, and the Hakka, both here in Mandalay and in Rangoon.

The demographic landscape among ethnic Chinese in Burma has indeed changed. Most prominent and seemingly successful members of the communities that we encountered were from Yunnan, replacing their compatriots from a generation ago who were from Guangdong and Fujian. As a result, the dynamics in business and commerce have also changed, with a greater emphasis on cross-border trading activities and Chinese government–backed large-scale development projects (i.e., construction and mining activities).

The three major armed groups in the Burma-China border areas—the Wa, the Kokang, and the Mengla—all have offices in Rangoon. Bao Youxiang, the supreme leader of the Wa, had invested a significant amount of money in real estate in Rangoon, and it is believed that many other Wa leaders also might have investments in the city. Many family members of Kokang leaders live in expensive houses in Rangoon and maintain close relationships with high-ranking Burmese officials.

A relatively successful entrepreneur in Rangoon had this to say when asked what qualifications a person must possess in order to enter the drug trade: "The most important qualification is to know from whom to buy and to whom to sell. If you don't have this connection, you can't do it." The businessman went on to stress that drug-related violence is almost nonexistent in Rangoon. However, drug dealers there are vulnerable to state-inflicted harm: "No violence in the drug business here, but if you are a dealer and get arrested, you must tell the Burmese authorities who your suppliers are or you will suffer a lot. They always go after higher-level suppliers but the investigation stops if the supplier is in the 'hills' (meaning the various special regions in the Shan State)."

Up to now, because of the lack of reliable data on the Burmese drug market, outsiders have only been able to guess at its characteristics: that the market is huge; that the drug business is hierarchical and well-organized; that drug entrepreneurs are usually in possession of large inventories to take advantage of the economy of scale; and yet are concerned about state interdiction. Some guesses were contradictory: drug entrepreneurs were thought to be frequently engaged in violence to protect their turf, but they also were thought to have influence with state officials, and thus were able to monopolize the drug market. It has also been assumed that in a non-enforcement country like Burma, people in the drug trade are not marginalized, but are, in fact, mostly influential public figures who are active in both the political and legitimate business arenas. Finally, it was thought that revenues from the drug trade made up a substantial percentage of the country's overall economy.

Our recent fieldwork in the Shan State (excluding the Wa, Kokang, and Mengla regions), Mandalay, and Rangoon challenges virtually all these assumptions. Although we did not spend a long period of time conducting fieldwork in these sites, our brief stay in these places indicated that the characteristics of the opiate market in Burma are not much different from the opiate market in countries with strict enforcement. We were not aware of any well-organized drug cartels in operation in most of Shan State, Mandalay, and Rangoon. The opiate market in these sites was also small scale and fragmented, and drug entrepreneurs were mostly Chinese who preferred to maintain a low profile. Drug-related violence was almost nonexistent, and the level of drug-related corruption was not as rampant as outsiders had believed.

The Drug Market in the Burma-China Border Area

As previously reported by other researchers, there is mounting evidence that expansive economic activities along the border regions have provided ample opportunities for the growth of the illicit enterprise of drug trafficking.[66] It was clear to us during our field activities that China has indeed become a country with high levels of drug importation both for transshipment purposes and for a growing domestic addict population. Because of geographical proximity, most heroin and methamphetamine trafficking activities take place along the Burma-Yunnan borders. Once inside China, traffickers use three main routes to move the drug into the interior of the country—one to the north through Sichuan Province, one through Guizhou Province toward the heart of the interior, and one through Guangxi and then Guangdong along the southern coastline heading toward Hong Kong for export to the international market.[67] The development of the Chinese route can be attributed to two main facilitators—geographical proximity and vibrant cross-border commerce. According to journalist Larry Jagan, between 1999 and 2009, more than 200,000 Chinese have crossed into northern Shan State in search of work and financial opportunity.[68] Moreover, the business life of hundreds of small towns and villages along the border is dominated by Chinese immigrants who have migrated to the area over the last ten years.

China and Burma share more than 2,000 kilometers of a common border, most of which is loosely guarded. Local villagers have for centuries traversed back and forth without regard to which country they might step on while carrying out commercial, agricultural, as well as family activities. Chinese farmers lease land from their relatives or friends on the Burmese side to grow and harvest crops. Local women and children comb the hills straddling the two countries to gather mushrooms and herbs each year. During our border visits, we sat in bamboo huts perched on the Burmese hillside that Chinese farmers had built to watch their crops during harvest seasons.

Because of dense vegetation in this near-tropical region, it is often difficult to tell where Chinese territory ends and Burmese territory begins. Local people use official border crossings because they are on main roads and are easier to cross when transporting heavy goods. Otherwise, unguarded pathways over the hills are just as convenient for those who want to avoid the border police. While traveling along the border, we often wondered how China could possibly stop drug traffickers from crossing into the country.

During the first few decades of Communist control, China's tight residential registration system and restrictions on population movement largely prevented any drugs from entering China. Yunnan Province now plays a pivotal role in the overall economic development and commercial activities in and around the Golden Triangle region, the so-called Mekong River subregion. The current trade between Yunnan and

Burma represents about half of all Sino-Burma commercial exchange.[69] With economic development comes greater movement of goods and people. China's rapid economic growth in the past two decades has quickly opened up venues for drug traffickers to exploit.

Drugs are transported into China via several means. In most cases, traffickers on the China side, upon receiving orders, arrange for the drugs to move across the border into a safe location somewhere close by. Crossing the border without being detected is relatively easy if one knows the terrain. According to a key informant in Bangkang, the headquarters of the Wa State, drug producers in Burma typically just sell the drug to buyers from China. They trade drugs for cash, but they are not involved in transporting the drug over the border. Buyers from China are responsible for the movement of drugs from Burma into China. Some of the major towns along the border areas that are notorious for drug trafficking are as follows.

Muse-Ruili

Drug trafficking between Muse (Burma) and Ruili (China) has expanded in recent years because traffickers are using the booming cross-border trade to conceal their drug activities. Not only do large numbers of fully loaded trucks cross the Muse-Ruili checkpoint in both directions every day, but many warehouses are available in the area to hold the commodities before they are transported to their final destinations. As a result, according to the people we interviewed in Muse, it is a place not only where all kinds of drugs (mainly opium, heroin, and methamphetamine) are produced, but also a place where drugs produced in other parts of Burma are warehoused and where drug deals are made. After drugs from Burma arrive in Ruili, they will continue to move on to Mangshi, Longling, Baoshan, and Dali, before arriving in Kunming. Drugs are also smuggled into China between Burma's Kachin State and China's Dehong Prefecture. As a result, drug trafficking activities in places like Longchuan, Fushan, Yingjiang, and Lianghe, all located within the Dehong Prefecture, are reported to be rampant. Muse is also host to large numbers of gambling casinos that cater to gamblers from China, where gambling is illegal but very popular. Many of the workers in the casinos in Muse are from China, and commute to their jobs.[70]

We also visited an area in Muse where many new, big houses are located. According to a high-ranking drug enforcer, it is the area where known drug entrepreneurs live, but he could not do anything about these people because he had no evidence against them. According to the officer: "Before we arrest someone for drug trafficking, we have to take into consideration who is protecting this drug dealer. We know those in Muse who are involved in the drug business, but we dare not arrest them at will. We have to be extremely careful in the process." He also told us that "Most drug dealers are ethnic Chinese, be they Burmese or Chinese citizens. Other ethnic groups do not have the brains or the connections to get involved in the drug business. If you are not smart enough, you can't be a drug dealer; and if you do not know the right people, you don't know how to get into this business."

We are not convinced that drug dealers in Muse are actually as smart and well-connected as this Burmese drug enforcement official would like us to believe. When we visited the drug enforcement headquarters in Muse to talk to officers there, we observed a wall filled with pictures of recently arrested drug traffickers along with the drugs and motor vehicles seized by the authorities. It is true that most of the drug offenders appeared to be ethnic Chinese, but they also looked like ordinary people who were merely taking advantage of the trading opportunities available there. There were pictures of both male and female, young and old, and they all appeared to be living under the same roof and belonged to a kinship network because the pictures were taken in front of the traffickers' homes. Most of them were arrested with a few kilograms of heroin or opium, or a certain amount of precursor chemicals used to produce heroin or methamphetamine.

In Ruili, many drug dealers are ethnic Han Chinese, as one local drug enforcement police officer observed:

> The majority of the big drug dealers are Chinese Han. However, they are not Ruili people. Most of them migrated to this city from other Yunnan cities, like Baoshan, for example. The big drug dealers here normally do not maintain a high profile life-style. Most of them are uneducated,

> former opium growers who later became opium traders and eventually heroin traffickers. They don't go to nightclubs or expensive restaurants. However, you can't help but notice that they like to live in big, nice houses and drive good cars.

Because of the reputation that heroin is cheap and abundant in Ruili, many heroin users from all over China came to Ruili to take advantage of cheap heroin and low cost of living. One informant told us that a heroin addict could survive in Ruili for as low as $1.20 a day; 40–70 cents for heroin and the rest for food. As a result, there was a sizeable retail heroin market in Ruili. However, according to a police officer in Ruili, the heroin retail market is dominated by the Burmese:

> Besides many cross-border traffickers, there are also large numbers of street-level dealers in Ruili. If you go to XXX Road at night, you will find many Burmese, including a small number of Indians from Burma, selling drugs on the streets. They will approach you and show you their four fingers, meaning they got No. 4 heroin. The purity rate here is about 90 percent or higher. You can get a bag of heroin (0.1 gram) for 25 to 50 cents. Of course, some of them also sell other drugs like methamphetamine tablets and Ketamine powder. There is not much we can do about these Burmese. First, they do not have Burmese IDs, so after we arrest them and try to send them back to Burma, the authorities there will not take them back unless they have Burmese IDs. Second, the majority of them have diseases like AIDS. Most of them do not receive medical treatment, so they are very weak and prone to illness. Many times, after they are arrested and detained for only one day, they get sick. We don't want them to die in our jail, so if we find out that they are sick, we let them go. Once I arrested a Burmese for selling drugs on the street. After he took a physical test, we found out he had AIDS; he became very sick after we detained him. For the next two days, we were all bogged down by this one, small-time drug dealer. Finally, I got permission from the court to release him. It was a nightmare.

In the early 2000s, the Burmese authorities, under pressure from the Chinese, arrested several big-time drug traffickers active in Muse and turned them over to the Chinese. The Chinese authorities executed all of them including Tan Xiaolin and Shang Chaomei. According to a Burmese drug enforcer, many big-time drug traffickers fled the area after those arrests, and the mid-level traffickers remaining in Muse tried to keep a low profile.

In response to law enforcement crackdowns on major heroin traders, drug producers in Burma and drug traffickers in China also use mules to move the drugs from Burma to China. A deputy chief of the drug enforcement unit in the Ruili Municipal Police Department had this to say about the changing patterns of drug trafficking in his jurisdiction:

> Three types of drug trafficking groups in this area: family, armed groups (overseas), and individual. Over the past several years, there is a dramatic increase in the number of body-packing drug traffickers [*rendijandu*]. In the past, this city was basically a transit point; nowadays, it is both a transit point and a local market. This makes our job all the more difficult. In the 1980s, it was mainly opium, now it is heroin. Over the past two years, there's also the trafficking of methamphetamine. Because of the increase in border trade and the development of this area as a tourist attraction, it provides many people a chance to use border trade and sightseeing to cover their drug trafficking activities. The local drug market is dominated by drug pushers from outside, especially people from Burma. They represent 70 percent of the retailers. The second largest group is the Xinjiang people. The majority of the Burmese retailers are non-users, and the majority of other outsiders in Ruili are involved in retailing drugs to support their drug habit.

Pangsai (Kyukoke or Jiugu)-Wanding

The Pangsai-Wanding area, located only a few miles south of Muse-Ruili, is another major gateway for cross-border trading. Wanding is one of the smallest border towns in China, with a population of less than 20,000. However, it is also a major tourist attraction because the small bridge that connects Pangsai and Wanding—Wanding Bridge—is a historical landmark; it was used by the British during World War II to transport supplies to China. The old, wooden bridge is still in existence, but the Chinese authorities built a new steel bridge alongside the old one to facilitate border crossing.

Even though the Pangsai-Wanding connection is not as significant as the Muse-Ruili connection as far as drug trafficking is concerned, traffickers still take advantage of the ease with which they are able to enter Wanding from Pangsai. On one occasion, drug enforcement police in Wanding arrested seven men and women (all Burmese nationals) who had swallowed packets of heroin. On November 2008, officials in Wanding stopped a car after being tipped off and uncovered 15 *joi* (weighed 24 kilograms) of opium.[71] On August 2010, a man on a motorcycle was arrested near the Wanding Bridge with three units of heroin that weighed 1,050 grams. The man said he agreed to transport the drug into China because he owed someone a huge gambling debt. Two retired police officers who once led the Wanding drug enforcement unit were arrested for drug trafficking after they became addicted to heroin. Methamphetamine use is allegedly rampant in Wanding, as the tablets from Burma began to show up in Wanding in the late 1990s.

Laukkai-Nansan

Before 2002, Kokang, located north of the Wa territory, was also a key opium cultivation area for many decades. As the first armed group to break away from the Communist Party of Burma and to sign a cease-fire agreement with the Burmese authorities in 1989, the Kokangese were allowed by the Rangoon government to remain armed and autonomous. However, when there were conflicts between the Yang clan and the Peng clan in the mid-1990s, it gave the Burmese an opportunity to move into the Kokang area. By 2004, there were about 6,000 Burmese soldiers in the Kokang area, and many checkpoints there were manned by Burmese soldiers.[72]

In 2002, Kokang's leaders declared that their farmers were no longer allowed to grow opium; the region was transformed into an opium-free area in 2003.[73] However, many people we interviewed, including the Wa leaders, believed that, as late as 2005, opium cultivation was still occurring in certain parts of Kokang. Moreover, many active heroin refineries are located in the Kokang area. Opium production there is not as massive as in the Wa State; heroin producers in Kokang often buy large amounts of opium from traders in the Wa State. Besides buying opium, Kokang's opium traders also travel to Wa villages to buy opium directly from the farmers.[74]

Laukkai is the "capital" of Kokang, and also a major drug-producing area where opium is refined into heroin, and where methamphetamine tablets are mass produced. Nansan is a small town located across from Laukkai, and belongs to Zhengkang County of Lincang Prefecture on the Chinese side. Many so-called *beiducun* or "drug backpacking villages" are located in Yongde County of Lincang Prefecture. Besides Zhengkang and Yongde, the other counties in Lincang include Fengqing, Shuanjiang, Kenma, Canyuang, and Lincang. Drug trafficking is a major concern for law enforcement in all these counties.

In August 2009, Burmese troops overran Kokang and thousands of refugees entered Nansan. The Peng clan was ousted and believed to be hiding in the Wa area, while the Burmese authorities promoted Bai Shoucheng, another Kokang leader, to be in charge of Kokang but to act as a puppet of the Burmese authorities. The refugees from the Kokang area created a nightmare for the Chinese authorities. After what had happened in Kokang and the subsequent influx of refugees, the Chinese came to realize that whatever occurs on the Burmese side of the border area could have a major impact on the Chinese side. As a result, the Chinese started paying close attention to the relationship between the Burmese junta and the United Wa State Army (UWSA), the most powerful ethnic armed group, with an estimated 30,000 troops.[75]

Bangkang-Menga

Bangkang is the "capital" of the Wa State and the headquarters of the United Wa State Army (UWSA). It is separated from Menga, a small Chinese town, by a tiny river. People from both sides can simply walk across a bridge to get to the other side, and the soldiers manning the checkpoints are not particularly concerned with the local people crossing the border. Unlike Muse-Ruili, there are not many trucks crossing Bangkang-Menga, so the officers on the Chinese side of the border only check the cars with some care.

The Wa area, located in the Shan State, is divided into the Northern Wa State and the Southern Wa State. It has a population of approximately 600,000 people, including the Wa, Lahu, Shan, Chinese, and other ethnic groups. There are an additional 350,000 Wa people on the Chinese side of the border, primarily in the counties of Cangyuan, Ximeng, Lancang, and Gengma of Yunnan Province.[76] Over the past two decades the drug trade has remained one of the few viable businesses in this historically poor area, and it is the most reliable means for Wa leaders to raise the money needed for state-building.[77]

Before opium cultivation was banned in the Wa area in 2005, almost every Wa family grew opium because it was the best (and only) cash crop and because they were required to pay an annual opium tax, in kind, to the Wa leaders. After the farmers collected the opium, some of it flowed into the private markets where traders of all levels bought and sold opium (just like any other commodity) before it ended up in heroin refineries. The opium collected by Wa leaders as opium tax was also eventually obtained by heroin producers. It was no secret that heroin producers—mostly Chinese entrepreneurs—were not operating independently from the Wa leaders, even though producing or trafficking heroin was a crime by Wa law.

Compared to the Muse-Ruili route, the Bangkang-Mengla route is not a major drug trafficking route, despite the fact that there are many heroin and methamphetamine factories in the Wa area and the roads between Bangkang and Kunming are relatively good. According to a Wa leader we interviewed, after the Chinese authorities caught a group of traffickers in Guangdong Province with 590 kilograms of heroin in 1996 and found out that the drugs belonged to a Wa leader, the Chinese summoned two Wa leaders to China and made them promise that there will be no more major drug trafficking from Bangkang to the Chinese side. Not long after the two leaders returned to Bangkang, a meeting was held among Wa leaders, who issued a statement on June 20, 1997, proclaiming harsh sentences for anyone caught selling heroin to buyers from China.[78]

Wa leaders are fully aware that they need the goodwill and support of China to survive and to remain connected to the outside world because Burmese authorities have historically shown little interest in furthering Wa's economic and political development. Wa leaders and their partners in the drug business are doing their best not to use the Bangkang-Menga route to move heroin just to avoid upsetting the Chinese authorities.

Mengla-Jinghong

Mengla is the "capital" of Special Region 4 of Shan State, and Jinghong is the commercial center of Xixuanbanna, a Dai autonomous prefecture of Yunnan Province that borders Burma and Laos.[79] At one time Mengla was known as the Las Vegas of the Golden Triangle because of the large numbers of well-established casinos that dotted the streets of Mengla. Gambling is illegal in China: therefore, Chinese must travel overseas or to neighboring countries such as Burma or Russia or special administration regions such as Macau to gamble in the legal casinos there. There were many gambling casinos in the Wa, Kokang, and Mengla areas, but the casinos in the Mengla area were considered to be bigger and better, and casino operators there were very aggressive in attracting high rollers from China to visit their casinos. As a result, the gambling industry in Mengla was, during its peak, significantly much more developed than the gambling industries in the Wa and Kokang. However, the business took a hard hit when the Chinese government banned cross-border gambling in 2005.[80] The Chinese authorities began to prohibit their citizens from traveling to other countries to gamble after several of their officials lost huge amounts of public money at the gambling tables of Mengla.

Even though the leaders of Mengla proclaimed their area to be drug-free in the late 1990s, many observers, including Chinese law enforcement officials, believe that drug laboratories still exist in the area, and that drugs are still being trafficked into China via Mengla. Drug experts in China also suggest that drugs produced in the Wa and Kokang areas are trafficked into China via Mengla.

The leader of the Mengla government, Lin Mingxian, is the son-in-law of Peng Jiasheng, the longtime leader of the Kokang government who was ousted by the Burmese junta in 2010. Leaders in the Mengla government, like officials in the Wa and the Kokang governments, are believed to be heavily involved in the drug business; it is not unusual for leaders in the three special regions to work together on an ad hoc basis to complete a drug transaction.

Drug Trafficking from Afghanistan to China

According to Chinese officials interviewed for this study, drug trafficking into China still occurs primarily through the Golden Triangle. Despite the fact that Afghanistan borders Xinjiang Province in China's northwest corner, little heroin or opium has come through Central Asia. According to one senior drug intelligence official in Beijing we interviewed:

> The Golden Crescent region is not much of a threat to China. Most drugs produced in the region—which includes Afghanistan, Iran, Pakistan, and several of those countries with names ending with "-stan"—are going to Europe, North America, and Russia. I have visited the border region between Xinjiang and Afghanistan; it is a very tiny strip of land about 92 kilometers long and 4,000 to 5,000 meters (about 12,000 to 15,000 feet) above sea level. It would be extremely difficult for humans to walk across. This natural barrier actually helps prevent this region from becoming a major drug trafficking route. Most narcotics from Afghanistan are still transported to Russia and Europe. Therefore, we still consider Afghanistan only as a potential threat.

However, since then, some observers have suggested that more and more drugs from Afghanistan are being transported into China. For example, Niklas Swanstrom and Yin He of Johns Hopkins University suggested that "the Golden Triangle in Southeast Asia has been, and still is, China's major source of narcotics supplies, even though Afghanistan in the near future may take over this position."[81] According to the United Nations Office on Drugs and Crime, "the Chinese heroin market is no longer supplied exclusively from the Golden Triangle, but may now be supplied also by Afghan heroin, which is trafficked via Pakistan, Central Asia, Africa and Gulf countries. . . . On the basis of tentative estimates, Afghan heroin may now command a 25 per cent share (15–17 tons) of the Chinese opiate market."[82]

After reviewing the Chinese law enforcement literature on cross-border drug trafficking between Afghanistan and China, Murray Scot Tanner of the Center for Naval Analyses (CNA) reached the following conclusion: "Between 2005 and 2009, Chinese police sources estimate that Golden Crescent heroin rose from a very small percentage to nearly one-third of all the illegal heroin seized by Chinese police nationwide."[83] According to Tanner, Chinese police confiscated just 14.2 kilos of Golden Crescent heroin in 2005, equivalent to less than 1 percent of heroin seizures nationally. It increased to more than 65 kilos in 2006, 147.4 kilos in 2007, 381 kilos in 2008, and 1,500 kilos in 2009.

Despite these claims by Western sources, our sense is that the Golden Crescent remains a minor but growing source for the China market. While the Chinese government keeps a wary eye on its northwestern frontier, data from police seizures continue to suggest that the Golden Triangle remains China's top concern. In the 2012 annual report, Chinese authorities admitted that more and more heroin had been trafficked into China from the Golden Crescent region, but there was a decline from the peak year of 2009. According to the report: "The infiltration of 'Golden Crescent' heroin was intensified, 10 'Golden Crescent' drug cases were cracked in Xinjiang in 2011, 4 of which had a seizure of heroin over 1 kg, and there were totally 610.9 kg of heroin seized in these 10 cases, which increased by 20 times than 2010."[84] The amount of heroin from the Golden Crescent seized—610.9 kg—represented 8 percent of all heroin seized in 2012.

Characteristics of the Burmese Drug Market

The opiate market in the border areas between Burma and China, especially on the Burmese side where a number of armed groups are operating as quasi-states, is unique in the sense that up until very recently, opium cultivation was not only legal, but also aggressively promoted by armed group leaders through the implementation of an opium tax.[85] As a result, the buying and selling of opium, from a few *kang* to hundreds of *joi*, was a major component of the local economy; almost everyone in these special regions played a role in the opiate market and benefited from it. People in these regions were also not afraid or ashamed to admit their participation in the small-scale cultivation or trading of opium.

Even though the opium market was completely legitimate in the Burmese side of the border areas and the existence of the opium trade there was mainly fueled by the heroin market, the latter did not enjoy the same level of legitimacy as the former, regardless of the size. Because the heroin market was illegal in these border areas, the size and organization, the operating methods and market structure, and the sociopolitical impact of the heroin market were significantly different from the opium market. As a result, when we examine the characteristics of the opiate market, it might be a good idea to separate opium from heroin because they are not considered the same in terms of legality in parts of the world.

Paoli et al. considered Burma, along with Afghanistan, to be the two non-enforcement countries.[86] Burma has been in turmoil for many years, and there are more than a dozen quasi-states run by different ethnic groups who have little in common with the ruling Burmans. The military junta, before its demise, was in control of only a small area of the country, and there was always the possibility that armed groups in the border area might overrun the authorities in Rangoon or Mandalay. It is therefore not accurate to conclude that drug enforcement in Burma is nonexistent and that it is the stated policy of the Burmese government tolerates or even promotes the production of and trade in opiates. The government's stated policy is that opium cultivation and drug production are illegal, and the Burmese authorities have indeed conducted many military operations against drug producers and traffickers in the border area. However, because the Burmese authorities allowed Lou Xinghan and Khun Sa (before their deaths) to reside in Rangoon after they publicly announced their retirement from the drug trade, and because many businesses in Rangoon and Mandalay were alleged to be funded by drug money, Burma is considered an exemplar of a narco-state by many drug experts in the West. These experts have also claimed that high-ranking Burmese officials are either directly involved in, or at least directly benefit from, the drug trade. We believe such an assessment by Western researchers and policy analysts lacks empirical support and is misconstrued.

In the special regions such as the Wa, the Kokang, and the Mengla, opium cultivation by farmers was legal, according to the laws of these special regions. In fact, at the time when opium cultivation was legal, the leaders of these special regions tacitly encouraged their people to grow opium by installing an opium tax system that required farmers to pay an opium tax with opium only. Under pressure from the

Burmese government and the world community, Mengla banned opium growing in 1997, and Kokang and Wa followed suit in 2003 and 2005, respectively.

During the time when ethnic armed group leaders allowed, and even encouraged, their people to grow opium, it was easy for anyone there to observe that the valleys of the entire area were covered with poppy plants. Farmers also often brought their small amounts of opium to the markets to sell to opium buyers in the open. However, the massive cultivation of opium, and the buying and selling of opium in the open markets, can hardly be viewed as a de facto legal commodity, as Paoli et al. have suggested.[87] Once a certain amount of opium was packaged into a *joi*, it became a controversial commodity because of its presumed relationship with the illegal heroin business, and the majority of the people there rarely had the opportunity to handle, or even see, the opium they produce in *joi* units.

There are many levels of opium traders in Burma, ranging from buying and selling a few *kang* in the open markets to trading hundreds of *joi* behind closed doors. It is relatively easy for anyone with some start-up money to enter and exit the opium market. Almost everyone in some parts of Burma is engaged in the growing, selling, or buying of opium, so it is not possible for any group or local government to actually regulate or monopolize the opium trade. People in power (i.e., armed group leaders and their relatives) and people with good connections to those people in power (i.e., Chinese drug entrepreneurs) are more likely to engage in opium trade on a larger scale.

Most opium transactions are completed on the spot, the buyer paying the seller cash or another commodity. Many small-time opium buyers with a load of household utensils and clothes will comb the remote areas during harvest time to barter with opium growers. Verbal argument during these transactions is possible, but physical altercation, not to mention murder, has never been observed or reported. Many mid- and high-level opium traders we talked to, many of them female, also told us that they had never engaged in violence in their opium business.

A major portion of the opium cultivated in Burma is refined into heroin, and a major portion of the heroin is produced for foreign rather than local consumption. As a result, there is also a network of people—mostly local ethnic group leaders, local Chinese drug entrepreneurs, and buyers from overseas—who are engaged in producing, trading, and transporting heroin. Unlike the opium market, the heroin market is not easy to enter; it is highly secretive, and most of the people living in the area who are in touch with opium on a daily basis have never had a chance to come in contact with even a small amount of heroin, not to mention heroin entrepreneurs or heroin laboratories. Our key informants in the Wa area often shared with us stories about how innocent people were killed by Wa soldiers simply because they inadvertently crossed paths with a heroin laboratory hidden in a remote area. Thus, compared to the opium market, the heroin market is significantly more covert, difficult to enter, involves a smaller number of participants, and is more likely to attract law enforcement responses from both the local and the central authorities.

Heroin-related open violence is also rare. A shootout between heroin producers or dealers is unheard of, regardless of the fact that many people in the drug-producing areas carry guns and many in the drug trade are protected by heavily armed soldiers. Killing of government authorities by drug dealers is also uncommon; on a few occasions, however, police have shot and killed a drug entrepreneur.

Even though the heroin market is better guarded than the opium market, the existence of a heroin market in Burma, especially in the Shan State, is an open secret. Most people there know that most of the harvested opium is used to produce heroin for export. The methamphetamine market, on the other hand, is a completely different story. Methamphetamine tablets produced in Burma are mostly exported to Thailand, and the influx of the drug into Thailand has resulted in a drug epidemic that is deeply troubling to the Thai authorities. The Thai government launched a war on *yaba* (Thai popular name for methamphetamine) in 2003, which ended with the death of thousands of *yaba* dealers, presumably shot to death by Thai authorities as a form of extrajudicial killing. Seen as the number one national security threat by Thai officials, the yaba trade has also created several major crises between the authorities in Bangkok and Rangoon.[88] In the methamphetamine market, violence is much more common than either the opium or heroin markets.

In sum, the drug market in Burma can be categorized into the opium, heroin, and methamphetamine markets; the characteristics of these markets are diverse. Consequently, we should not generalize about the Burmese drug markets based on one of these three drugs. It is also fair to say that the Burmese drug market is relatively violence-free, most drug dealers in Burma maintain low profiles, and most drug transactions are carried out quietly behind closed doors.

3

Wholesale Heroin Trafficking

The process of moving heroin from the manufacturer's warehouse in Burma to addicts on the streets of China consists of multiple stages. Overall, these stages fall into four general categories: (1) crossing the border between Burma and China; (2) forwarding to Kunming or other locations in Yunnan Province for transshipment to other parts of China or overseas; (3) transportation to major transshipment hubs in China for further distribution; and (4) further distribution from wholesalers to mid-level dealers, street vendors, and eventually to users.

In the literature on drug trafficking, there is a tendency to view most cross-border drug trafficking activities as high-level, especially if the drug is transported from a source country to a transit or a destination country.[1] Our interviews in China, however, suggested that drug trafficking between Burma and China often consists of multiple layers. On the face of it, whoever is the closest to the source of the supply (or the manufacturer) should be ranked higher in the trafficking chain. However, the process of ranking the level of drug traffickers is no easy task. As we discovered in the field, while the cultivation and harvesting of opium poppies are largely self-regulated by the farmers scattered in impoverished locations in northern Burma, the sale of raw opium for processing and refining into heroin is tightly controlled by local warlords. In a sense, these warlords may be considered the "original" suppliers of heroin because all the manufacturers and the warehouses are essentially under their control or carry out their businesses in regions under warlord control. But, unlike their predecessors, current warlords themselves typically do not get involved directly in the drug business. Instead, they levy charges for the protection of the drug trade within their controlled territories as a way to fund their military and government operations. In principle, the highest level of traffickers includes those who can acquire any shipments from the warehouses on the Burma side regardless of the weight. In practice, however, we have come to realize that the weight of a drug consignment says a lot about how close the trafficker is to the source, particularly at the earlier stages. From an operational point of view, it would be difficult for a warlord to allow multiple "mules" to come and pick up a consignment from a warehouse. The exposure to potential risk is simply too high. Large quantities of drugs are often signs of the significant status a trafficker commands in the trafficking chain.

As discussed later in the book, while the ants-moving-house strategy is widely practiced by drug traffickers these days, whereby multiple mules are hired to break up a shipment of drugs, this often occurs at the mid- to lower levels of the trafficking business. When mules complete their courier duties and the total consignment becomes whole, the weight matters again. Moreover, from a legal point of view, weight is directly related to the severity of punishment. In the Chinese context, hundreds or tens of kilograms could be considered as high-level trafficking; several kilograms could be ranked as mid-level; and less than two kilograms could be viewed as low-level. Many low-level traffickers who are hired as couriers normally carried just a few hundred grams of heroin or less. In this chapter, we focus our discussion on the wholesale heroin trafficking (high and middle markets). In the following chapters, we will explore low-level heroin trafficking and the retail market. The trafficking of opium and methamphetamine from Burma to China, believed to occur on a much smaller scale than heroin, will be omitted here.

In the mid-1980s, several years after China opened its doors to the outside world, heroin from Burma began to show up in China on a massive scale.[2] Heroin users we interviewed in Kunming told us that, at the beginning of the heroin epidemic, drug users from China, especially those who were living in Yunnan Province, simply went over to Burma or traveled to the Chinese side of the border area to buy heroin and brought the drug back to Kunming. Because law enforcement authorities were not familiar with the drug at that time, chances of being arrested for possession of heroin were almost nonexistent. Within a few years, however, Chinese authorities came to realize the huge impact of heroin use and began to pay attention to the movement of heroin from Burma to China; this led to the trafficking of heroin by drug entrepreneurs who were non-users.

Major Trafficking Cases

On April 12, 1986, authorities in Yunnan seized 22 kilograms of heroin. The drug case, masterminded by drug traffickers from Thailand and Hong Kong, is considered the first major case since China came under Communist control in 1949.[3] Chinese authorities executed two defendants, including one Thai citizen. The same year, police in Zhenkang (a Chinese town located across from Burma's township of Kokang) arrested 13 suspects and confiscated 13.1 kilograms of heroin. Three traffickers were sentenced to death, and four received life sentences. It is safe to say that the trafficking of heroin from Burma to China began to develop shortly after China adopted the open door policy and began its economic reform.

After various ethnic armed groups in Burma signed cease-fire agreements with the central government in 1989, opium cultivation and heroin production in Burma, especially along the border area near China, began to increase significantly. As a result, there was also an increase in the number of major cross-border heroin trafficking cases. For example, in March 1990, Chinese authorities arrested more than 50 suspects for drug trafficking and seized 221 kilograms of heroin, about $185,000 in cash, several guns, and motor vehicles. The head of the group, Ma Yonghua, was executed by the authorities in Lanzhou. At that time, it was the largest ever heroin trafficking case in China. A month or so after that incident, Chinese drug enforcers dismantled another drug trafficking ring and arrested 140 drug traffickers. About 34 kilograms of heroin and about $88,500 in drug money were also confiscated. At the end of 1990, two more major heroin trafficking cases were uncovered: one case involved about 40 kilograms of heroin and the other, about 22 kilograms.

In 1992, the Chinese government decided to go after drug traffickers in Pingyuan, a border town in Yunnan dominated by Muslim people.[4] The Yunnan provincial government organized an 83-day drug elimination operation in Pingyuan. The vice mayor of the town and 854 other defendants were arrested on drug charges. Almost a thousand kilograms of heroin and 353 illegal weapons were also seized. In 1994 and 1995, two drug kingpins from Kokang—Yang Maoxian and Lee Guoting—were arrested and executed by the Chinese authorities.

However, the war against drug traffickers in Pingyuan and the execution of drug lords from Kokang appeared to have little impact on the heroin trade. Key informants in Kunming told us that Muslim drug dealers simply moved their operations from Pingyuan to other Muslim towns closer to Kunming. In March 1996, authorities in Guangzhou seized 221 kilograms of heroin from the Golden Triangle. A month later, another 600 kilograms were confiscated by Guangzhou authorities; the heroin was believed to have originated in the Wa area in Burma. Thirty-nine traffickers, including seven from Hong Kong, were arrested. Wang Shijiang, the leader of the group, was executed. The seizure was then hailed as the largest since 1949. That year, Khun Sa, a powerful drug kingpin active in the Thai-Burma border area, also surrendered to the Burmese government and agreed to live in Rangoon and be placed under constant government surveillance.[5]

For the next five years, no major heroin trafficking incidents were reported in the media. But then, in 2001, two major heroin cases were widely publicized in the Chinese press. The first case involved the arrests of two suspects in Baoshan with 102 kilograms of heroin hidden inside the handrails of a truck. The suspects confessed that the heroin was to be delivered to a man in Guangzhou. In the same year, law enforcers in Luoping in Yunnan discovered 672 kilograms of heroin hidden inside timbers in two trucks headed for Guangzhou.[6] A large amount of drug money was also seized after authorities broke up the trafficking ring.

In April 5, 2002, 14 suspects (two in Shenzhen, eleven in Burma, and one in Thailand) were arrested and 360 kilograms of heroin were seized. The drugs were destined for Hong Kong via Yunnan and Guangdong. The following year, drug enforcers at the Mukang Checkpoint discovered 284 kilograms of heroin inside two trucks filled with salted fishes. The same year, police in Mengting (Lincang County) confiscated 463 kilograms of heroin. The mastermind—Liu Yikang—was arrested in Thailand and brought back to Kunming to stand trial.

In June 2004, authorities in Kunming uncovered 501 kilograms of heroin inside a truck that originated in Baoshan and was headed for Chongqing. According to Chinese government reports, a Mr. Li gave a Mr. Yu and a Mr. Yang (both from Longling, Yunnan, the two were cousins working in Ruili) about $36,000 to buy a secondhand truck equipped with a large water tank. They found the truck in Baoshan.

Under Li's instruction, Yu and Yang made two trial trips from Ruili to Kunming. On June 5, Li and his people installed a huge water tank onto the truck near the border (probably between Ruili and Muse) and he asked Yu and Yang to drive the truck to Chongqing (later, Li wanted the truck to go to Guangdong instead). Li promised to give the two about $180,000 after the delivery. Yu, Yang, and the two drivers of the truck were arrested near Kunming. After the police pried open the water tank, they found 806 bricks of heroin weighing 501 kilograms. The fate of Mr. Li and his boss was unknown.

No major heroin trafficking cases were reported in the Chinese media after that incident, even though there were reports that large consignments of heroin were seized in Burma or Thailand. For example, in September 10, 2005, 496 kilograms of heroin destined for Thailand were seized in Kentung, Burma. About 70 United Wa State Army (UWSA) soldiers were arrested, including a promising new leader. In January 25, 2009, 89 kilograms of heroin were seized in Rangoon. In July 10, 2009, Burmese authorities seized about 1,000 kilograms of heroin in a truck on the outskirts of Tachilek.

These sorts of trafficking cases, reported in the media, make it clear that there are well-organized, high-level heroin trafficking rings active in Burma, Thailand, Hong Kong, and China. These traffickers were able to move hundreds of kilograms of heroin out of Burma and, more often than not, their drugs were transported into China via Yunnan Province over land on trucks. We do not know what percentage of the drugs imported into China every year was detected by the Chinese authorities. According to our field contacts and interviews with police officials, intelligence played a key role in most of those uncovered heroin cases.

To provide a more nuanced understanding of these high-level drug traffickers, we present in the following sections one high-level and one mid-level heroin trafficker.

Tan Xiaolin: A Heroin Kingpin

Tan Xiaolin was born in a remote village in Lezhi County, Sichuan Province, in 1962. His father, a college graduate, was forced to quit his government job in a city and return to his hometown after being labeled a "rightist" by the Chinese communists. Not long after Tan's father was purged from the government, the first wife of Tan's father committed suicide, leaving behind three children. Three years later, Tan's father married again and Tan was later born. Both Tan's father and mother did not have a regular job; he made some money by helping people to write letters, and she knit. His 54-year-old father died when Tan was only 13. The family struggled, eating only yams at every meal.[7]

Tan quit school after realizing how hard his mother had to work to raise four children on her own. Tan worked odd jobs for a while, and then he began to travel to Guangdong, Zhejiang, and Shanghai to bring back merchandise to sell in his hometown. Starting in 1982, he bought plastic sandals in the Zhejiang area and sold them in the Sichuan area. Within a few years, by the age of 21, he had made a small fortune.

Later, when Tan's friends invited him to join their herb business, he invested all his money in the newly established company. Tan and his friends began to transport poppy shells and fake bear claws from Yunnan to Sichuan. One day, several of his business partners were arrested, and their commodities were confiscated. Tan was not arrested because his partners did not mention him to the authorities, but the incident ruined him financially.

After wandering in Yunnan for two years, he met a man named Chen, who was then manager of an import-export company in Ruili. In 1992, Chen invited Tan, by that time known as "Little Sichuan," to cross the border to attend the birthday party of an influential figure. There, he met the daughter of Yang Guodong, a major drug producer and the financial minister of the Mongu Special Region in Burma, one of many special regions in the Shan State. Tan eventually married Yang's daughter and moved to Mongu. With the help of his father-in-law, Tan started his own small business. His wife gave birth to two daughters.

One day, Tan returned home and discovered his wife's badly beaten body. Two drug addicts who had burglarized Tan's place looking for money had killed her; the two children were home when their mother was murdered. Following his wife's murder, Tan quickly lost interest in his small business and began to engage in the drug business to get rich quickly.

Tan's first drug deal was carried out in Tachilek. He and his partner bought 80 kilograms of heroin in a place called Naimou Mountain and transported the drug to Tachilek. The two of them paid $240 per kilogram in Burma, and sold it for about $3,650 per kilogram in Tachilek. After splitting the profits with his partner, Tan pocketed about $136,000 on that single deal. As Tan began to make tens of thousands of dollars from the heroin trade, he also began to invest in a variety of legitimate businesses in Burma. In time, he became the finance minister of the Guardian Unit of Mongu Special Region and vice president of an overseas Chinese association in Burma.

Tan's hero was Alberto Fujimori, the former president of Peru who was of Japanese descent. After making tons of money from both legitimate businesses and the illicit drug economy, Tan quickly established a close relationship with Burmese generals by frequently visiting and donating money to famous Buddhist temples often visited by the generals. At one point, when the Shwedagon Pagoda in Rangoon was raising money for a major renovation, Tan donated about $200,000. According to Chang Ting, author of *China Always Says "No" to Narcotics*:

> With the help of Yang Guodong, Tan Xiaolin quickly followed the drug trafficking road, which was very common in the locality. At first, he traded drugs mainly in the border area between Thailand and Myanmar. He changed his status constantly, going from a hired hand for making drugs to a drug lord. Just when his business was growing, something went wrong with the route on which he depended for transporting his drugs. After 1994, because of the incessant wars on the border between Thailand and Myanmar, his drug transportation route was often cut off, and the drug lords also bullied each other in the process. Tan Xiaolin decided to find another route to get his drugs through. In 1995, he left the place where he had lived for three years and moved his family to Muse town in Myanmar.[8]

After Tan moved to Muse, opposite the town of Ruili, he began to transport heroin into China via the Muse-Ruili route. He was alleged to have established a well-organized drug trafficking organization with a clear division of labor. Tan's organization "set up a number of bases inside and outside of Myanmar, established a warehouse, rebuilt camouflaged vehicles, used code words for communication, supervised each other, transported drugs in sections, had a single line of contact and used other devious means to avoid police and customs inspections."[9] According to Chinese authorities, Tan's organization was responsible for the trafficking of three tons of heroin into China between 1995 and 2001, including the 490 kilograms of heroin confiscated by the authorities in Guangzhou City in November 1999.[10]

Tan Xiaolin appeared on the radar of the Chinese drug enforcement authorities as soon as he arrived in Muse in 1995, and he knew it. However, he decided to carry on with his drug activities, often conducting trial runs to evade the Chinese authorities. He also stopped going to China after the November 1999 drug bust, believing that if he stayed on the Burmese side, the Chinese could not touch him.

On November 4, 1999, authorities in Guangzhou City confiscated more than 100 kilograms of heroin transported by truck from Muse to China. It belonged to Tan Xiaolin. In the process, Chinese authorities accidentally discovered more than 12 tons of amphetamine inside the warehouse where Tan's heroin was found. The 554 boxes of amphetamine belonged to Tan's partner in China who was producing amphetamine with a group of associates while simultaneously working with Tan to import hundreds of kilograms of heroin into China.[11]

On April 12, 2001, the Chinese authorities made a formal request to the Burmese authorities to arrest Tan Xiaolin for drug trafficking. Eight days later, the Burmese authorities arrested Tan, and the Chinese authorities followed by apprehending 18 associates of Tan in the cities of Kunming, Diqing, Baoshan, and Chongqing. On April 23, 2001, Chinese officials arrived in Muse to bring Tan back to China. Tan was found guilty of drug trafficking and executed in Kunming on June 25, 2004.[12]

One high-ranking drug enforcement official in Beijing who was directly involved in overseeing the investigation and capture of Tan commented on how the big players in the drug trade differed from the rest:

> When the major players are arrested, they behave very differently from the commoners in the drug trade. They are ready to accept their fate. For instance, when we finally caught Tan Xiaolin, I felt like I had known him for a long time, because I had been in charge of his case. When I talked to him, he was quite calm and fatalistic. He knew his luck ran out. He was quite honest about his business operation and told us about

> his organization. He took responsibility for what he did. He could not hide it anyway, since we had gathered his information for years and knew the people around him. Smaller-scale traffickers, however, would lie to the end, and try to get away with as much as possible at every turn during interrogations.

It is interesting to note that, since Tan's case in the early 2000s, there have been no other cases of similar significance either in the size of the trafficking organization or quantities of the drugs transported. Either the big traffickers have greatly improved their operations and learned how to avoid detection and apprehension, or the drug trade has become more fragmented and dominated largely by mid-level or smaller operators whose capabilities are only in the hundreds of grams at most. When a large trafficking organization is broken up, it encourages many small operators to enter the system and replace the large organization. In any case, it has been more than a decade and there have been no cases as spectacular as Tan's.

Jiang Jiatian and Yang Jufen: A Family Business

In December 2010, when a young woman who was sentenced to death for heroin trafficking announced that she was willing to donate her organs after her execution, the news shocked China, as few Chinese volunteer their organs after death—let alone drug trafficker. Because she was also a mistress of a major crime figure who was also sentenced to death for his role in the drug trade plus a variety of other serious crimes, her story, along with his, was widely reported in the Chinese media. In this section, we provide a picture of a relatively typical mid-level heroin trafficking organization in China by reviewing the news reports about this couple's engagement in the heroin trade.

Yang Jufen, a 29-year-old woman, once said that when she entered the heroin trade, she knew she would have to face the death penalty. She was born in Pingda Township of Yunnan's Longling County in 1981. Pingda is close to Burma. People in Pingda often walk over to the Burmese side without having to go through any checkpoints. It is also relatively easy for people in Pingda to take a bus to Nansan Township of Zhenkang County and cross a checkpoint to arrive in Laukkai of

Kokang on the Burma side, one of the major drug production and distribution centers of the Golden Triangle.

After graduating from elementary school, Yang Jufen stayed home and helped her family with house chores and farming. In 1997, when she was 16, she went to Ruili to work. There, she met a man who in 2002 invited her to move to Kunming to work for him in his foot massage parlor. One source said the man's business in Kunming was actually a "hair salon," a euphemism for a front for prostitution in China. Two years after she arrived in Kunming, she met Jiang Jiatian, a 51-year-old married man who was three years older than her father. After Jiang rented her an apartment and gave her a bank card with a $1,200 credit, she agreed to be his mistress. A year later, Yang gave birth to a baby girl. She also began to develop a gambling habit.

Jiang Jiatian was born in a small village in Sichuan Province in 1953. After attending school for only two years, he dropped out and stayed home to become a farmer. In his twenties, he married and had three children. After realizing he was barely able to support his family as a farmer, Jiang went to Kunming in 1990 at the age of 37 to look for work. He found a job as a construction worker, but quit after becoming convinced that hard work was not for someone with a brain like his. Later, he became a scalper in the Kunming Train Station, which also happened to be a major retail heroin market in the city.[13] In 1998, he began to sell heroin bags to drug users in the "villages within a city" (*chengzhongcun*) near the train station.[14] A year later, Jiang had established himself as a major player in the heroin retail business around the train station, supplying $12 heroin bags to small hotel operators in the area who in turn would sell them at their hotels. Jiang would pay a $1.20 commission per bag to the hotel operators. According to the Chinese authorities, because of Jiang, heroin retail activities around the train station were rampant in 2001. Police in Kunming formed a task force to go after Jiang, and on September 2001, they caught him with 30 grams of heroin and sent him to jail for 11 months.

Upon his release from jail, Jiang Jiatian stopped dealing heroin for a while. However, when Yang Jufen's father, Yang Guoyin, came to visit his pregnant daughter in Kunming in 2004, Jiang was back in the heroin trade. Mr. Yang's second son was arrested for heroin trafficking and received a suspended death sentence. Because Jiang and one of Yang's family members were arrested for drug crimes, and because Jiang and Mr. Yang were about the same age, Jiang and Mr. Yang quickly established a close relationship. Mr. Yang told his "son-in-law" that he knew some drug distributors in Burma and that he would like to bring heroin to Kunming for sale. Jiang told his "father-in-law" that if he could bring heroin to Kunming, he could hook him up with buyers there.

Knowing that Jiang would help her father sell heroin in Kunming, Yang Jufen gave her father $960 to take to Burma. After Mr. Yang arrived in Burma, he found a person from his hometown who sold him 80 grams of heroin for $8.40 a gram. With the heroin in hand, Mr. Yang first went back to his home in Longling, and then traveled to Kunming. When Mr. Yang showed up in Kunming, Jiang Jiatian introduced a buyer to Mr. Yang and his daughter; the buyer paid the Yangs $36 per gram for a total of $2,880. After that first successful deal, Mr. Yang began to make regular bus trips from Kunming to Nansan with a bag of cash, walk across a checkpoint and arrive in Laukkai, where he would buy a small amount of heroin to take back to Kunming. Often, Mr. Yang would go back to his home in Pingda Township in Longling County to take a break before returning to Kunming. Whenever Mr. Yang was back in Kunming with the heroin, he would keep it at his wife's place in Kunming. His daughter would then contact Li Wencai, a female drug dealer, to go to Mrs. Yang's home for the transaction. Ms. Li would arrive by motorbike, carrying a black plastic bag filled with cash. According to Mrs. Yang, she had never seen so much cash in her whole life. Ms. Li would then leave with the heroin in her backpack. During that time, Mr. Yang brought back only a few hundred grams of heroin each trip; the most he ever carried at one time was three units (one unit equals 350 grams) for a little more than a kilogram.

Around October 2007, Yang Jufen told Jiang Jiatian that she would like to operate a long-distance passenger bus between Nansan and Kunming. Xie Mingxiang, a bus driver, helped the couple buy a bus for $142,000. The bus was registered under Jiang's name. Ms. Yang told Jiang that Mr. Xie suggested that they should be bringing heroin from the border area to Kunming for resale because every other bus running between Nansan and Kunming more or less did so. Jiang agreed, and he and Ms. Yang took a trip to the border area just before the 2008 Chinese New Year to find a seller.

After the couple arrived in Nansan, they met Jiang's contact there, a woman known as "Big Sister from Lincang." In a hotel in Nansan, the Big Sister then introduced the couple to a woman carrying a baby. That woman was from Kokang, and she was known as Lao Shun. Jiang told Lao Shun he wanted eight units of "commodity," and Lao Shun said it would cost $8,500 for a pair of units. Jiang was able to negotiate the price down to $7,800. Later, Xie Mingxiang, the bus driver, transported the "commodity" back to Kunming—hiding the heroin in a toolbox in the bus. The couple flew back to Kunming from Lincang. According to Xie Mingxiang, Yang gave him $440 a month to work as a bus driver and $220 per unit for transporting the heroin from Nansan to Kunming. Another bus driver worked along with Xie, but that driver was never told that the bus was being used to transport heroin.

Later, Jiang told the Chinese authorities: "I was responsible for setting up the connection to the source, and after the 'bridge' was built, I let Yang Guoyin (Jufen's father) be in charge. The first trip was an exploration, and we did not know whether it was going to be successful or not, so that's why we did not ask Yang Guoyin to come along."

Not long after the 2008 Chinese New Year, Jiang and Ms. Yang decided to traffic heroin a second time. Jiang later admitted to the authorities: "Jufen and I each gave Yang Guoyin $15,500, and he went to Laukkai [Kokang] to buy drugs from the dealer that we'd met the first time. He was gone for a month before he came back to Kunming." On this trip Yang returned with 12 units of heroin, and the drugs were again transported to Kunming from Nansan by Xie Mingxiang, the bus driver. Yang took another trip to Burma in June 2008, with the same amount of money, and bought the same amount of heroin as the previous time. Yang's daughter, Yang Jufen, regularly dealt with four dealers in Kunming: Xiao Shuan, Lao Liao, Li Wencai, and Li Xiayun. She would sell a unit for $14,000 to the first two dealers, and $12,000 a unit to the other two dealers and front them the drug if they wanted her to, because they were considered by Ms. Yang to be regular business partners.

On June 12, 2008, when Ms. Li Wencai returned home from Mrs. Yang's place with 347 grams of heroin and was about to sell it to another dealer, she was arrested by the police. After Li's arrest, Jiang and Ms. Yang stopped their drug dealing activities for a short while. However, on August 27, 2008, Ms. Yang decided to ask her father to take another trip to Burma; this time, he left Kunming with more than $70,000. He went over to Kokang from Nansan, bought 19 units of heroin from Lao Shun, the regular supplier, and walked back over to the Chinese side with a handbag of heroin that weighed about seven kilograms. Shortly after he set foot on the Chinese side, he was arrested by the authorities who were likely watching his every move since the arrest of Li Wencai two months earlier.

According to Yang Jufen, between 2004 and the time she was arrested in September 2008, she and her family had trafficked a total of 60 kilograms of heroin. She admitted that she was involved in seven major drug deals, in which 85 units of heroin changed hands. Because each unit weighed about 350 grams, the seven drug deals amounted to almost 30 kilograms.

Around 2008, before he was arrested, Jiang Jiatian had invested his drug money in 11 business entities, including three teashops, three restaurants, two small hotels, a transportation company, and a wedding company. He was also in possession of more than 20 luxury cars. The Chinese authorities accused Jiang and his associates of using their teashops and hotels to extort money from their customers, and the restaurants as cover to launder the drug money.

Eventually, 41 defendants (14 of them female) were arrested and charged with engaging in a mafia-like organized crime group, drug trafficking, extortion, fraud, and other crimes.[15] Many family members of Yang Jufen were implicated, including her father, mother, brother, and sister-in-law. From the Jiang family, Jiang's son, one of his mistresses, and mother-in-law were also arrested. On December 7, 2009, Yang, Jiang, Yang's father, and Xie Mingxiang were sentenced to death. Jiang Manyin (Jufen's mother) received a life sentence, and Jiang Tailai (Jiatian's son) was sentenced to 18 years. Li Wenchai (the buyer in Kunming) received a suspended death sentence. On August 27, 2010, the court turned down Yang Jufen's appeal. Yang and the rest of the defendants all denied that they were members of a mafia-like criminal organization.

The Jiang Jiatian and Yang Jufen heroin case provided us with a rare window into the social organization of mid-level drug trafficking in China. Some of the characteristics associated with the Jiang and Yang organization are relatively typical of other mid-level drug trafficking organizations. First, the Jiang and Yang group was primarily a family business. Jiang and Yang were lovers (and very much like a married couple), and all the key figures in their drug business were either immediate family members or close relatives. Jiang and Yang were the investors and masterminds, Yang's father was the one who traveled to Burma to buy the drugs, Yang's mother was responsible for providing a place to store the drugs, and Yang's brother and Jiang's son played major roles in their drug trafficking activities. Only the bus driver Xie Mingxiang and the buyers in Kunming were not blood relatives of Jiang and Yang. According to the defendants, because most of them were related by blood, not only did they trust one another; they were also able to share, or not share, the profits from the drug business without any animosity. For example, Yang's father said he did not make any money from the drug business; he was doing it for his five-year-old granddaughter, a child of Jiang and Yang. Many of the other drug trafficking groups we met in China were family-based.

Second, people at this level normally do not use drugs. Unlike the retailers we examine in chapter 6, mid-level heroin traders not only refrain from experimenting with the drug they are trading; they also despise those people who are addicted to the commodity they are trading. For example, there was only one person in the Jiang and Yang organization who used heroin, and that was Jiang's son (Jiang Tailai). However, according to the senior Jiang, after he found out his son was using heroin, he beat him up so badly that the son later quit using heroin.

Third, violence is rare at this level of the heroin trade in China. In the 74-page indictments of the Jiang and Yang mafia-like criminal organization, not a single violent incident was mentioned. The prosecutors also stressed that Jiang was not a violent man, even though he was dubbed the "Godfather of Nanhou Village" in the media. None of the defendants who were accused of drug trafficking had ever armed themselves, nor were ever implicated in a violent incident. The buying of heroin in Burma, the transportation of the drug into China, and the selling of the drug to buyers in China all proceeded quietly and peacefully for the Jiang and Yang group for a period of four years, between 2004 and 2008, without any drug-related conflict between them and the sellers in Burma or the buyers in China.

Drug Trafficking in Southern China

To shed more light on the issue of high-level drug trafficking between Burma and China, we examine heroin trafficking in Southern China, focusing on Guangdong Province. The province is a major destination for Burmese heroin, not only to satisfy the demands of large numbers of heroin users living there, but also to meet the needs of heroin distributors in other parts of China or from overseas.[16] For example, a drug enforcement official in Fuzhou City told us that heroin in Fujian Province mostly comes from Guangdong.

During the 1980s and 1990s, traffickers from Guangdong Province and Hong Kong made trips to border regions in search of suppliers of drugs. Some of them made trips into the Wa State on the Burmese side and tried to find suppliers on their own. This practice has largely stopped, according to drug enforcement officials and drug dealers. Drug traffickers in southern China or elsewhere either hire mules or contract other traffickers to bring the goods into their territory. Trafficking routes from any given two points are typically well protected and nurtured once they have been developed. Traffickers rarely venture outside their transportation zones because such a move is often risky. According to one incarcerated trafficker from Guangdong Province:

> The reason is simple. If you are from Guangdong or Hong Kong, what business do you have coming to the border area or even to Yunnan? In the border area, people like me stand out because of our identification cards and our accents, which attract attention in hotels, restaurants, or even at bus stations.[17] Military police at checkpoints pay particular attention to non-native travelers, question them, and search their belongings. You can make up excuses like looking for business opportunities or exploring local products for export to Guangdong. But soon you will run out of such excuses. Even local contacts you have established cannot be trusted these days; there are many government informants. They will take your money, then turn around, and report you to the police to get another cash award.[18]

Coastal provinces in southern China, such as Guangdong and Fujian, have always attracted drug traffickers and dealers alike because of vibrant commercial activities and rapid economic development. Guangzhou, for instance, has become a major illicit drug transshipment center in southern China.[19] According to senior drug enforcement officials in Guangzhou, the size of the addict population has remained largely stable over the years but the city of 12 million people has become increasingly cosmopolitan, with not only a large domestic "floating" population but also an increasing number of foreign visitors seeking economic opportunities. One senior drug enforcement official of the provincial government openly acknowledged that Guangzhou has become a favorite gathering place for drug traffickers home and abroad. He noted,

> Guangdong Province leads the nation in economic development and ranks far ahead of other provinces in terms of its GDP output. As its capital city, Guangzhou attracts people of all stripes, including drug traffickers. Most people in China will agree that Guangdong enjoys a reputation for business efficiency and reliability. You don't hear much about people in Guangdong trying to sell shoddy products or businesspeople ripping off customers in their pursuit of profits. In fact, Guangdong dominates the country in the manufacturing of high-tech and high-end consumer products, from automobiles to electronics, and from air conditioners to furniture. Anything that is made in Guangdong is typically thought to be high in quality and fair in pricing.
>
> In a strange way, this good business reputation has also extended into the underworld of drug trafficking and distribution. For instance, we recently seized a large consignment of ice in Guangzhou that was destined for Hunan Province. However the lab report came back to indicate that the chemical signature of this consignment matched the drugs manufactured locally in Hunan. This was not an isolated event. There have been several seizures of drugs that were transported to Guangdong just so they could be sold back to Hunan and other provinces.

Such a roundabout trafficking scheme would seem not only inefficient but also expensive because consumer products stamped with "Made in Guangdong" labels typically command higher prices. This senior drug enforcement official offered two possible explanations as to why traffickers chose to send drugs this way.

> First, these events may be purely coincidental because drug trafficking is like other illegitimate business activities where the dealers carefully guard their trade secrets and try to cover their tracks. No one knows where the drug consignment may be heading to next. Therefore, although drugs are manufactured in Hunan or other places, they are shipped to Guangdong because dealers here have received purchase requests from interior China. Drugs made in Hunan, for instance, are then sold back to the same place where they were produced. Unlike legitimate products that can be researched and cross-referenced in an open market, illicit drugs are manufactured and transported under utmost secrecy. Illicit drug makers may not have venues to unload their products locally. Another explanation is that manufacturers of illicit drugs prefer sending their merchandise to Guangdong for a good price. Buyers elsewhere like to purchase drugs from Guangdong because they can count on the quality and quantity.

Another senior police official concurred with this observation that "Guangzhou is now used by drug dealers as a major transshipment location for drugs from Yunnan and other parts of China. The city is like a big wholesale distribution center. Heroin is transported from Yunnan Province and out to other places. Hong Kong is not the only outlet, not even the major one."

Despite proximity to Hong Kong and Southeast Asia, provinces in southern China are primarily used by traffickers to move drugs to local distributors or export to neighboring provinces. Although it is possible some drugs may eventually find their way into the North American market, by most accounts from drug enforcement officials in Guangdong and Fujian as well as Beijing, drugs transported into mainland China from the Golden Triangle are largely intended for domestic consumption, with limited quantities going abroad to nearby countries.

Dongguan is a manufacturing center located between Guangzhou and Shenzhen, and the many towns within Dongguan are home to thousands of factories owned by foreign entrepreneurs. A small factory owner in Hojie (a town within the jurisdiction of Dongguan) who claimed that he used to have a bunch of "followers" (insinuating that he was a gang leader) told us how he once was involved in the heroin business:

> Besides this factory, I also collect debt, but I only get involved if the amount is $12,000 or more. In the past, I also "gambled" in the drug business. This means, whenever a drug trader is planning to move a consignment of drug but does not have enough capital, I will give him $2,500, and if the deal goes through, I may get back as much as $12,000. If the deal fails, this means my money is also *paotang* (soaked or wasted). A few days ago, someone called me and asked me whether I am still interested in doing this, and I said not anymore.
>
> Now (January 2010), the retail price of a gram of heroin in Hojie is $52; in the border area, you get a gram for about $11. A mule is paid $3,000 per trip, and he or she will transport between 500 to 1,000 grams per trip, and the person who is hired to watch the mule is paid $1,500. The main purpose is to make sure that the mule will not run away with the commodity, not to alert us when the mule is arrested. I personally experienced three times when the mule disappeared with the drug.

Drug traffickers and dealers in Guangdong resemble those in Yunnan and other parts of China—they are a mixed bunch; they come from diverse backgrounds. However, a few patterns have emerged that are unique to the Guangdong context. In Guangdong, drug traffickers typically fall into three categories: they are usually ex-convicts, failed businessmen, or foreigners. One senior drug enforcement official in Guangdong Province described how ex-convicts have become a major recruitment pool for drug traffickers:

> Most drug traffickers do not have decent careers or employable skills. However, not having a career or any employable skills is not a sufficient condition for entry into the drug trafficking business. These people feel frustrated by the lack of opportunities to become rich quickly. For instance, many traffickers were ex-offenders who were exiled to Xinjiang Province in 1983.[20] After completing their sentences, many have now returned to Guangdong. Guess what? These people, after being exposed to prison subculture, have become seasoned criminals and are less amicable to conformity. They have few reasons to abide by the law. Besides, when these people returned to their hometowns and saw their peers all having made money and accumulated sizeable material wealth, they wanted to be just like them. With few money-making venues available

> to these ex-convicts, drug trafficking becomes a natural choice. Similarly, those who have served time in prison for other reasons are another main source of prospective traffickers. These people are usually looked down upon in society and have few legitimate employment opportunities. Drug trafficking becomes a way of survival.

In addition to ex-convicts, entrepreneurs who are down on their luck in legitimate business ventures, are desperate to make a comeback, and are unwilling to give up a lifestyle that they have grown accustomed to will enter the drug business. Most of these people are merchants by trade who buy and sell consumer products and whose social networks often include contacts with the underworld. Since few legitimate opportunities can bring about sizeable fortunes as quickly as drug trafficking can, its risk and consequence somehow become acceptable in a time of desperation. A third characteristic of drug traffickers in Guangdong, particularly in Guangzhou, is the number of foreigners involved in the business. According to local senior police officials, the number of foreigners residing in Guangzhou has increased steadily in recent years, and so has the number of foreign drug traffickers. These foreign traffickers, many of them of African descent, have shown up in Guangdong's investigations with increased frequency. One senior drug enforcement intelligence analyst from the provincial government noted:

> I am talking about people from Nigeria, Kenya, Congo, and South Africa, places that we don't normally think of as source countries or destination regions. As we look deeper into the kind of transactions they engage in, we have come to realize that these are no ordinary traffickers. They are merchants who treat drugs as hard currency to buy other things. They smuggle drugs into China mostly in exchange for money to purchase and export consumer products back to their home countries. Chinese products are hot items in these countries. They have figured out that a quick and convenient way to acquire hard currency is through drug trafficking. We have arrested quite a few of these people. Although there are increased efforts to monitor the movement of foreigners living in Guangzhou, in reality there is little we can do.
>
> Usually, Chinese police officers tend to go easy on foreigners because of language and cultural difficulties. Furthermore, Chinese police

> consider cases involving foreigners sensitive and not worth the trouble. There is a common saying: nothing is trivial when it comes to matters involving foreign countries. We are talking about international incidents if we don't handle foreigners carefully. Most police officers simply want to avoid such cases. Unfortunately, foreign drug traffickers know this weakness of ours. So whenever they are confronted or questioned, they will speak their native languages. They know well that our police officers are reluctant to deal with foreigners.

Despite their reluctance, Chinese authorities catch and convict foreign drug traffickers from time to time. However, the extradition process with foreign countries is often complicated, for legal as well as political reasons. One senior official in the Ministry of Public Security in Beijing explained: "We follow stricter procedures when it comes to foreign nationals caught trafficking drugs in China. For instance, the threshold for the death penalty in China does not require much, and foreign nationals living in China are subject to our legal procedures. But if a foreign national is sentenced to death, this decision must be reviewed by the Supreme Court.[21] In other words, the death penalty for a foreigner is reviewed with far greater scrutiny than that for a Chinese citizen."

Other drug enforcement officials in Guangdong and Fujian also claim to have noticed an increase of foreign drug traffickers trying to break into the Chinese market. One senior police academy instructor in Fujian said: "I can tell you that members of a drug cartel in Colombia have recently begun to explore the Chinese market. On at least two occasions, drug traffickers from Latin America smuggled several kilos of cocaine into China to test the market and see if they can find a local buyer. It turned out that these traffickers did not make any money. The several kilos of cocaine were just used to try out the market."

Characteristics of High-Level Drug Trafficking in China

No Monopoly or Cartel

Compared to high-level drug markets in other parts of the world, the high-level heroin business in China is unique in many ways. First, there is neither a drug cartel nor plaza (drug trafficking corridor) in China.

Howard Campbell, a sociologist, characterized the drug trade in Mexico as follows:

> Transportation routes and territories controlled by specific cartels in collusion with police, military, and government officials, as noted above, are known as plazas. Control of a plaza gives the drug lord and police commander of an area the power to charge less-powerful traffickers tolls, known as *pisos*. Generally, one main cartel dominates a plaza at any given time, although this control is often contested or subverted by internal conflict, may be disputed among several groups, and is subject to rapid change. Attempts by rival cartels to ship drugs through a plaza or take over a plaza controlled by their enemies has led to much of the recent drug violence in Mexico.[22]

This characterization of the drug trade in Mexico is not applicable to the high-level drug trade in China. In China, drug cartels that we know of do not exist, especially after Tan Xiaolin, and no drug group there is powerful enough to claim a particular drug route as their own or charge other drug traffickers a toll for using a particular drug route. All the major roads connecting Burma and China are heavily guarded by the Chinese authorities, and high-level drug traffickers can only hope and pray that their trucks will not be searched while traveling on these roads. Many high-level drug traffickers are active in China, but the concept of "turf" has yet to develop among these drug entrepreneurs.

Because of the government's relentless pursuit of drug kingpins, high-level drug traffickers are extremely cautious in choosing who to trust and who to work with. As one ranking police official in Yunnan elaborated on the government's pursuit of drug kingpins:

> Cross-border drug trafficking activities are always organized. There is always a network for these traffickers. Because of the risk and money involved, it is not possible for drug traffickers to operate like street vendors. The big kingpins are mostly behind the scenes. They must know who is working for them and often investigate in many ways their own people. Sometimes, a boss would walk around a member of the trafficking group to get a sense, or observe from a distance and sometimes

> follow their own people around. They must be able to trust those working for them. To reduce risk, drug trafficking organizations are mostly well defined in their division of labor. Even within the same task, such as transportation, there are multiple individuals involved in different stages of the shipment. That the planning is meticulous and careful and secrecy is a must.

Despite their appearance of organization, as suggested by the Chinese police official quoted previously, high-level drug traffickers in China are not in a position to monopolize any segment or region of the heroin market, not to mention maintain a monopoly over the entire Chinese heroin market. These high-level heroin entrepreneurs are also not capable of encroaching on other types of drug markets, such as the amphetamine-type stimulant market or ketamine powder market. After the arrest of Liu Zhaohua, the man who was responsible for the production of the largest amount of ATS in China's history, he was asked about his relationship to Tan Xiaolin, the heroin kingpin described previously. Liu said: "Of course, I know him; we did meet a few times. However, I did not have a close relationship with him; he was in the no. 4 [heroin] business, and I never have a high opinion of people who are in the no. 4 business."[23]

Even though an ATS producer like Liu Zhaohua was not impressed with high-level heroin dealers, most of the people we talked to in China agreed that these heroin dealers were not ordinary criminals. According to a longtime Kunming businessman:

> The big dealers in Kunming are not street thugs or gangsters. If you see them, you won't know that they are in the drug business. They all dress nicely and speak and act in a sophisticated way. The police know who these people are, but they can't or won't do anything about them. Actually, the police strategy is to attack poison with poison (*yidugongdu*). That is, the police will allow the big dealers to keep on doing their business as long as they provide the police with a certain amount of confiscated drugs and the identities of a certain number of small-time dealers when the nation's anti-drug campaign is observed on June 26 every year.[24]

Thus, as far as monopoly is concerned, the high-level Chinese heroin trade is very different from the high-level drug trade in Mexico or Colombia.[25] It is important to point out that upper-level drug businesses in Canada, Britain, and the United States are also not monopolized by a few powerful drug cartels. For example, after interviewing 50 incarcerated high-level drug traffickers in Canada, criminologist Frederick Desroches concluded: "There is no evidence in this study of a Mafia-style monopoly, near-monopoly, or cartel in the Canadian drug market."[26] According to Desroches, "high-level traffickers work in small groups, are flexible in their organization and division of labor, deal with a small number of clients, insulate themselves from their illegal activities, maintain a low profile, collect tremendous profits, and function as independent entrepreneurs."[27] Studies of high-level drug traffickers in Britain[28] and the United States[29] report similar findings.

Lack of Violence and Corruption

In the literature on high-level or cross-border drug trafficking, some researchers have suggested that violence is inevitable in the lucrative and competitive but illicit drug trade.[30] For example, Howard Campbell, a professor at the University of Texas at El Paso, described drug-related violence in Mexico as follows:

> Drug hit men also engage in intricate attempts to disguise their identities and activities, although many drug killings in Mexico and on the border have been conducted brazenly—with automatic weapons in broad daylight—with no attempt at camouflage or subterfuge. Besides physically eliminating enemies, drug killings are meant to intimidate rivals, law enforcement, government officials, and the public through richly choreographed rituals of brutality with specific symbolic meaning.[31]

After the Mexican authorities began to crack down on drug trafficking in 2006, there was a dramatic increase in the numbers of drug-related murders. The media was quick to put a spotlight on drug violence in Mexico by constantly coming up with in-depth reports of the brutal murders, often illustrated with shocking pictures of bloody corpses with their heads or arms missing. In the public imagination, violence and drug trafficking were inseparable. And there are widespread reports that Mexican law enforcement is infiltrated by Mexican drug cartels.[32]

In an in-depth study on drug trafficking in five countries in Central America (Belize, Guatemala, Honduras, Costa Rica, and Panama), Julie Marie Bunck and Michael Ross Fowler, two political scientists, also found that drug traffickers there often used violence: "Family members of even low-level, expendable employees have stood as collateral, readily killed by the organization if the employee were to try to cheat it or reveal its secrets to competitors or the authorities. Drug groups have also used bribes, bullets, and threats to suborn, dispense with, or intimidate judges, police officers, prison wardens, and a host of others who might stand in their way."[33]

Contrary to what we have learned from the literature on drug trafficking in Colombia,[34] the U.S.-Mexico border,[35] Central America,[36] the *favelas* (shantytowns) of Brazil,[37] or the retail drug markets within the United States,[38] violence is almost unheard of in the Chinese heroin market. One ranking Chinese police official attributed the absence of violence among high-level traffickers to their intelligence and class status: "Compared to regular street level crime, drug trafficking involves people with greater financial resources and connections. These people also have high levels of intelligence. They have to, in order to organize and plan your operations. By and large, drug trafficking related murders are rare on the China side."

Some researchers have also observed that violence is virtually absent in high-level drug markets in the United States, Britain, and Canada. According to criminologists Scott Decker and Margaret Chapman, the boat smugglers they studied who transported large consignments of drugs into the United States refrained from using violence: "None of the boat smugglers mentioned resorting to violence when faced with law enforcement, not even when the Bahamas adopted a shoot policy."[39] After reviewing the literature on middle-market drug distribution in the UK, Pearson and Hobbs concluded: "Business principles are predominant in the potentially lucrative drugs market, which means that 'violence-avoidance' is the more general rule. Violence attracts attention and is 'bad for business.' . . . Little evidence is found for so-called 'turf wars.'"[40] In a study on the Canadian drug market, University of

Waterloo professor Frederick Desroches found: "The most unanimous consensus among high-level dealers is that violence in largely unnecessary and that market forces, not coercion, govern business relationships in the drug trade."[41]

In the drug trafficking literature, corruption is often mentioned along with violence as one of the two main methods that upper-market drug dealers adopt to enforce their will on others or to achieve their goals.[42] High- and mid-level drug traffickers in China did engage in corruption, but their bribery of government and law enforcement officials was restricted to protecting themselves after being arrested, not to seek cooperation from officials in their drug trafficking activities. In other words, drug-related corruption in China is mainly reactive rather than proactive. During the course of our study, we heard many stories about family members of an arrested drug dealer trying to bribe officials so that the sentence of the defendant would be shorter or, better yet, the defendant would receive no punishment. On our way to Ruili from Mangshi, a female taxi driver shared this story with us:

> I had a very good friend who married a man from Yingjiang. My friend is a Dai woman from Kajung village, located between Ruili and Mangshi. They had a child and lived a relatively comfortable life. They had a house and a savings of about $15,000. One day, he was arrested for drug trafficking. Someone asked him to transport eight kilograms of heroin from Yingjiang to Kunming. The drug was hidden in his car, and he was arrested near Baoshan. Someone must have tipped off the police; otherwise, this would not have happened. He received the death penalty initially, but after spending about $20,000 ($3,750 for a lawyer and another $16,250 for the Chinese authorities) his sentence was changed to a suspended death sentence. If he could have afforded to pay the authorities about $62,500, he could have walked away, but his family didn't have that kind of money.

Although corruption is a common concern when it comes to drug control, law enforcement officials we interviewed in China told us that it is almost impossible for drug traffickers to ask government officials to protect their drug businesses or allow their drugs to go through checkpoints, but the traffickers certainly could reduce their sentences if they had the money and the connections to bribe the right officials. Occasionally, there are reports in the media of drug enforcers complicit in the drug business, but these events are rare, and the officials engaged in trafficking were doing it on their own and not in cooperation with other drug traffickers.

On the issue of official corruption in drug enforcement, Chinese officials acknowledged China's share of the problem, but claimed that in comparison to other developing countries, particularly those in Latin America, China is running a relatively clean operation. One high-ranking Public Security official in Beijing stated,

> I can proudly claim that our drug enforcement agencies are the cleanest in the world. I cannot say that we never have corrupt drug officers. But these are rare cases. Unlike some other countries where drug traffickers have infiltrated into many aspects of society and even managed to influence their political and law enforcement affairs, drug traffickers have never been able to systematically corrupt any of our government or law enforcement agencies. This will never happen in China, because after all we are still a one-party country and our government will not tolerate this kind of threat to its regime. In a sense, our political and legal system ensures that corruption of our government officials or police officers by drug traffickers will not become a major issue in China.

Desroches, in his study of the Canadian drug market, found that the vast majority of high-level drug traffickers in Canada made no attempt to bribe or corrupt public officials because they "held the belief that police and customs officials were difficult and dangerous to bribe and that business can function without official corruption."[43] Patricia Adler, Nicholas Dorn and his associates, and Peter Reuter and John Haaga also suggested that official corruption was rare in the high-level drug markets they studied.[44]

In sum, the Chinese high-level drug market is very similar to the high-level drug trades in the United States, the UK, and Canada, but very different from the high-level drug markets in Mexico and Colombia, especially in terms of monopoly, violence, and corruption. As discussed in chapter 1 on the work of Letizia Paoli and associates, drug market characteristics around the world are determined by level of effective illegality.[45] Drug markets in countries like the United States, Great Britain, Canada, and China, under strict enforcement, tend to be small, nonhierarchical, poorly organized, with less violence and corruption, and exist on the margins of society. Drug trafficking organizations in lax enforcement countries such as Mexico and Colombia tend to be larger, better organized, more likely to use violence and corruption, and members of these organizations "can lead very comfortable lives, publicly enjoying their wealth and circulating in high society in the company of high level politicians."[46]

4

Low-Level Heroin Trafficking

Ants-Moving-House

The Golden Triangle, infamous for its opium cultivation and heroin production, has gone through significant changes in recent years.[1] Shifts in global opium and heroin supply, the struggle for political legitimacy by regional warlords, and the hostile international sociopolitical environment hastened the decline of large, armed organizations in the trafficking of heroin. Although active players are still buying and processing opium poppies in the region, the business of transporting and distributing heroin and other drugs in the region is increasingly dominated by loosely affiliated entrepreneurs, mostly ethnic Chinese.[2] Through multiple networks, often tied to one's close social contacts, these traffickers move their merchandise in small quantities to other equally fragmented networks of traders and distributors. People of diverse backgrounds participate in the drug trafficking business. Most are poorly educated and have few opportunities in life. All are aware of the risks in the business. Many strategies are devised to evade authorities, the most common of which is the use of "mules" to transport drugs in small quantities, resembling the work of ants. According to political scientists Julie Marie Bunck and Michael Ross Fowler, many smuggling organizations in Central America also used "ant traffic"—couriers or mules carry only a small amount of drugs—to move considerable amounts of drugs.[3] This chapter is about the social organization of the "ants" or "mules" in the Chinese heroin market.

In China, tens of thousands of ordinary men and women are arrested every year for drug offenses, especially for trafficking, transporting, or distributing heroin. However, only arrests with large amounts of heroin (several kilograms or more) make the news. By law, a person who is caught with 50 grams of heroin could be sentenced to death in China. Many drug traffickers receive a suspended death sentence for their offenses; they then spend the next 20 years or so in prison after their sentence is commuted to a life sentence, typically because of "good conduct," and is then further reduced to a 21-year sentence.

Little is known about these ordinary citizens who are caught with a few hundred grams of heroin and then languish inside a prison for many, many years. Who are they? Where are they from? Why are they willing to risk their lives for such a relatively small amount of money (at least by U.S. standards)? As mentioned earlier, in China, dealing drugs is called *shatou shengyi* (head-chopping business) because one could easily be executed for getting caught doing this business. However, many drug traffickers are actually mules hired by someone to move a small amount of drugs for a small amount of money. The question is: why are mules willing to engage in such a high-risk activity? How much are they being paid? Are they being tricked into the drug business and unknowingly transporting drugs from one point to another? We also do not know much about the social organization of these mules. How are they organized? What is the relationship between the mules themselves and between the mules and their employers?

In 2005, we conducted a survey of convicted drug offenders inside a major prison in China. The prison was segregated according to gender. Our local contacts assisted us in gaining entrance to both male and female quarters of the prison. The survey was based on convenience sampling—whoever happened to be in the literacy classes or on breaks from the nearby workshops. No prescreening or subject selection took place by either the prison officials or the researchers. We do not purport to have acquired a representative sample of the convicted population in the prison. Nor do we pretend that findings from this survey can be generalized. However, our sample represented more than 10 percent of the prison's inmate population at the time. The random nature of participation, albeit based on convenience instead of a sampling frame, gave us some confidence that our respondents were not much different from those who did not participate in the survey. Subsequent conversations with prison officials and our local law enforcement contacts suggest our sample should reflect closely the larger prison population. However, we had no way of verifying such claims. Because few researchers have ever attempted such surveys of drug traffickers inside China, we can at least offer some glimpses of the people who were caught conducting cross-border drug trafficking along the Burma-China borders.

Individual Characteristics

Gender

As shown in table 4.1, we oversampled females, thus making the two gender categories roughly equivalent for comparison purposes. According to prison officials, the actual male to female ratio was 3 to 1, suggesting that transnational crime such as drug trafficking—similar to another type of transnational crime—human smuggling, is not predominantly a male phenomenon.[4] Sociologist Howard Campbell, in his study on drug trafficking between Mexico and the United States, also found that women played an active role in the drug trade.[5] It was not uncommon to come across women either in prison or on the street who were active in the heroin trade in the years of our field observations. Many of these women were poor ethnic minorities from northern Burma. We will discuss women's participation in the drug trade further in chapter 7, where we explore how certain market conditions make gender a salient factor in this illicit business.

Age at Arrest

At the time of their arrests, the average age of our prison subjects was 30 years old; the median was 29, and the mode was 28. Females were slightly older than males, with an average age of 31 years compared to the average age of 29 among the males. Age difference was not noticeable by country of birth or by ethnicity (i.e., Chinese Han versus other ethnic minorities such as the Dai/Shan or Jingpo/Kachin), except that the Yi in the sample were significantly younger.

Our subjects were not particularly young at the time of their arrests. Of the 578 subjects, only three were 16, four were 17, and thirteen were 18. In general, those who were arrested for cross-border drug trafficking or domestic drug transportation were about 29 and those who were charged with drug distribution or sale were about 33 years old when they were arrested. There was also an age difference in terms of the type of drug involved. Inmates who were arrested for methamphetamine or

Table 4.1. Demographic Characteristics of the Incarcerated Drug Traffickers ($N = 578$)

Variable	N	%
Sex		
Male	281	49
Female	297	51
Age at arrest (mean = 30, median = 29, mode = 28)		
16–20	60	11
21–30	264	47
31–40	153	28
41–68	76	14
Marital status		
Single	169	31
Married	244	44
Divorced	97	17
Separated	21	4
Widowed	20	4
Country of birth		
China	453	78
Burma	121	21
Vietnam	4	1
Education		
None	107	19
Elementary	217	38
Middle School	180	31
High School	49	9
College	18	3
Employed?		
Yes	275	49
No	286	51
Ever arrested?		
Yes	35	6
No	527	94
Ever used drugs?		
Yes	93	16
No	471	84

Note: Percentages are rounded and represent valid cases.

ice were younger, with an average age of 26, compared to the average age of 30 for subjects who were engaged in the heroin business and 35 for opium-related offenders. In the border between Burma and China, age and types of drugs involved are closely related. During our fieldwork in the area, we observed that a grandfather was engaged in the opium business, but his son was involved in the heroin trade, and the grandson was active in the distribution of methamphetamine.

Marital Status

Thirty-one percent of our subjects were single and 44 percent married; 17 percent said they were divorced and another 8 percent said they were either separated or widowed. Female subjects who were born in Burma and were older were more likely to be married, and male subjects who were born in China and were younger were more likely to be single.

Place of Birth

Of the 578 subjects, 453 (78 percent) were born in China, 121 (21 percent) in Burma, and 4 (about 1 percent) in Vietnam. When we were conducting the survey, we also met several female inmates from Laos, but because of language problems, they were not able to complete the questionnaire and thus were excluded. The majority of the subjects from Burma also were not able to read Chinese, and they were helped by the first author, born and raised in Burma, who translated the questionnaire sentence by sentence and assisted in administering the survey. These subjects were also instructed to write their answers in Burmese if they chose to. One noticeable pattern about the group of subjects from Burma was that they were almost all female, 119 in total; there were only 2 Burma-born males.

We asked our subjects to tell us the provinces and cities where they were born. Of the 485 subjects who identified the province where they were born (mostly those who were born in China), 270 (56 percent) were born in Yunnan, 44 (9 percent) in Sichuan, 32 (7 percent) in Guizhou, 15 (3 percent) in Hunan, and 12 (2.5 percent) each in Henan, Hubei, and Ningxia.[6] For our sample of drug inmates, 7 out of 10 were born in the three provinces closest to the source area in Burma: Yunnan, Sichuan, and Guizhou. Only 3 out of the 270 subjects born in Yunnan Province were born in Kunming City, where the majority of our subjects were arrested. Rather, most of our subjects were born primarily in the border towns where drug trafficking activities were reported to be rampant: Baoshan ($N=21$), Longling ($N=20$), Zhenkang ($N=20$), Luxi (or Mangshi) ($N=19$), Yongde ($N=15$), Dali ($N=13$), and Fengqing ($N=12$). Baoshan City is located between Ruili and Dali, and it is believed that heroin is trafficked from Muse (Burma) into Ruili (China), and then transported to Baoshan via Luxi.[7] After Baoshan, drugs are delivered to Dali before they are forwarded to Kunming. Han Chinese who are born in Baoshan have always been very active in the heroin business. Longling County is located just northeast of Luxi, and drugs headed to Baoshan from Luxi must pass through Longling. Many subjects were also born in Luxi, a gateway to Ruili because its airport is nearest to Ruili and Muse. Dali Autonomous Prefecture is a Bai Minority area, and Dali City is not only a major tourist attraction but also a key link between drugs from Muse and consumers in Kunming. Many Hui (Muslim) people from Weishan County, especially Yongjiang Town, are alleged to be active in the heroin business. In sum, Baoshan, Longling, Luxi, and Dali are all located along the most important drug route between Burma and China: Muse–Ruili–Luxi–Longling–Baoshan–Dali–Kunming.

Most people from Kokang enter China via Nansan, a town in Zhenkang County. Heroin from Kokang normally passes through the following counties of Lincang Prefecture: Zhenkang–Yongde–Shuanjiang–Cangyuan–Fengqing–Lingcang, before arriving in Kunming. The airport in Lincang County is the nearest airport to the Kokang area. Within Yongde County, there is a village called Panglao, which is dubbed "drug backpacking village" in the Chinese media because so many people from that village are working as mules in the drug trafficking business. The route from Kokang to Kunming via Lincang Prefecture is considered to be the second major drug trafficking route between Burma and China.

For those 44 subjects who were born in Sichuan Province, six were from Chongqing and five were from Xingwen. Chongqing is one of the four province-level municipalities in China (the others are Beijing, Shanghai, and Tianjin), and with its strategic location and a population of more than 33 million, the city is a major distribution center and consumer market for illicit drugs.

Out of the 32 subjects from Guizhou, six were from Zhijin and five from Panxian, two areas in Guizhou that are well known in China for drug trafficking.[8] According to a report prepared by researchers at the Guizhou Police College, of the 32 towns and townships in Zhijin County, only two remote towns were drug-free. It was estimated that, at any given time, there were 400 people from Zhijin who were engaged in the drug business. Panxian County is adjacent to Qujin of Yunnan Province, and is located between Kunming and Guiyang, the capital of Guizhou Province. Panxian was once listed by the Chinese authorities as one of the country's 17 "drug disaster areas" or "drug intensity regions." Subjects from Ningxia Province were predominantly born in Tongxin City, another city considered by Chinese officials to be a home of drug traffickers.

One interesting phenomenon was the regional networking of drug traffickers. Drug traffickers were often migrants from one specific region. In this informal economy, it makes perfect sense. People of the same hometown, once established in the drug trade, tend to bring along others from the same village when additional people are needed. Conversely, when villagers and relatives learn about the quick wealth made by a trafficker, they will ask to be involved. In other words, entry into the trafficking business is a process of referrals based on one's close social networks; such familial and social connections help reduce barriers to joining the drug trade and facilitating the establishment of trust among associates.

As a result, anti-narcotics officials have reported from time to time that traffickers seem to originate from the same geographical region. Drug enforcement officials thus pay particular attention to changes and shifts in the geographical backgrounds of those arrested, because such intelligence often foretells the stream of traffickers to come. Once traffickers from one region begin attracting police attention, all people from the region become suspect any time they are stopped along well-known trafficking routes in China. Intensified police efforts soon disrupt the movement by these region-specific traffickers. Traffickers from other regions soon fill in the supply lines vacated by these targeted groups. In mainland China, all citizens are issued an ID card that identifies their registered residence and ethnicity, in addition to their name and date of birth. One ranking police official at a border town made the following observations:

> Many years ago the Hui (Muslim) ethnic minority people in Yunnan dominated the drug trafficking business. Now there are few of them. Most drug traffickers of Hui ethnicity have either been executed, or put in prison, or have changed their career. For many years, Hui travelers would automatically invite greater scrutiny from police and border inspectors. There was so much harassment and profiling against the Hui people who

> traveled to border regions that their involvement in this business was greatly reduced. These days most traffickers come from provinces such as Hubei, Sichuan, and Hunan.

Such observations also seem to coincide with what we have heard from traffickers themselves. One trafficker, who had already spent more than 14 years in prison at the time of the interview, noted the changes in the inmates coming through his prison.

> Traffickers, mostly mules, tend to come from specific geographical regions. Many of the inmates these days come from Liangshan Prefecture (a region in Sichuan Province, north of Yunnan, where most people belong to the ethnic Yi group) and Mengcheng in Anhui Province (an interior province to the east where most people are ethnic Han). Most of them are mules hired from the same villages. It is like the domino game. When one or two individuals took risks and made handsome profits, many others wanted to follow suit; then more and more villagers would join in as more stories of success circulated back to the hometown. Death and imprisonment did not seem to deter these people much.

Ethnicity

The vast majority of our sample (about 70 percent) were Han Chinese (N=394), followed by Dai/Shan (N=42, or 7 percent) and Hui/Muslim (N=38, or almost 7 percent; see table 4.2). There were also quite a few Kachin/Jingpo (N=19), Wa (N=14), Bai (N=13), and Yi (N=12) in our study. We grouped the rest of the 19 ethnic groups into "Others," including Hani, Zhuang, Lili, and Miao. Even though some minority groups are often depicted in the media and police reports as "very active" in the drug trade,[9] our data suggest that the drug business in the border area is actually dominated by ethnic Chinese; at least the vast majority of the drug traffickers arrested and incarcerated are Han Chinese and not members of other ethnic groups.

Even those who claimed to be born in Burma were mostly Han Chinese. Of the 121 subjects born in Burma, at least 62 were Han Chinese, 24 Dai/Shan, and 14 Kachin/Jingpo. Only two subjects born in Burma identified themselves as Burmese (or Burman). Most of the Han

Table 4.2. Country of Birth by Ethnicity ($N=569$)

Ethnicity	China	Burma	Vietnam	Total
Han Chinese	331	62	1	394
Dai/Shan	18	24	0	42
Hui/Muslim	36	2	0	38
Kachin/Jingpo	5	14	0	19
Wa	9	5	0	14
Bai	12	1	0	13
Yi	12	0	0	12
Others	24	10	3	37
Total	447	118	4	569

Chinese who were born in Burma came from Kokang, Wa, or other parts of northern Burma such as Lashio.

The Hui/Muslim in the sample, as well as the Bai, the Yi, and the Wa, were predominantly born in China. Most of the Hui/Muslim in the sample were born in Weishan or Tongxin, Wa in Lancang or Cangyuan, and Bai in Dali or Yunlong. Dai/Shan subjects in our study were more likely to be born in Burma than China. The majority of the Dai/Shan, Hui/Muslim, Kachin/Jingpo, Wa, and "Others" were female. More men than women were presented among the Han Chinese, the Bai, and the Yi.

Education

Almost one out of five subjects did not receive any education. About 38 percent of the sample received only elementary school education and another 32 percent, middle school education. Only 9 percent attended high school and 3 percent, college. It was clear that people arrested for drug trafficking offenses were mostly from the lower end of educational attainment; this is especially true if the prison inmate is from a neighboring country such as Burma. When we compared our prison sample with a sample of sex workers from China ($N=164$), we found the drug inmates to have significantly less education than sex workers. Eighty-nine percent of the drug inmates received middle school education or less, whereas only 49 percent of the sex workers were in the same category.[10]

Employment

Almost half of the inmates said they were employed at the time of their arrest. Male and female subjects were equally likely to be employed, as were subjects from different countries. Those who were working said they were most likely to be farmers ($N=78$), individual entrepreneurs ($N=61$), laborers ($N=47$), or drivers ($N=25$). Several school teachers ($N=5$), restaurant owners or workers ($N=6$), and casino workers ($N=7$) were also in the sample. The ones who said they were employed did not make much from their legitimate jobs, as more than 70 percent of the employed said they were making less than $120 a month.

Arrest Record

Although the prison where the survey was conducted kept only serious offenders, it was interesting to note that the vast majority (94 percent) had never been arrested before. One may question the truthfulness of the survey response; however, we tend to believe these figures, as the prison officials also vouched for these findings. Because drug trafficking relies heavily on one's social and familial relationships, people of dubious backgrounds or prior arrest records would not likely be accepted into a trafficking circle unless of course these people are already connected. Of the 35 subjects who had been previously arrested, 28 were male and 34 were born in China. But for many of these subjects, their first encounter with the police would probably be their last because of their lengthy sentences.

Offenses and Sentences

The offenses charged against our subjects fell into three general categories, with 45 percent ($N=223$) charged for drug transportation (transporting drugs within China), 39 percent ($N=193$) for cross-border drug trafficking (trafficking drugs from Burma into China), and the remaining 16 percent ($N=78$) for distribution or sale of drugs within China. Although ATS has become increasingly popular among young people in coastal as well as interior China, heroin accounted for 95 percent of the drugs transported by our participants. As shown in table 4.3,

Table 4.3. Offenses and Sentences ($N=578$)

Variable	*N*	%
Offense charged		
Domestic drug transportation	223	45
Cross-border drug trafficking	193	39
Distribution or sales of drugs	78	16
Drugs involved		
Heroin	516	95
ATS*	10	2
Opium	10	2
Morphine	6	1
Place of arrest		
Street	171	35
Hotel	77	16
Car or bus	63	13
Checkpoint	55	11
Railway station	41	9
Home	34	7
Airport	29	6
Other	13	3
Sentences for current offense		
Suspended death	234	42
Life	172	31
10 or more years	123	22
Less than 10 years	30	5

Note: Percentages are rounded and represent valid cases.
* ATS = Methamphetamine or ice.

ATS-related offenses only accounted for 2 percent of the sample. This skewed concentration of heroin was most likely due to Yunnan's geographical location, as the Golden Triangle remains the main source of heroin for China as well as for Southeast Asia.[11] Although the production of ATS in Burma has been on the rise in recent years,[12] there are many domestic manufacturers and distributors who can supply local markets with cheaper, homemade products.[13] But when it comes to heroin, Burma remains the major source of supply for the entire region.

Drug Use

Another interesting finding was that only a small number of the drug offenders we surveyed, 16 percent ($N=93$), were reported to have used drugs. In contrast, of the 40 drug smugglers interviewed by criminologists Scott Decker and Margaret Townsend Chapman in the United

States, 85 percent ($N=34$) reported that they had used drugs.[14] Male subjects were more likely to have used drugs than female, and subjects who were born in China were more likely to have drug use experience than those subjects from Burma. As we later found out through interviews and field observations, drug addicts in general get involved in the trafficking and sales business for two reasons. First, they can have access to the drug of their choice; and second, they can make money to support their habit. But the trafficking business by and large shuns the participation of anyone who uses drugs, particularly at levels close to the source of the drugs or along high-risk routes. As a result, most drug users were able to engage only in retail sales near where they live and were unlikely to be recruited by drug entrepreneurs to engage in cross-border drug trafficking or long-distance drug transportation. We will discuss the retail market in chapter 6.

Reasons for Entering the Drug Trade

Although all of our subjects were motivated by the prospect of quick money, the pathways to the business and their circumstances varied widely. Every subject we talked to had their own story. While some subjects did not seem to have thought much about the danger and risk, others claimed to have pondered for months before they finally took the plunge. One prisoner, who was sentenced to death but won an appeal that led to a "stayed" death sentence, said it was a hard decision for him and his business partner to enter the drug trade:

> My business partner and I were hesitant at first. We spent a lot of time talking and calculating. Months later, we decided it was worth the risk to make some fast money. I knew if I put my $250,000 in savings into one deal, I could reap profits in excess of $2.5 million. At the time, my partner and I had combined assets of less than $600,000, which took us more than ten years to accumulate through hard work and frugal living. The potential profit in drug trafficking simply was overwhelmingly attractive at the time.

With an investment of $250,000 in a drug deal, this subject could not be labeled a typical, low-level drug mule. The majority of the subjects who participated in our survey were arrested while transporting drugs for others, and they offered a variety of reasons for their engagement in the drug trade. As often depicted in the news media, many of our subjects said they entered the drug trade because they were addicted to gambling. According to a 47-year-old divorced woman:

> Because I was a heavy gambler, I came to know people in the drug business at the gambling joints. I lost a lot of money in the gambling places, and I was divorced. I regretted that I lost my family because of gambling, but I also felt that I did not have anything and I wanted to make money to get those things back. I heard that the drug business was very lucrative, and that's how I got involved in this.

Some subjects who were born in inland China became heavy gamblers after they moved to the borderland between Burma and China. These people migrated to the border area with the intention to work hard and make an honest living, but soon fell prey to the lure of the many gambling casinos in the area. When a gambling habit developed, they also became vulnerable to being recruited into the drug business as mules. A 42-year-old man from Liaoning Province who received a suspended death sentence for transporting 370 grams of heroin had this to say: "I lost a lot of money in a gambling joint and then I was taken advantage of (by a drug trafficker). I met a man from my hometown and he gave me money to continue gambling after I lost everything. Later, he asked me to move some stuff to Guangzhou, and that's the beginning of the story."

As mentioned earlier, about 93 subjects were drug users; their engagement in the drug business could be the result of their drug habits. For example, a 32-year-old woman from Guizhou Province, who received a life sentence for transporting 108 grams of heroin, said she entered the drug trade after using heroin for a long period of time and was completely broke. Another subject, a 33-year-old woman who received a 15-year sentence for distributing 340 grams of heroin in Kunming, explained how she entered the business: "In 1997, I was in Chongqing while my husband was doing business in Kunming. After two months in Kunming, my husband became addicted to heroin. At that time, I did not say anything about his drug habits. Later, my 3-year-old son and I joined my husband in Kunming. After I became acquainted with a few 'people in society' (*shehui pengyou*), I also began to use heroin. My husband and I both used heroin, and to support our habits, we got involved in the heroin business." Most of our subjects, however, were non-users who were simply unhappy with their economic conditions; when an opportunity to make quick money arose, they grabbed it. One female subject described her experience this way.

> I was working in Guangzhou, making more than $120 a month. I went there with my husband in 1991, and for a while, we lived a peaceful and happy life. However, I was not satisfied with my economic situation. At that point, something also happened in my family and I was in need of money. That's why, when a friend asked me to go to Kunming in 2001, I did. I agreed to help that friend transport drugs. (This subject was a 35-year-old Sichuanese female who received a life sentence after being arrested with 416 grams of heroin.)

In sum, most of our subjects said they entered the heroin trade because they were (1) heavy gamblers, (2) heroin addicts, or (3) desperate for money because of a failed business, sickness in the family, child support, and a variety of other reasons. A small number of subjects insisted that they did not intend to become engaged in the drug business; before they were arrested, they did not know they were moving drugs. Most of our subjects came from poor, rural areas, had little education, and for whatever reasons were desperate for money. Thus, they were vulnerable to drug entrepreneurs who were always looking for drug mules. A man from Banlao, a village near the border where many drug mules came from, had this to say when asked why so many people from his village were engaged in drug trafficking:

> Who doesn't want to live a comfortable life? Who's willing to smuggle drugs and take a risk? The problem is that we are poor. People in this village work nonstop all year long, and yet half the people do not have enough food to eat. That's why many young people are getting together and going over to Burma with their back baskets to transport drugs.[15]

According to various sources, some drug traffickers go back to their villages after making good money in the drug trade and throw lavish dinner parties for their friends. They then become the heroes of the village. Many poor farmers followed in their steps and became drug traffickers and thus sustained the vicious cycle. In Ningxia, a northern province where large numbers of mules came from, there is a saying: "I am going down to Yunnan as if I am going to the front line. I go back and forth in one trip and make tens of thousands of yuan, so even if someone chops off my head, I am willing to give it a try." In the areas where many drug mules lived, there was another saying: "After a father is executed, his son continues; if a husband is executed, his wife carries on."

Size and Organization

The social organization of the drug trafficking business resembles mostly informal social groups of individuals. In our effort to examine the structure of drug trafficking organizations in the Golden Triangle and in Yunnan Province, we looked for key players and their roles within the smuggling activity, and studied the way they were organized. We found that trafficking organizations often started with just a couple of people who were either blood-related or knew one another in the same neighborhood or village. Despite high risk and dire consequences, entry into the trafficking business usually takes place amidst a combination of personal situations and fortuitous opportunities. Generally, the only requirement for entry into the drug trade is sufficient *trust* between the recruiter and his prospective partner. When blood-related relatives (and in-laws too) are in the business, it is usually easy for additional members of the family or clan to join in. One convicted prisoner recalled how he entered the business: "Both my sister and her husband were in the drug business on the Burma side. Later, my brother-in-law came over to coordinate trafficking operations on the China side. He traveled back and forth all the time. Many of my friends in Burma were in the drug trade. So it was not hard for me to gain access to heroin."

In reference to the most recent arrest that had put them behind bars, we asked our subjects how many other people had been tagged, as well. Of the 538 subjects who responded to this question, 186 (35 percent) said they were the only ones arrested. Another 118 (22 percent) said they were arrested with one other defendant, another 113 (21 percent) said there were three defendants, and another 69 (13 percent) said there were four defendants. Only 52 subjects (10 percent) said they were arrested with four or more others. Of those who said they were arrested with one or more co-defendants, about 60 percent said they were arrested with one or more friends, 16 percent said a relative was involved, 8 percent said a family member was implicated, and 6 percent said a boyfriend or girlfriend was detained as well. Our data suggest that a substantial number of our subjects were engaged in their drug offenses with a friend, a relative, a family member, or an intimate partner.

Our data suggest that most low-level drug trafficking, transportation, or distribution cases in China involved a relatively small number of people, as reflected in the number of people arrested. Of course, it is possible that large numbers of people are involved and only a small number of people are caught, but judging from the number of people arrested for drug offenses, it is safe to say that most of these drug operations are relatively small. As observed by criminologists Peter Reuter and John Haaga, "Successful operation does not require the creation of a large or enduring organization."[16]

In the absence of a blood relationship, informal social networks often play a vital role in screening and monitoring new recruits. Over the years, drug traffickers have also adapted to the changing market and to law enforcement activities. According to law enforcement officials as well as drug traffickers, the trafficking business is becoming increasingly dichotomized, with the mules on one end knowing little of whom they are working for, and the organizers (mostly entrepreneurs themselves) on the other end who coordinate operations from behind the scenes.

Operating Methods and Market Structure

Amount of Drugs

Of the subjects who were arrested for heroin offenses, 37 percent said they were engaged in cross-border drug trafficking, 46 percent said they were involved in drug transportation within China, and 17 percent indicated they were charged with drug distribution within China.[17] Subjects who were engaged in the heroin trade said they were arrested with an average of 2,484 grams or 2.484 kilograms. Traffickers were arrested with an average of 3,208 grams, and transporters with 2,000 grams and distributors with 2,181 grams respectively. More than half of the total number of heroin offenders were arrested with less than 380 grams, and about 71 percent of them with less than a kilogram. Only 5 percent of our heroin offenders were arrested with more than 10 kilograms. Such a skewed distribution in weights probably reflects the reality of the prison population, for two reasons. First, as we have argued in several places, the drug trade is mostly supported by a multitude of mules or couriers who were hired to ferry smaller quantities from one location to another. Second, the greater the weight, the more likely the convicted will be executed, thus leaving only the "less" serious offenders in prison. As discussed later, the weight of the seized heroin was clearly related to the severity of the sentence.

Table 4.4 shows the relationship between the amount of heroin the subjects were arrested with and other variables such as gender, ethnicity,

Table 4.4. Amount of Heroin Seized ($N = 516$)

Variable	*N*	Grams
Sex		
Male	254	3,182
Female	225	1,303
Country of birth		
China	397	2,479
Burma	80	1,461
Vietnam	2	341
Ethnicity		
Han Chinese	337	2,682
Non–Han Chinese	135	1,421
Place of arrest		
Hotel	66	3,687
Street	148	2,887
Home	27	4,546
Checkpoint	51	2,359
Airport	21	471
Train station	35	335
Car or bus	54	1,133
Other	12	1,371
Number of defendants arrested		
1	156	1,141
2	98	2,171
3	101	3,308
4 or more	95	3,530
Sentence		
Years or life	260	1,475
Suspended death	208	3,413

etc. Male subjects were arrested with significantly more heroin (an average of 3,182 grams) than female subjects (an average of 1,303 grams). Subjects who were born in China were likely to engage in significantly larger consignments of heroin than those who were born in Burma or Vietnam. Regardless of country of birth, Han Chinese in our sample were arrested with almost twice as much heroin as non–Han Chinese subjects. Place of arrest was also related to the amount of heroin seized. Subjects who were caught in hotels or homes were more likely to be in possession of larger amounts of heroin than those who were arrested on the streets or at checkpoints. Defendants who had been stopped in airports, train stations, cars, or buses were carrying the smallest amount of drugs, usually just a few hundred grams. If a subject was arrested alone, the amount of heroin confiscated was about 1,141 grams on average. If the number of defendants arrested increased, the amount of heroin also increased. Punishment meted out by the Chinese authorities was also related to the size of the heroin consignment. Subjects who received a prison term or a life sentence were arrested with an average of 1,475 grams of heroin, whereas subjects who received a suspended death sentence were seized with an average of 3,413 grams of heroin.

Even though a person caught with 50 grams of heroin in China could receive a death sentence according to law, law enforcers we interviewed told us that this harsh law was almost unenforceable, especially in the border areas where the drug business was rampant. According to an anti-narcotics police officer in Ruili: "Here in Ruili, if a person is arrested with one or two thousand grams of heroin, he or she is highly unlikely to receive the death sentence, even though by law a person could receive the death penalty for possessing 50 grams or more with the intent to sell. If we were to follow the law strictly here, the entire Ruili River would turn bloody red."

Modes of Trafficking and Transportation

One way for mules to transport drugs from one destination to another is to simply carry the drugs in their backpacks or back baskets and walk the whole distance. According to some of our key informants, this is probably the safest way to transport drugs because the mule is less likely to be stopped and searched while walking and he or she can avoid checkpoints by walking around them.

Since walking is not feasible if a mule must transport drugs a long distance, many mules rely on public transportation. However, this also enables law enforcers to set up checkpoints along the major drug routes and screen passengers for drug mules. For example, when we were about to fly from Kunming to Rangoon to work on this research project, we met a Chinese woman at the Kunming airport who was on her way to Rangoon. According to her, "I took a bus from Ruili to Kunming. The bus was searched four times on the way to Kunming, and at the last checkpoint, the police arrested a young man for drug trafficking. He had with him hundreds of grams of heroin. At the last checkpoint, our bus was thoroughly searched for about four hours. Other buses were not searched like ours, and my guess was someone must have tipped off the authorities about our bus."

Train is another type of public transportation often utilized by mules. Chinese public security officers are also very active in searching train passengers for drugs, especially on those trains arriving in Kunming from the border areas or leaving Kunming for other urban centers.

A small number of mules use commercial airlines. In a newspaper article published on July 30, 2006, 30 women, mostly from Xingjiang, were arrested at the Kunming Airport after they arrived there from Mangshi (or Luxi) and heading for Guangzhou. Nineteen women were pregnant, and others were carrying babies. A total of about 5,800 grams of heroin were found among these women. Each woman was carrying only about an average of 200 grams. Pregnant women or women with babies are often recruited to engage in drug offenses because Chinese authorities are reluctant to incarcerate these women, especially if they belong to a minority group.

Income

A woman in her twenties, from a rural area near Liuzhou City of Guangxi Province, told us she was promised to receive $2,300 for moving 2,000 grams from Kokang in Burma to Chongqing, a mere $1.15 per gram. According to her:

> I went to Kokang because I couldn't find any job in my hometown. After I got there, a friend of my husband treated us very well for a month. Then, he asked me to help him smuggle 2,000 grams of heroin to Chongqing. He promised to pay me $2,300 for my service. After I was arrested, I was sentenced to death. When my family paid a certain amount of money to the court, my sentence was changed to a suspended death sentence. You don't understand; $2,300 was a lot of money for people like us in Guangxi.

Another subject said he agreed to be paid $2.30 per gram. Very often, our subjects were arrested before they were paid for their services. That's why one of our key informants had the following to say about working as a mule in the drug business:

> It is not worth it. Many young and poor people are being exploited as mules by the traffickers. The mules normally move just a few hundred grams, so they do not make much. Because they are moving only a small amount of drug per trip, they are not going to make much even if they are successful. However, if they get arrested, they could be executed or sentenced to life. If they want to take such a high risk, they should move a large amount of heroin in one trip, and if they make it, they can live a comfortable life forever.

As for the income one could derive from the trafficking business, the majority of the surveyed subjects declined to provide any specific information. Of those who answered (*N*=116 or 20 percent of the sample), the majority (76 percent) claimed to have made $1,200 or less, while 17 percent said they had made from $1,200 to $12,000. Eight individuals claimed to have made more than $12,000 from the drug trade. These figures should be viewed with suspicion as most drug dealers and traffickers do not like to discuss financial matters, either inside or outside the prison. These figures nonetheless provide some reference for future studies.

The Stories of a Trafficker, a Transporter, and a Distributor

In addition to the survey with drug inmates inside a prison in China, we also held lengthy face-to-face interviews with several drug offenders inside the same prison. Here, we include a story each for a trafficker, a transporter, and a distributor. The first subject was a 30-year-old Hui (Muslim) man from Pingyuan Town arrested for *heroin trafficking*:

> I was born in 1974 in Pingyuan, and dropped out of junior high school. By the age of 17, I was already doing business along with my father. Later, I arrived in Dehong Prefecture. When I was about to go over to Muse to have fun, I met a 26-year-old woman when I was trying to change Chinese yuan into Burmese kyat. The woman told me she could bring me over to the Burmese side without any documents because she knew how to get to the other side through a hidden path. She also told me she owned a karaoke store in Kyukoke (or Pangsai). After we got there, the woman said it's not easy to make a living in Pingyuan and suggested that I take some "stuff" back to my town. She said I can make a lot of money.
>
> In Ruili, when a stranger shows up, they will ask the person whether he or she needs white drug (white powder). If you say you do not use drug, then they will ask you whether you want to deal drug.
>
> That woman in Kyukoke later asked me to follow an old man and deliver a certain amount of drug to a place in China. She promised to pay me $300. She said there were only a few hundred grams of heroin involved, but after we were arrested, we found out that the old man was carrying 2,580 grams of heroin. The old man said he had been running this route for more than twelve years and now that he was about to retire, he wanted to train a few young people to take over his job. We set out: the old man, me, and another young man. We left Kyukoke around midnight, from the home of that woman. We were planning to take small roads to deliver the drug to Longling. It was estimated that the three of us would have to walk for one-and-a-half days to get to our destination. We walked around Mangshi to avoid the two checkpoints there. After we did that, we got separated from the old man. That woman gave us $35 each before we took off, so the young man and I kept on walking toward Longling to meet the woman and her aunt (in her forties). Only later did I learn that the old man had been arrested at a checkpoint. The old man brought a group of police officers to our meeting point in Longling. When the police arrived, the young man escaped and the rest of us were all arrested.

I was initially sentenced to death, with a two-year suspension. Later, it was changed to life, and then to nineteen years. I need to serve another fourteen-and-a-half year. The younger woman and her aunt were both executed. I don't know how long the young woman in Kyukoke had been in the drug business, but after I was arrested, the police told me that they had been watching her for a long time and that she was on their black list. That woman was born in China. After she arrived in Kyukoke, she got herself a Burmese ID card. At any rate, if you have money, you can get yourself a Burmese ID.

When we took off from Kyukoke, it was the old man who was carrying the drug. He also brought along some opium to smoke. That other young man was a heroin user. While we were traveling, he took some heroin out of the package to smoke, but the old man would not allow the young man to examine how much drug was there. However, that young man told me the old man had more than a few hundred grams with him.

I don't think that woman and her aunt were by any means big-time drug dealers. They were also helping others to move drugs, and that's why they needed to be in Longling to meet us. If they are not personally involved, it will be very hard for them to remain in the business. That night when we left Kyukoke, that woman took the drug out from her bedroom.

Another subject was a 58-year-old gambler, and a career criminal from Guangxi Province, who was charged with *heroin transportation* within China. He was having difficulty walking when we interviewed him; he said he hurt one of his legs while working there.

I came to know a boss (*laoban*) in Guangzhou. The boss asked Ah Zhou to bring three men with him to Mangshi of Yunnan. The four of us got to Mangshi from Guangzhou by car. After we arrived in Mangshi, we checked into a hotel. The following day, I hid 383 grams of heroin in my shoes and took a bus to Tenchong with one of the other men. I did not know that other man at all. We were planning to take a bus to Tenchong and then from there fly to Guangzhou. All three of us each carried more than 300 grams of heroin in our shoes. Ah Zhou was the exception; he had more than 1,000 grams of heroin wrapped around his body. Ah Zhou asked me and the other man to go ahead while he and another man followed us in another bus. When our bus arrived at a checkpoint, the *wujin* (armed police) there asked the two of us to step out. Very quickly, they found the drug in our shoes. When we were interrogated, we told the police about Ah Zhou and the other man who were following us in another bus.

Ah Zhou was executed and the three of us all received suspended death sentences. Later, my sentence was changed to life imprisonment. This November (of 2005), I believe my sentence will be further reduced to eighteen or twenty years. I was arrested in 2001, and transferred to this prison in 2003.

The boss promised to pay me $950. Before we left Guangzhou, he gave me $120 to make sure that I had money to return to Guangzhou in case I got separated from the others.

I arrived in Guangzhou in 1991. I like to gamble, and I owe the boss more than $120 gambling debt. After I arrived in Guangzhou, I never had a regular job. I stole to survive.

I was arrested in 1983 during the strike-hard campaign and spent two months in jail. My parents died when I was a kid. When you don't have parents, people will look down on you. That's why I am still single—no woman would marry me.

I had never been to Burma and I was arrested the first time I got involved in this. I was thinking that I won't be caught. I did not use the drug myself. I know this thing is not a good thing.

Another subject, a Wa man from Mengtin, a Chinese town near Kokang, was arrested for *distributing heroin*. According to him:

I was arrested in 1996 for being a middleman in a drug deal involving 1,800 grams of heroin. Initially, I received a commuted death sentence, later it was changed to life, and eventually to nineteen years.

The whole thing was a trap by the *gongan* (police). There was a Wa man in Xuanjiang who asked me whether I know anyone who got *foa* ("commodity"). At that point, I happened to know a guy from Nansan who had the stuff. So I brought them together and they talked. Then the guy from Nansan went to get the drug and the Xuanjiang man went to get the money. When the Xuanjiang guy saw the drug, he took his hat off and flipped it into the air. All of a sudden, six or seven police officers stormed at us. At that point, I realized that the Wa guy from Xuanjiang was an undercover cop.

The guy from Nansan was executed. My sentence was commuted from death to life, and then to nineteen years. I was once married, and my wife was also a Wa person. However, we did not get along, so she went back to her parents. After that I was wandering in society, and that's why I ended up like this. I was spending most of my time in Mengtin. I was also arrested in that town. I had never been to the Wa State, nor am I in the drug business. I was only introducing a buyer to a seller and I did not know it was a crime.

Conclusion

Every year, thousands of mules are arrested in China for moving drugs, mainly heroin, from Burma to China or within China from a drug distribution center in cities such as Kunming or Guangzhou, to a drug consumption market such as Fuzhou, Wuhan, Shanghai, or Beijing. In this chapter, we examined the individual characteristics of these mules, the reasons for them to enter the drug trade, and the social organization, market structure, and operating methods of low-level drug trafficking, transportation, and distribution. We also provided the stories of three incarcerated low-level drug offenders: a trafficker, a transporter, and a distributor. In the following chapter, we will discuss in greater detail how these low-level drug traffickers, along with mid- and high-level drug traffickers, constitute a generation of entrepreneurial traffickers unrelated to mafia-like criminal organizations and how these entrepreneurs strive to conduct drug transactions in a strict enforcement country like China.

5

The Social Organization of Entrepreneurial Traffickers

Unlike Latin America, Mexico in particular, where the drug trafficking business is controlled by a few large-scale cartels, the market for heroin and other illicit drugs in China is fragmented and controlled mostly by groups of entrepreneurs. Neither our field interviews nor government officials turned up evidence that any large criminal organizations were in charge of any transportation process. Over the past few decades, there were a few high-profile individual drug traffickers who were apprehended and executed by the Chinese authorities. Although the Chinese government does not release its death penalty statistics, our conversations inside the jails, interviews with anti-narcotic officials and street-level drug dealers, and published news media reports suggest hundreds, if not more, are sentenced to death each year. It is unlikely that any large trafficking organizations can survive or sustain themselves for long in such a harsh penal environment. Furthermore, in a totalitarian society, formalized associations or organizations are not to be tolerated—not to mention criminal cartels—without the approval of the authorities. However, there appears to be no shortage of individual risk takers who find the enormous profits hard to resist.

Organized Crime and Drug Trafficking

As mentioned in chapter 1, we are guided primarily by two theoretical paradigms in our analysis of drug trafficking activities—(1) the traditional corporate model,[1] and (2) the enterprise model.[2] Under the traditional corporate model, criminal organizations possess a clear division of labor and chain of command. Tasks and responsibilities are assigned according to members' skills and abilities. Rules and regulations govern members' activities. Examples of these corporate-like crime syndicates include the Italian Mafia and Japanese Yakuza. Such structured organizations are thought to fulfill certain social functions, such as inefficiencies in government services, demand for fringe goods and services (e.g., gambling, prostitution, and controlled substance), and cultural tolerance of informal business dealings and unconventional solutions to personal problems unique to different countries. Despite their shady reputations, many criminal organizations nonetheless have existed in some societies for centuries if not longer and are believed to provide "useful" services to their host societies. In these criminal organizations, membership is restricted and criminal entities are often visible in the community, such as in Japan.[3]

The same cannot be said of the enterprise model, which suggests flexible and adaptive networks that expand and contract to deal with the uncertainties inherent in an illicit marketplace. These organizations are made up of loosely affiliated individuals who come to know each other through their social and business networks. They are more disorganized than organized from an organizational perspective.[4] These entrepreneurs are organized only to the extent that they can effectively carry out business transactions. There is no clear hierarchy and no formal recognition of either membership or leadership.

Over the years, we have applied both paradigms in our studies of various criminal enterprising activities such as transnational human smuggling and cross-border drug trafficking activities. We have come to appreciate the complex relationships among enterprising individuals. Many of these relationships represent largely temporary associations of individuals for whom the only qualification for entering the business is some valuable contribution such as money or access to hard-to-acquire services/products. Others occasionally possess a few rudimentary hierarchical features, in which some individuals have more say than their partners in how and when an operation is to be executed. In these organizational features, the hierarchical structure and horizontal differentiation (i.e., division of labor) do not evolve in the same direction (i.e., the greater the hierarchical differentiation, the greater the division of labor). The relationship between hierarchy and division of labor in many criminal organizations is diagonal rather than on a continuum or parallel. Such a diagonal relationship may better explain criminal organizations when they adopt various forms in response to the constraints of market conditions.[5] In this study, we are continuing this *adaptive enterprise perspective* to examine the features of drug trafficking organizations in the Golden Triangle, e.g., their structure (if any), risk management strategies, and business practices.

Traditional Chinese criminal organizations, such as Hong Kong–based triads and Taiwan-based crime syndicates, have long been accused of playing active roles in international drug trafficking activities in Asia and Oceania.[6] Throughout this project, we attempted to explore the nexus between drug trafficking and traditional Chinese criminal organizations, such as those based in Taiwan, Hong Kong, and the United States, and tried to understand how traditional criminal organizations may participate in the drug trade, at what stage, and the roles they play.

We made a conscientious effort to look for evidence and asked front-line drug enforcement officials from China and surrounding countries as well as American anti-narcotics agents to describe or explain this widely speculated association between triad-type criminal organizations and international drug trafficking. Throughout the many months of fieldwork and hundreds of interviews and conversations with drug traffickers, dealers, and addicts, as well as law enforcement officials, we have thus far found little evidence to suggest any systematic linkage between drug trafficking and traditional criminal organizations. This observation does not suggest that no individual members of triad societies were ever part of the drug trade. However, we are fairly certain that triad-type criminal organizations in China, Hong Kong, Taiwan, and the United States are not active players in cross-national drug trafficking operations. In a study on all drug-related sentencing files in Yunnan, Guangdong, Guangxi, Fujian, Hong Kong, and Macau between 2006 and 2007, Chinese criminologist Kaicheng Huang and his colleagues concluded that "no sufficient evidence in the current study supports the general conception that drug smuggling, trafficking, and transportation are typically organized crime."[7] Of the 856 drug cases they analyzed, only two cases involved criminal organizations from Taiwan.

Law enforcement agencies and government officials in Southeast Asia also suggest the same. None of the subjects in this study knew of anyone who acted on the order of their gangster "big brothers" to partake in any trafficking operations. Despite its tremendous profit potential, we believe cross-national drug trafficking does not fit the organizational requisites of traditional criminal organizations. In a previously published paper, we have argued that most transnational criminal activities are fraught with risks and uncertainties. With their emphasis on permanency and sustained profitability, traditional crime families are structurally unfit for fluid situations with unpredictable outcomes.[8] On the contrary, individual entrepreneurs seem capable of thriving under these precarious market conditions.

Three factors may have contributed to this often-cited connection between traditional criminal organizations and cross-border drug trafficking. The first is the preoccupation of U.S. drug enforcement policies that have targeted well-known drug cartels or trafficking organizations in Colombia and Mexico. Decades of drug enforcement in the Latin America have influenced U.S. views on drug trafficking organizations in general. Second, drug trafficking is an organized behavior, although there are different degrees of organization. Therefore, the term is used loosely to describe any groups of individuals involved in this enterprise. Third, triad societies have long fascinated Western scholars and policy makers alike. Any organized criminal activity, from human smuggling and counterfeiting to drug trafficking and pirating, gets labeled as being orchestrated by triads when in fact there has been little evidence to substantiate their involvement in any of these activities.

Even U.S. drug enforcement officials in the field have acknowledged that there are no drug kingpins, or at least they have not seen any in China or Southeast Asia. One U.S. law enforcement representative in the region stated:

> Big drug kingpins are rarely found in Hong Kong or Southeast Asia, but there are significant players. We don't really call them groups or organizations. They can only be described as loosely connected syndicates. Hong Kong Chinese are not as structured as the Colombians. The main players may be calling the shots, but it mostly has to do with one's expertise. To give you an example, the four of us get into a venture. You have an expertise in providing transportation. We may just collaborate on one shipment. On the next shipment, you and I may stay in one deal. But the other two collaborate with someone else. It makes law enforcement penetration a lot more difficult. Investigations must be carried out on a case-by-case basis.

This assessment of the relationship between traditional criminal organizations and drug trafficking has been widely shared by law enforcement officials in Hong Kong and mainland China. One senior Hong Kong police official agreed with the U.S. drug enforcement officials:

> One would like to believe that triad societies like Sun Yee On and 14K are controlling drug trafficking. Triad societies are no doubt involved in all sorts of criminal activities. If they are involved in drug trafficking, they are involved in low-level retail sales. They are not as organized as one would like to think. In large transnational shipments, you may arrest people who happen to be members of 14K, but that doesn't mean their involvement in the drug business was endorsed by the head of 14K. A lot of drug criminals may have membership in the triad societies but they are not working for their groups. Large international cases may make a good story, but the triad connection is a myth.

In 2006, the U.S. government officially acknowledged for the first time what drug enforcement agents in the field have known for years: that the Hong Kong drug trade is primarily dominated by loosely connected individuals and there is no evidence to suggest any direct link between regional drug trafficking and Hong Kong triads.[9] In fact, regional law enforcement agencies in Hong Kong as well as surrounding jurisdictions have long ceased to search for evidence to pin the blame on triad societies. Oxford University criminologist Federico Varese also concluded that "Hong Kong triads control low-level drug dealing in the city [Hong Kong], but they have never become the dominant players in the international trade."[10]

However, entrepreneurs of Chinese descent remain active in drug manufacturing and distributing activities in Southeast Asia.[11] During our numerous visits to Southeast Asia and China's Yunnan Province, it was apparent that Chinese nationals were among the most active players in the regional drug trade. Law enforcement sources in the region seem to agree that one will find Chinese nationals in almost all major drug raids. Our contacts in Burma claimed that almost all major traffickers and distributors of illicit drugs are Chinese. One ranking intelligence official with the Australian Federal Police noted: "Most major drug manufacturing and trafficking activities in Southeast Asia and elsewhere in the Pacific region are linked to Chinese criminals. Chinese criminal entrepreneurs have long demonstrated their ability to develop new market opportunities and forge business partnerships with people of different ethnic backgrounds."

Our findings about the lack of Chinese organized crime groups' involvement in cross-border drug trafficking support the work of many other researchers in this respect. In her pioneering study of an upper-level drug dealing and smuggling community in San Diego, California, sociologist Patricia Adler concluded that: "This is not an arena dominated by a criminal syndicate but an illicit market populated by individuals and small groups of wheeler-dealers who operate competitively and entrepreneurially."[12] Mexican researcher Luis Astorga, after conducting a study on drug trafficking in Mexico, "characterized efforts to describe drug trafficking as highly organized or as similar to organized crime as 'myths.'"[13] After reviewing the research on trafficking cocaine from Colombia to the Netherlands by criminologist Damian Zaitch, Decker and Chapman summarized:

> Zaitch concluded that cocaine smuggling lacks many of the features typically associated with organized crime. Indeed, he argued that most smuggling involves small groups that are isolated from each other, that smuggling lacks vertical organization, and that "families" (individuals with familial ties or long histories of working with each other) are the primary social organizations involved in drug smuggling. Zaitch argued that "cocaine enterprises in themselves are heterogeneous and mutating product of fragile agreements between people and flexible articulation between legal and illegal enterprises." Indeed, he described drug smuggling from Colombia to the Netherlands (Europe's second most popular country of destination) as informal, small, and decentralized.[14]

However, the connection between the drug trade and the contemporary "dark societies" in mainland China remains unclear. Contemporary criminal organizations, or the so-called dark societies (the Chinese equivalent of mafia-type of organizations), are a recent development in China. Although China's one-party political system does not tolerate any organizations that it does not approve of, these dark societies have been acknowledged for years by law enforcement officials as well as academics.[15] The government refuses to acknowledge that China has an organized crime problem, as is perceived in the West. However, it does acknowledge there are organizations with "dark society characteristics."[16] Our fieldwork failed to find evidence that substantiates any connection between any organized crime entities and drug traffickers.

Even in Guangdong, where anything goes, criminal organizations are not known for their involvement in the drug trafficking business. For instance, in the past few years, the Communist government in Beijing stepped up its effort in cracking down on official corruption and dark societies. In one such event, two mafia-type organizations were broken up in Yangjiang, a coastal city of 2.4 million in Guangdong Province.[17] The two godfathers (Lin Guoqin and Xu Jianqiang) built their empires in the old-fashioned way, by running gambling dens, brothels, and extortion schemes. Over a decade or so, the two criminal organizations had grown into massive empires in the region, controlling 20 different types of businesses, with 30,000 followers. Businesses such as cement production, wholesale fish markets, taxis, restaurants, and hotels reportedly were monopolized by the two organizations in the city. The local law enforcement and other government agencies were thought to be on the take and providing protection for years. The central government in Beijing had to resort to using special investigative forces from other regions to crack the case. In November 2007, hundreds of police from outside the city were mobilized to assist in the arrests of the two mafia bosses and their top lieutenants during a banquet. After three years of lengthy legal wrangling, Xu Jianqiang's death sentence was carried out in December 2010, while Lin was put on a stayed death sentence.[18] Police reports widely accused the two mafia organizations of practically monopolizing all vital economic sectors of Yangjiang City and raising prices at will. However, one thing ostensibly missing from any of the reports was their involvement in the transportation and distribution of illicit drugs.

According to our field interviews with government and law enforcement representatives in mainland China, several factors seemed to hinder the convergence of these two groups of players. First, drug trafficking and consumption still provoke strong negative emotions in a country that fought wars and lost dearly over drugs (i.e., the two Opium Wars in the nineteenth century). Second, any criminal organizations that rely on bribery to facilitate their racketeering activities will lose their protection from government or police officials if they begin to get involved with illicit drugs. As one ranking Chinese police official proclaimed, "no one can save you if you are caught dealing drugs. Corruption exists in many parts of the society, but not in the drug business."

We found this to be true in our review of the news coverage in China on official corruption and drug seizures. Stories about government anticorruption efforts typically produce a laundry list of charges against arrested officials and criminal organization figures, such as operating gambling dens, keeping mistresses, taking bribes, extorting local businesses (or collecting protection fees), controlling restaurant and entertainment businesses, and conspiring in collective bidding for government projects. But not drug trafficking. Government officials and even police officers were arrested on drug trafficking charges, but they were always acting on their own in the drug trade. Rarely were there any reported implications on political corruption. After examining the main charges against 74 "organizations with an underworld nature" in China between 1992 and 2009, Federico Varese found that only six organizations were charged with drug trafficking or drug crimes.[19]

Another sign suggesting a lack of involvement by traditional criminal organizations in the drug trade is the relative absence of violence. According to criminologist Diego Gambetta, the key characteristic of organized crime is its protection service, the ability to broker and ensure contacts in an underground economy where legitimate market regulatory functions are absent.[20] Violence serves several instrumental functions in the drug trade, such as deterring unscrupulous dealers, eliminating police turncoats, and guarding one's stash.

By most accounts, either from drug enforcement officials or drug traffickers themselves, violence is not a common occurrence in the drug trade in China. We inquired frequently in our field activities about how and when violence occurred among drug traffickers or whether there were contract killings for getting back at a snitch or taking out competition on one's turf. Compared to drug trafficking in Latin America and along the U.S.-Mexico border, the drug trade in China is rather quiet. Even when we encountered cases where members of a trafficking group ratted on each other or informants sold out their own friends for cash rewards, we did not hear of any revenge killings or murders by contract inside China. Some police officials explained that the lack of violence was partly due to the difficulty in acquiring firearms in China. Others point to the general preference among illicit enterprises of all types to stay out of sight of the authorities. One ranking prosecutor in Hong Kong reflected on why Chinese drug traffickers were less likely to resort to violence: "It is already a dangerous business without the violence. Once you open fire at each other, you attract all kinds of attention. It is just too much hassle. One could have used the time to plot new trafficking routes or find some officials to bribe. It is just not the Chinese way of doing business."

However, some drug enforcement officials along the Burma-China border differed in their assessment. They claimed to have encountered an increasing number of armed drug carriers crossing the border. These mules, traveling in packs, carried firearms to guard their shipment from bandits as well as the police. Scaring off the bandits was easy to understand, because the border region was porous and frequented by smugglers and opportunists of all kinds. Confronting the police with firearms was a recent development. In fact, these police officials in the border region blamed drug traffickers for the influx of illegal firearms in the black market. A police chief in a small border town described the occasional drug interceptions that turned violent:

> Violence is not common, but we have encountered traffickers who resorted to violence when they are cornered by police. Most of the firearms that we confiscated were from drug raids. There are two reasons that traffickers carry weapons. First, traffickers must protect themselves against unscrupulous buyers or sellers. In this business, trust is a rare commodity. Second, when a trafficker carries enough drugs to warrant the death penalty if caught by the police, he will fight to the end. There have been several cases in which our police officers have been killed or wounded by drug traffickers during routine checkpoint inspections. Our officers had no idea that they were about to uncover a large cache of drugs, and the traffickers acted first.

Gun control is extremely tight in China. For decades, even police officers were not allowed to carry weapons while on routine patrols. Guns are still strictly controlled these days, although police officers in most places are equipped with handguns. All guns must be stored in locked cabinets during off-hours and registered whenever they are checked out. The police chief at a border town complained:

> In the early years, our officers joked that drug traffickers were better equipped than the police. It was true. In those years, our officers often chased armed drug traffickers with only a baton in their hands. Things are different now. Our drug enforcement officers are well-equipped. But that doesn't mean they are safe from physical harm. Unlike soldiers in a war who can shoot first to eliminate the enemy, our police can only react to violence, and shoot only when shot at. Moreover, our officers are always in the open while the traffickers are always in disguise. You never know whom you are approaching until it is too late. Some traffickers carry grenades small enough to fit into their hands and you cannot see them until it is too late. When traffickers carry enough drugs to qualify for the death penalty or a life sentence, they will likely use every weapon at their disposal trying to escape. These dead-enders have nothing to lose.

Besides the question of whether there is a link between traditional organized crime and drug trafficking, there is also the question of whether drug traffickers are also engaged in other transnational crimes such as human smuggling, human trafficking, arms trafficking, counterfeited goods smuggling, etc., either concurrently or separately. In other words, are these different types of transnational crimes dominated by different groups or networks of offenders, that have their own pathways, processes, and structures, or do they work in concert and there is overlapping in terms of offenders and activities involving transnational crime?

Even though we did not ask our subjects specifically about this question, none of them, be they incarcerated drug traffickers, retail drug dealers, key informants, or government officials, mentioned the overlapping between drug trafficking and other forms of transnational crime. None of the drug traffickers and heroin retailers we interviewed said anything about engaging in crime other than drugs. Both authors had conducted several projects on human smuggling, human trafficking, and transnational organized crime in Asia, and none of these studies had found any overlapping of offenders or activities in the transnational crime scene.[21] Even though American authorities had speculated about the same group of offenders engaging in a wide variety of transnational criminal activities, our research suggested that transnational crime networks are highly specialized. It is relatively unlikely for a human smuggling organization to be involved in drug trafficking, or for a drug-manufacturing group to participate in the trafficking of women for prostitution.

A Fragmented Drug Trade

Law enforcement officials, drug traffickers, as well as street vendors all claim that multiple, mutually independent stages stand between drugs in the warehouse in Burma and the vendors on the street hundreds or thousands of miles away. These segments along the trafficking and distribution routes are separated from each other and are engaged by different groups of individuals who may have further contacts with other trafficking individuals. Even when large consignments are seized by the authorities, the traffickers are often only aware of the stage in which they play a role. They usually have no idea how the drug was obtained in the previous stage and where the drug is going in the next stage. One female drug distributor in Kunming, who routinely traveled to another city once or twice a month to pick up her heroin orders (normally in the range of 50 grams up to 100 grams), said she had no idea how her supplier obtained the drug: "We all observe the custom that one dealer does not ask how another gets his merchandise. Nor should anyone ask me about my customers. The only exception is when your existing supplier cannot provide you with enough quantity and you want more, so you ask for referrals."

As a result, transactions in the drug trade are carried out mostly on a one-on-one basis, with rarely anyone else knowing any of the transportation details. Furthermore, transactions in the drug trade are mostly carried out in a public space or places where one can easily disappear into the crowd. One incarcerated trafficker in Kunming explained:

> There is so much misinformation and images of drug traffickers and dealers in movies and TV shows. I always find it funny how the movie

> industry portrays drug traffickers as seedy people making transactions in some old and dilapidated warehouses or remote hillsides late at night. I don't think any real trafficker would want to go to these places. Traffickers are all wealthy people. Why would anyone go there? In my days, we always discussed businesses and made decisions in five-star hotels, like this last time when my partner and I were contemplating whether we should invest all our money in a drug deal. We went to a five-star hotel in Guangzhou and talked about it over a lavish dinner.

Findings from our prison survey, as discussed in chapter 4, match this assertion. Most of our prison subjects, 90 percent, were arrested in public places such as in a hotel, on a bus, or on the street. What's more, the vast majority of drug traffickers spent little time on their drug business, and almost half of our prison subjects said they were employed before their arrests.

After decades of relentless crackdowns by governments in the Golden Triangle, large-scale drug manufacturing and trafficking activities in the Golden Triangle region have significantly decreased. Warlords who previously engaged in open production and transportation of illicit drugs are now seeking political legitimacy and refrain from direct involvement in the drug trade. Armed patrols along miles of opium transportation caravans and fights between rival drug lords have long faded into folklore. However, the demand for illicit drugs remains. Small-time entrepreneurs have thus risen to meet the market demand. The drug trade and distribution system appear to take the shape of a fan, with a geographically concentrated location for drug production (i.e., northern Burma) branching out through increasing numbers of small groups of entrepreneurs forwarding the drugs from one stage to the next before reaching the street vendors. Chinese nationals remain the most active players in the trafficking and distribution of heroin and other illicit drugs in Southeast Asia.

As discussed earlier, multiple groups of individuals are involved in multiple stages of the drug trade, with transactions at any given stage always occurring between two terminating points. Even when seizures of large amounts of heroin were announced by law enforcement agencies, they were mostly caught at some stages along the trafficking routes. Thus far we have not been able to locate any cases or reports on any traffickers capable of orchestrating transactions from the point of manufacturing to the street vendors. Even within two points of a transaction, the job of delivering the drugs is increasingly done by "mules" or couriers, as discussed in chapter 4, whereas the traffickers are distancing themselves from any direct handling of the drugs. As one ranking police official described the current drug trafficking business:

> Large drug consignments are becoming rarer these days. Drug traffickers realize the penalty for small drug carriers is less severe and the potential loss is also small. They hire "mules" to pick up and deliver drugs at predetermined locations within specified time frame, and their only connection is a mobile phone number. We have captured many of these "mules" but rarely can we reach the organizers behind them. As soon as an arrest is made and the delivery is disrupted, the mobile phone number becomes invalid. These organizers are watching the mules from a distance.

This finding led us to believe that the drug trade as a whole is largely a fragmented marketplace, with numerous segments of point-to-point transactions. The distance between two transaction points may vary, for instance from Kunming to Guangzhou by air freight or long-haul trucking. But all transactions appeared to commence and terminate between two points by any trafficking groups. In other words, the activity of moving drugs from the production region in northern Burma into interior China resembled a series of independent or even disjointed relays, with each successive stage involving one or two people who only knew where to receive and deliver the merchandise. Drug traffickers typically only take care of one specific section. It is not their business to learn about where the drugs were originated or where they are heading.

As shown in figure 5.1, such disconnected and mutually independent trafficking entities seemed well suited to carry out one lap and to pass the baton to the next stage. Because all parties involved in moving a drug consignment must minimize their exposure to possible law enforcement detection and safeguard their own financial interests, each stage represents a complete business transaction. The individuals in one trafficking group would not have any idea nor do they care where their consignment would travel in the next stage. Despite such a restricted communication process and lack of collective actions among trafficking

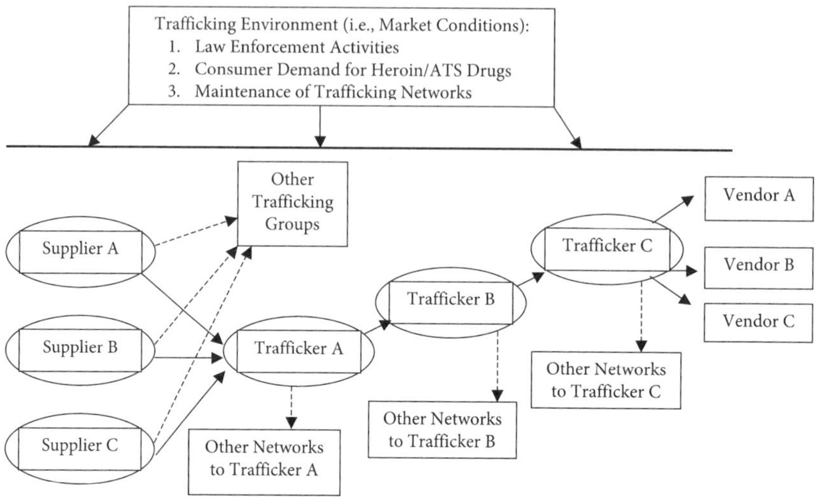

Fig. 5.1. A conceptual diagram of exploring cross-border drug trafficking networks. *Notes*: The solid lines represent the direct connections in a trafficking network, whereas the dotted lines indicate that each trafficker within one network may maintain additional linkages to other trafficking groups. We assume both suppliers and traffickers respond to similar market conditions along the Sino-Burma border regions, such as law enforcement activities and price fluctuations resulting from imbalance between supply and demand.

groups, the drug market as a whole manages to function effectively, with drugs flowing continuously from the manufacturers into the hands of the users.

Organizational Characteristics

The often disconnected and mutually independent trafficking activities seem rather inconceivable and precarious for any organized enterprise. But they are a rational response to a hostile market environment where the top priority for all parties involved is not to get caught by the police and not to be ripped off by unscrupulous partners. We found similar business practices in transnational human smuggling activities.[22] In our effort to map out the web of social connections that link a drug trafficker to his or her primary as well as secondary contacts in the business, we have once again observed the *dyadic cartwheel network* at work. Each drug trafficking group or individual maintains his own contacts in the business; and these contacts again have their own additional resources. The one-on-one transactions seem most optimal and effective in fulfilling the two fundamental principles of this illicit enterprise: (1) risk management, and (2) profit maximization.

Based on official reports and interviews with incarcerated subjects, it appears that behind each trafficking operation, there is always a core group of individuals actively involved. Often times the core members of a trafficking group are either family members or close friends. Most trafficking groups are small and they are often unaware of others in the same region. Monopoly does not exist in the drug trade inside China. It is unlikely that any trafficking groups will ever grow to any visible sizes because they will attract attention and invite immediate crackdowns from the authorities. As one top drug enforcement official in Beijing said,

> The drug trade is a bit like a thug roaming the street. If the thug is weak, no one will listen to him. But if he tries to assert himself by beating up people and claiming a territory, people will be afraid of him. But then the police will go after him. This is why most trafficking groups in China are small so that they can evade the authorities. As soon as any organization grows in size and operation, it will attract attention from the police. The Communist government will not tolerate the existence of any organized criminal groups. It is possible that there may be a few big-time drug lords who continuously stay ahead of the police. In reality, such a scenario is highly unlikely. We would have heard something through our intelligence operations. The word will get around, and sooner or later we will come across references or informants who will lead us to the big players.

HIERARCHY AND DIVISION OF LABOR

Despite the fact that traffickers come from diverse backgrounds and form tenuous alliances, the actual movement of drugs is always planned to the best ability of those involved. Compared to other transnational enterprise crimes such as human smuggling or piracy, greater efforts go into the planning and concealment of drug trafficking activities because of the serious consequences if authorities find out. Great emphasis is placed on staying below the law enforcement radar while securing payment upon delivery.

Drug trafficking tasks are clearly defined and delegated to different players in an organization. Some of the tasks, such as transportation, often require multiple individuals (or mules). Traffickers can be placed in three general categories: the core members (including financers and coordinators), the associates (assistants and specialists who are peripheral to the core members), and mules or laborers. The core members, mostly entrepreneurs themselves, finance and coordinate trafficking operations. These people typically stay behind the scenes. They know those who are carrying out the smuggling plan. It does not mean that core members only make phone calls from remote locations. They often participate directly in the trafficking process, except they almost never reveal themselves. For instance, they disguise themselves as bystanders to witness the handover of a consignment, or follow their own people around to see if they have been watched by the police. The actual transportation of drugs is done by mules—mostly poorly educated people, from rural areas of the country. One senior police officer in a border town in Yunnan observed,

> The mules are paid for the pieces they carry. They usually swallow packets of drugs wrapped in condoms. The more one can swallow, the more he gets paid at the destination. In most cases, these mules can swallow between 100 to 200 grams of heroin in one trip. The most that we have ever caught was one man who swallowed 600 grams of heroin. These mules have no distribution channels themselves. They are mules only. They often don't even know whom they are working for. They are given a cell phone number or a piece of paper with a simple description of a location where there are public phones. These mules give little thought to the fact that what they are doing is actually life threatening. There have been many incidents of ruptured condoms inside the stomach causing death to the carriers.

Although the core members of a trafficking group give instructions, there is no clear hierarchical order within a trafficking organization. Therefore, mules are not entirely powerless, although they probably receive the least financial reward in any transactions. Mules do not always follow instructions, although such deviations frequently result in exposure of an operation. Mules follow the trafficker's instruction because of their belief in its eventual success. If they sense the risk is too high, they will not take the offer or will bargain for more money or even chart their own transportation route. One senior drug enforcement officer in Guangdong said that the mules are fully aware of what they are carrying and they choose to participate in trafficking operations because they know they can get away with it:

> Drug traffickers are usually quite clever. If not, they will not last long. In general, people who can survive two or three years in this business are usually very intelligent and think really hard in order to stay ahead of the police. For instance, ethnic minority women pregnant with babies from Xinjiang Autonomous Region have been heavily recruited to transport drugs by concealing them in their body cavities or wrapped around their body. These are Muslim women. Now we are talking about sensitive political issues when it comes to ethnic minorities. We can't conduct strip searches even by our female staff. Even when we have concrete evidence against them, by law, they cannot be incarcerated because of their special status as pregnant Muslim women. So we have to let them go, after confiscating the drugs.

Core members also negotiate among themselves based on their expertise, perceived risks, and mutual needs. In this business, no one can afford to follow orders blindly from anyone regardless of the pay. Because of the multiple stages involved in the drug trade, core members are buyers as well as sellers. In addition to worrying about financing and coordinating trafficking operations, these core members are also responsible for maintaining and repairing the network, as this is a trade that receives frequent blows from law enforcement activities. One incarcerated drug offender on a stayed death sentence commented on how to connect the chain once someone is arrested:

> If one link is broken, the common way of repairing the network is to talk to the guy while he is still in the county detention center where visits are still allowed. He will usually tell the "visitor" where to find the next person to dispose of the shipment. People at my level (of trafficking) are usually sentenced to death or at least spend decades in prison. Why not help out your partner to get rid of the goods. It is a lot of money. Also, it

> is customary in this business that when your partner is caught, his wife and children will be taken care of. I can only help by telling my partner how to continue the business. He will be able to make more money and give some to my family. We take care of each other when one falls. Now I am here, I know my partner is taking care of my family. He sends my share of the money to my wife each month.

Role differentiation in drug trafficking also shows patterns of regional characteristics. Financiers and organizers of drug trafficking operations tend to come from Hong Kong. Taiwanese criminals are involved at all levels, but their specialty is in the manufacturing process. They seem to have developed much expertise in the production of synthetic drugs in large-scale labs in places like China, Taiwan, the Philippines, Indonesia, and Malaysia.

MOBILITY IN THE HEROIN BUSINESS

Throughout our field activities, we tried to ascertain subjects involved in different phases of the drug business. We probed about their business activities, transaction characteristics, and distribution of power among partners. As described in earlier chapters, the illicit drug industry is made up of many levels of players. However, we are curious about how rigid is the structural hierarchy or whether upward mobility was possible. Our sense was that these levels of group players were closely knit and least permeable to outsiders, from those who are in charge of moving heroin across the border to those in the wholesale business and then to the lower levels of wholesalers and distributors. Each trafficking route seems unique in its operation and players. It is perhaps most challenging to explore and locate the multiple participants before the drug reaches the street vendors. From our conversations with law enforcement agencies and street vendors, it appears higher levels of traffickers or wholesalers, or the professionals, do not consume the product they sell. As one addict in Kunming told us, "Most wholesales are carried out by professional dealers. These professional dealers don't do drugs. I know that for a fact, because drug use will mess up their business."

During our many months of fieldwork, we have talked to enough vendors to realize that the retail business is dominated by addicts. For these heroin users/sellers, chances to move upward in the heroin trade are close to zero. A 34-year-old addict in Kunming was such an example. He tried for many years to enter a higher level of the drug business:

> Drug trafficking is a highly structured and closed system. No one can penetrate. Trust me. Every drug addict wants to get involved in the drug trafficking and wholesale business. The reason is very simple. We all want to somehow sustain our supply of drugs, and because of our contacts with the drug users. You would think we have the best retailing network. Other than *yifanyangxi* (i.e., retailing drugs to support one's addiction), addicts do not normally get to involve in the trafficking or wholesaling side of the business. No drug traffickers want to hire drug addicts. First of all, I don't know where these people are and no one will tell me. It is just like the fruit wholesale. Even if you go to Xishuanbanna, the center of major fruit production in Yunnan, you are not going to be able to buy fruits in bulk. The system of fruit growing and distribution is well established. As an outsider, you can't just arrive in Xishuanbanna and want to become a fruit wholesaler or distributor.
>
> Secondly, even if I am brave enough to travel to the border regions and ask for such connections, they will find out that I am a user. Traffickers do not hire drug addicts because drug users are known to be unreliable. Drug use and the problems associated with addiction will mess up the trafficking business. It is simply not safe to get drug addicts involved in the business. Thirdly, it takes a lot of money to become a drug dealer. The investment is so huge, few drug addicts can afford the price. At the wholesale and distribution levels, it is always cash on delivery. At the local level, occasionally you will find drug dealers who will give some heroin to an addict, without immediate payment. Usually these addicts have established enough trust with the street vendor and have done business with the dealer for quite some time and earned enough of a reputation for repayment. But at the wholesale level, nobody uses the delayed payment practice. The only possibility would be that a trusted friend, not a user, who convinces a distributor that he has enough retail network to move the product. The distributor may give him the drug and the dealer disposes the goods and returns the money for the first time. As you can see, the money required to start a business is well beyond a drug addict's capability.

> One last reason is the limited social network of a drug addict. Once I started using drugs, my social circle becomes smaller and smaller. My life basically was reduced to three basic activities. The first thing I could think of the minute I woke up was where and how to get money to buy drugs. I would steal, lie to my relatives, and swindle my friends out of money. As soon as I got some money, I would run to the drug dealer to buy drugs. Then I would rush home or a friend's place to consume the drug and relax. Without enough social network, how can one move drugs. What if the business is not good for a given day, I would inevitably consume my own investment. Trust me, no drug addicts-turned-dealers would last. But every drug addict dreams of becoming a dealer, so they could support their own drug use. As you can see there are many reasons that drug addicts cannot get into the drug sale business, other than *yifanyiangxi*.

Self-Preservation as a Trafficker

Drug traffickers exercise extreme caution because of the high risks involved in terms of safety as well as for financial reasons. Of the two major concerns in the drug trade, personal safety is much more important, because it does not take much (as low as 50 grams) to qualify for the death penalty in China. High levels of differentiation in roles and specialization in the drug trade can be viewed as a self-preservation strategy in response to law enforcement activities as well as possibly unscrupulous dealers. By separating the financing, coordination, and actual transportation of drugs, players at each stage can best protect themselves and minimize their exposure to authorities. In the event that any one stage is exposed, police will have little information about the other stages of the drug transaction. All subjects in this study clearly indicated that safety was at the top of their list of worries in the business. One long-term prisoner reflected why he was caught:

> In our business, there is a saying, "the police can make ten thousand mistakes, but we cannot afford a single one." The police get to go home each day, sleep and eat and carry on as usual if they don't catch any drug traffickers or if they let traffickers go undetected. But if a trafficker lets down his guard and makes one wrong move, it is often fatal. Let's look at the

> big picture. No drug traffickers can beat the police in the long run. We will always lose this cat-and-mouse game in the end. There are loopholes for traffickers to take advantage of. But sooner or later mistakes will be made. The risk of being arrested increases with each trip. If a trafficker wants to stay ahead of the police, he must be ten times more careful than the police in planning and executing every move. But in most cases, it is so easy to forget this basic principle when you are so close to finishing the job that you can almost smell the cash.

Law enforcement officials and drug traffickers interviewed in this study shared with us some of the ingenious strategies devised by traffickers to avoid detection. Frequent changes of contact information are a basic technique practiced by all people in the drug trade. One senior investigator in Guangdong gave one example:

> Last year, we caught a trafficker who used more than 100 cell phone numbers in eight months. Each phone number was typically used only once, definitely no more than three times before the SIM card and the phone were discarded. It is so cheap now to buy a SIM card and there are also used cell phones, probably stolen ones, for sale everywhere for very little money.

Concealment is a specialization in the drug trade that all traffickers come to rely upon. While some traffickers have developed clever ways to hide drugs on their own, others hire people with special talents at both ends of the trip, first to hide the drugs at the source and then to disguise them at the destination. Another drug enforcement official marveled at the many imaginative ways drug traffickers have devised to evade police inspections:

> You know the old Chinese saying—"while goodness advances a foot, evil advances a yard." Drug traffickers continue to create clever ways to hide their contraband. There are simple ways to hide drugs, such as Coke bottles, which are used to transport opium tar because opium is similar in color to Coca Cola. It is difficult to single out which bottles contain opium tar in a truck full of Coke bottles. We also have caught traffickers dissolving heroin and then absorbing it with their clothing. Then, after

> the clothing materials soaked with heroin arrive at their destination, they are washed with special chemicals and the water solution is refined back to its powder form. Other forms of concealment include mixing heroin or ice with dark-colored materials and molding the mix into various art crafts or common consumer products. There are many ways to dissolve heroin in chemical solutions. But such concealment strategies usually require specialists at both ends of the transaction.

One convicted drug trafficker, who specialized in retrofitting passenger cars to hide contraband, recalled his first experience in modifying a car:

> I spent ten days modifying the car. I had to rip out all the seats and cut open the floor. Then for the next six days I tried to pack as much heroin into the cavities as possible. Sixty kilograms were all I could pack into the space. It was a lot of work. I didn't hire anyone. I had to do this myself. You can't trust anyone for this type of work. I repainted the floor and body carefully to make it look like no work had been done to the car. We had all the equipment to do the job. My brother-in-law did this type of job a lot.

For financial safety, people in the drug trade frequently use what a trafficker called "the mine laying technique," whereby a buyer typically puts an agreed-upon deposit into a bank account set up by the seller, and the seller will deliver the merchandise to a password-protected locker at a supermarket.[23] These two people do not even have to see each other during a transaction, thus protecting one another's identity from law enforcement. The drug is often retrieved by a mule who is given the password and gets paid upon delivery while the retrieval process may be watched by the real buyer or an associate standing nearby to make sure the mule was not followed.

Conclusion

U.S. authorities have long asserted that U.S.-based tongs and gangs are actively involved in the transportation of Southeast Asian heroin into the United States. Over the years, a number of tong and gang leaders in

San Francisco, Chicago, Boston, and New York have been convicted of heroin trafficking.[24] However, there have been no known studies that examined how U.S. tongs and gangs are linked to drug producers and traffickers in China and Southeast Asia. We have attempted, in this study, to uncover the nexus between drug trafficking and traditional Chinese criminal organizations, such as those based in Taiwan, Hong Kong, China, and the United States, and have tried to understand whether traditional criminal organizations actively participate in the drug trade, at what stage, and how important their influence is in the transactions.

After months of fieldwork, we were unable to establish any clear linkage between transnational drug trafficking and any traditional Chinese criminal organizations anywhere in the world. This observation does not suggest that no individual members of these criminal organizations ever took part in trafficking activities. We simply do not have any evidence nor reasons to believe that triad societies in Hong Kong or Chinese tongs and gangs in the United States are meaningful players in the transnational drug trade. Representatives of law enforcement agencies and government officials in China and Southeast Asian countries agreed with our assessment when we probed these issues.

Despite its tremendous profits, we believe that transnational drug trade as a business does not fit well with the primary organizational requisites of the traditional criminal underworld. In one of our previously published papers, we presented our *structural deficiency perspective* to explain that most illicit transnational activities are fraught with risks and uncertainties that offer poor prospects for long-term and stable income.[25] Fluidity in transactions and unpredictable outcomes, not to mention likely exposure to law enforcement activities, are among the elements that deter established criminal organizations from entering into transnational enterprising activities. For these established crime families, the lure of enormous profits is not enough to outweigh the organizational tendency toward sustainable and predictable profitability. On the contrary, individual entrepreneurs have no such organizational baggage and are willing to venture into adverse conditions in the marketplace based on their personal calculus of risks and returns.

The social organization of drug trafficking in China is not unique. Research on drug trafficking in the United States,[26] the United Kingdom,[27] Canada,[28] the Netherlands,[29] and Central America[30] had revealed that drug trafficking organizations in these countries are, like the ones in China, entrepreneurial, small, fluid, and unrelated to organized crime groups. For example, in a study of drug trafficking organizations in five countries in Central America, political science professors Bunck and Fowler concluded:

> Even the largest and most profitable foreign drug organizations at work in Central America have had relatively few permanent employees, as compared to legitimate businesses. The degree to which a drug organization was vertically integrated varied from one group to another and from one period to another, but none was like a multinational corporation with a dense, hierarchically organized, Weberian bureaucracy at its headquarters. Rather, drug organizations tended to be lean, decentralized, and highly compartmentalized criminal groups.[31]

Criminologists Jana Benson and Scott Decker at Arizona State University conducted in-depth interviews with 34 high-level drug traffickers held in U.S. federal prisons to examine the organizational structure of international drug smuggling. They concluded that:

> Rather than being characterized as efficient or rational, drug smugglers work in groups that are horizontal rather than vertical. That is, orders or commands seldom come from a centralized authority communicated down an organizational structure. Instead, drug smugglers work in loosely connected nodes where communication is informal. Such groups of drug smugglers described their groups as having few rules, and seldom relied on a meritocracy for selecting, recruiting, or promoting members in the group. . . . These groups were highly adaptable to their environment. . . . This description of international drug smuggling groups itself must be regarded as dynamic and evolutionary.[32]

We began our study with the assumption that drug trafficking is an organized enterprise because all transactions must be carefully planned and executed or the consequences will be more than financial loss. While we still think the drug trade is highly organized, we are convinced that such organized behavior is accomplished through the collective commitment of the multitude of cooperatives, or small groups of entrepreneurs, who are bound by their shared desire to make money and fear of the consequences should any mishaps occur. There is neither organizational identity nor group culture to speak of; and the hierarchical order within any group is limited. Group leaders are mostly those who invest the most money in an operation or have the most crucial contacts necessary to get trafficking tasks accomplished. Leadership is not based on charisma, physical prowess, management experience, or any other exceptional skills. Membership of and loyalty to a group last as long as profitable transactions can be made with risks that are perceived to be acceptable.

Such transient membership and temporary alliance may contradict the images created by news media stories or official accounts of high-profile kingpins, such as Tan Xiaolin, who reportedly had scores of armed guards and operated one of the best known trafficking networks along the Burma-China border in the early 2000s. Despite the claims from the media or government reports, China's heroin trade consists mostly of highly fragmented stages and mutually isolated groups of entrepreneurs. In reality, all traffickers that came to our attention were involved in particular segments or specific stages of the drug trade, picking up their consignment at one point and moving it to the next. We are not aware of any organizations or traffickers that operated in multiple markets or exerted influence beyond their point of delivery. This is not to say that drug trafficking is not organized or coordinated among these entrepreneurs. Quite the contrary, careful planning and execution are fundamental to operational success; and redundancy is kept to a minimum since every task is carried out by "trusted" partners. However, such organized behavior should not be confused with the concept of a formal organization, which implies operational regularity and existential continuity.

We must also acknowledge that our observations were limited in terms of the cases and subjects that came to our attention. In other words, highly organized organizations or crime bosses were either executed or on death row, thus not available to be interviewed. Those available for interviews may be purposefully kept from the knowledge of the organization to protect the leaders or simply had no idea how the organization operated. It is therefore possible that our observations were systematically biased toward low-level operatives, thus appearing rather disorganized.

It is possible that the traffickers who came to our attention were members of larger trafficking or sales organizations—spokes on a wheel just as the manager of a local McDonalds may be an entrepreneur doing a good business but tied into a much larger sales organization. In our current study, we defined upper-level players on the basis of the amount of heroin trafficked rather than the extensiveness or number of individuals involved or the complexity of their trafficking network. This approach may indeed present an analytical bias—identifying the level of the operation by the weight of the heroin rather than the number of persons supervised or working under any drug kingpin. On the other hand, although not always accurate, the weight of the drugs transported does correlate well with the scale of a trafficker's operation.

6

The Retail Heroin Market in China

In the late 1980s and early 1990s, drug enforcers in the United States and Europe believed that most of the heroin transported into China was destined for the international market; these days, however, law enforcement can no longer make this claim. Some of the heroin from Burma might be transported overseas via Guangzhou and Hong Kong, but as the heroin market began to expand in the late 1990s, the bulk of the heroin imported into China has remained there to meet domestic demands.[1]

In this chapter, we will discuss how the heroin imported from Burma was retailed in one Chinese city—Kunming. We focus on Kunming not only because it is the heroin capital of China, but also because our research project was conducted with the participation of researchers from a police college located there.

In order to understand the social organization of street-level heroin sales, we hired former heroin user/sellers affiliated with a community-based rehabilitation center to conduct interviews with 25 active heroin dealers. The interviews were conducted with the aid of a standardized questionnaire. The authors themselves also conducted informal interviews with 14 heroin dealers without using the standardized questionnaire.

Kunming: The Spring City

Yunnan Province is China's most geographically and ethnically diverse province. It has an estimated population of 44.83 million; ethnic minorities in Yunnan account for about 34 percent of its total population. Major ethnic groups include Yi, Bai, Hani, Zhuang, Dai, and Miao.

Kunming is the economic, political, cultural, and transportation center of Yunnan Province and a gateway to Southeast Asia. After 1949, with the construction of large iron and steel and chemical complexes, Kunming developed rapidly into an industrial metropolis, alongside the cities of Chongqing, Chengdu, and Guiyang. When Kunming was selected as host of the 1999 World's Fair, the government took that opportunity to transform the city into one of China's best developed urban centers. As the authorities in Beijing turn their attention to the development of southwest China to take advantage of Southeast Asia's natural resources and markets, Kunming now plays an important role in China's drive to enhance its economic and political stature in the world. Kunming also attracts domestic and foreign tourists all year round.

Of the 6.25 million population of Kunming, 86 percent are Han Chinese and 14 percent are minority. The city's residents are proud of their laid-back attitude; they see themselves as people who enjoy life—sipping tea, munching *kwaji* (sunflower seed), playing cards, and chatting. They are not particularly concerned about having a successful career or a lot of money.

Kunming is also the largest Chinese city closest to the Golden Triangle. The physical proximity not only enables many armed groups to use Kunming as their stepping stone to the rest of China but also as a distribution center for heroin. The city has also become the capital of heroin use because many users from other parts of China have moved to Kunming so that they can gain access to cheap but high-quality heroin.[2]

Heroin Retail in Kunming

According to the street-level heroin dealers we interviewed, opium from Burma began to show up in Kunming in the late 1980s and then was quickly replaced by heroin, also from Burma. Mr. Su, a 50-year-old Han Chinese male who was a heroin user and retailer, had this to say about the beginning of heroin use in Kunming:

> After China opened its door and began to get involved in economic development, opium began to appear here in Kunming around 1987. Opium was brought to Kunming from Burma. A year later, heroin showed up. It was very cheap then, only $4.50 a gram. Around that time, not very many people knew what heroin was. I remember once I was inside a sauna place, and I became very uncomfortable because of heroin withdrawal. So I decided to smoke it right then and there. While I was doing that, three men came in, and one of them, a police officer, asked

> me what I was smoking. I said it was some kind of painkiller powder to treat my headache. The man said he had never seen anyone smoke something like that to cure a headache, but he would give it a try if and when he had a headache. Not long after, I went to a barber shop in Yiliang, and I also smoked it inside the store. When the hairdressers asked me what I was doing, I told them the same story; that the thing I was smoking was a fantastic painkiller for headache. Come to think of it, it was very funny.
>
> By 1990, people here began to understand what heroin was. The authorities began to pay attention to this problem and as a result, it wasn't that easy to bring heroin from Burma or the border area into Kunming anymore. Well, if something is hard to come by, it also becomes a valued commodity and someone will try to bring it to people for a profit. Before 1990, because heroin was abundant, there was no trafficking; people just brought the drug to Kunming on their own and shared it with other people and didn't bother to ask for anything in return. People living in Pingyuan (90 percent Hui Muslim), Dali, Banna (or Jinhong), and Weishan (also a Hui community), began to move the drug to Kunming. In 1992 and 1993, Kunming was a mess. Heroin addicts were doing all kinds of crazy things, and on each and every block you can find ten to twenty drug addicts wandering around. You can buy heroin on the streets in broad daylight. Outsiders began to call Kunming the Heroin Capital. By then, almost every family with a young person had a heroin user.

According to the heroin retailers we interviewed, in 1989 and 1990, heroin was basically brought to Kunming by people who went to a border area like Ruili to do business. Between 1989 and 1994, it was easy to buy heroin in Kunming; the quality of the drug was also very good. However, the crackdown in Pingyuan in 1992 and the anti-drug activities in other parts of China raised the price of a gram of heroin from $9 to between $47 and $52 by 1994. However, that did not last for long. Within six months, a large number of Yi ethnic people from Sichuan Liangshan showed up in Kunming and flooded the city with cheap heroin. The Yi sold their heroin on the curbside for $23 a gram. According to Huan Gao, author of *Women and Heroin Addiction in China's Changing Economy*, there were more people selling heroin than people selling cabbages on the street near the railway station.[3] In 1997, there was another police crackdown, which resulted in many people going into the hills to buy heroin. That lasted about a year. Between 1998 and 2011, there was not much of a change. The use of heroin decreased significantly, about 70 percent. However, before 2002, heroin was still the drug of choice in Kunming. After 2002, more and more young people were lured into the use of newly popularized drugs such as ketamine, ecstasy, and ice.

Nowadays, very few users go to the Yi-dominated area *Xiao Chang Cun* (Little Factory Village) to buy heroin because, according to Mr. Cai, a 46-year-old Hui Muslim who was born in Kunming and used to engage in both heroin use and sale:

> *Xiao Chang Chun* is dominated by Yi dealers. No Kunming users will venture into the area to buy heroin from Yi dealers because, one, their drug is not pure, and two, it is extremely dangerous to buy drugs in that area. The police are always keeping a close eye on people going into that slum area. Of course, if someone is desperate for the drug and can not find it elsewhere, he or she might take a risk and go there to find it.

The area is located near the Kunming Railway Station, a place where many cheap hotels, restaurants, and secondhand stores are situated. It is also a place where people go to buy stolen properties such as bicycles, furniture, and home appliances.

Mr. Cai, quoted above, characterized the social organization of the heroin trade in Kunming as follows:

> The heroin business is organized like this. There is a group of [upper-level] heroin dealers in Kunming who are providing the drug to low-level dealers who in turn are supplying the drug to drug addicts on a daily basis. These [upper-level] dealers will go to Weishan every month or every season.[4] If they have a lot of working capital, they will go every season because they can buy more in one trip. If they don't have a lot of money, they go more often. The more trips they make, the more risks they must take. Of course, they can also reduce the risk by asking people in Weishan to deliver the drug to them, but that will cost double. If they pick up the drug in Weishan, it could be $10 a gram, but if the drug is delivered to Kunming, it could cost $20 a gram. What are they going to

do? People in Weishan won't come to Kunming to retail, they just stay in their own territory and let people in Kunming dominate the drug business here. Why should they? The lower level you get involved in, the more risk. As we say among us, doing retail is like having a long tail (*ling shou wei ba hen chang*).

The role of Xundian in the drug business was not significant before 1996.[5] Only after drug networks in Pingyuan and Weishan were assaulted by the authorities in the early 1990s did the Hui move their drug bases to Xundian. In fact, it is significantly closer to Kunming than either Pingyuan or Weishan. The Hui are very active in the drug trade because they are ready to sacrifice themselves for the sake of their families. In their perspective, if my family can live a prosperous life, it's ok that I may lose my life.

Right now [2006], the price of a gram of heroin on the Burmese side is about $7.50 a gram. The supplier can get a gram of heroin for $14 to $16 if he or she picks up the drug in Weishan; if the drug is delivered to Kunming, it is going to be more than $25 a gram at the wholesale level. The dealer may buy the heroin from a supplier for $35 to $40 a gram, depending on the quality of the drug. And a street-level dealer will ask about $50 per gram from his addict clients.

From the previous quote, it is clear that after heroin is transported into China from Burma, the drug is warehoused in places like Weishan and Xundian, many of which are autonomous minority regions. Wholesalers from Kunming often travel to these places to buy heroin, and then bring the drug back to sell to heroin retailers. We will discuss the details later in the chapter.

Individual Characteristics

Table 6.1 is a list of the 25 heroin dealers we formally interviewed. We would like to emphasize that our sample is a convenient one, and we certainly could not claim that the individual characteristics discussed here represent the heroin retail population in Kunming. Two subjects claimed that they were HIV-positive, and one, handicapped. The average age of the subjects was 38, and it suggests that heroin retail in Kunming

Table 6.1. A List of Heroin Retailers Interviewed in Kunming ($N = 25$)

Case no.	Surname	Age	Gender	Ethnicity	Drug use?	Arrested	Impris- oned	Monthly income (yuan)
01	Ma	30	Male	Hui	Yes	3	2	4,750
02	Hu	40	Female	Han	Yes	6	2	3,000
03*	Lu	34	Female	Han	Yes	7	1	2,500
04	Yuan	31	Male	Han	Yes	8	2	3,250
05	Wang	41	Male	Hui	Yes	5	1	1,800
06	Zhang	36	Male	Han	Yes	3	0	1,000
07	Liu	40	Male	Han	Yes	5	3	7,200
08	Lin	45	Male	Han	Yes	10	0	450
09	Li	41	Male	Han	Yes	7	1	1,000
10	He	39	Female	Hui	Yes	5	1	6,000
11	Feng	30	Female	Han	Yes	3	0	4,000
12	Zhao	36	Male	Han	No	4	1	3,500
13	Chen	40	Female	Naxi	Yes	5	1	15,000
14†	Ting	35	Male	Han	No	4	0	8,000
15	Zhou	34	Female	Hui	Yes	2	1	8,500
16	Fang	37	Male	Han	Yes	6	5	20,000
17	Deng	41	Male	Han	Yes	2	1	50,000
18	Yang	33	Male	Han	No	0	0	10,000
19	Wen	52	Male	Yi	No	2	1	13,500
20*	Xi	36	Male	Han	Yes	5	3	6,500
21	Xu	46	Male	Han	Yes	6	1	2,500
22	Gao	28	Female	Han	Yes	3	0	5,000
23	Mao	42	Female	Han	No	2	0	6,500
24	Guan	39	Female	Han	Yes	5	2	4,500
25	Bao	42	Female	Han	Yes	8	0	4,000
		Average 38	60% male	76% Han	80% Yes	Average 4.6	Average 1.1	Average 7,698

* HIV-positive; † handicapped.

was not controlled by young (and thus potentially violent) people. Sixty percent of our subjects were male, and 76 percent of the sample was Han (Chinese). Table 6.1 also shows that the vast majority (80 percent) were heroin users, and they had been arrested for drug use or sale numerous times before, even though most of these arrests did not result in imprisonment.[6] Our subjects made an average of about $930 a month from dealing drugs, a significant amount of money if we take into consideration that most people in Kunming did not make more than about $240 a month.

Table 6.2 shows the demographic characteristics of the 25 heroin dealers we interviewed on a formal basis. As already noted, more than half of our subjects (60%) were male, and the mean age for the sample was about 38. The youngest subject was 28, and the oldest, 52. The 14 drug dealers we interviewed informally were very similar to the 25 dealers with whom we conducted formal interviews. Compared to street-level cocaine dealers,[7] crack dealers,[8] and heroin dealers[9] in the United

Table 6.2. Individual Characteristics of Heroin Dealers in Kunming, China ($N = 25$)

Variable	*N*	%
Sex		
Male	15	60
Female	10	40
Age		
Mean = 37.9, Minimum = 28, Maximum = 52		
Marital status		
Single	7	28
Cohabitated	6	24
Married	4	16
Separated	1	4
Divorced	4	16
Widowed	3	12
Ethnicity		
Han (Chinese)	19	76
Hui (Muslim)	4	16
Naxi	1	4
Yi	1	4
Education		
Elementary school	6	24
Middle school	11	44
High school	6	24
College	2	8
Drug use?		
Yes	20	80
No	5	20
Working?		
Yes	7	28
No	18	72

States, the street-level heroin dealers in China we interviewed were much older.

Most of our subjects were married, had been married, or maintained a stable relationship with a live-in partner. Nineteen out of the 25 (76%) were Han, and the other 4 Hui (Muslim), 1 Naxi, and 1 Yi minority. Hui people were overrepresented in our sample, considering that there were only 150,000 Hui in Kunming (out of a population of more than 6 million). A Hui drug dealer we interviewed explained why:

> Hui people are active in the drug business because according to the Koran, even if you commit a crime, as long as you are willing to donate 10 percent of your illegal gains to the mosque, Allah will forgive you, and you still will go to heaven after you die. I don't have the money to donate 10 percent of my drug income, but I will go to the mosque and donate some money once in a while.

Seventeen of them (68 percent) were born in Kunming City; the rest were born in Yunnan Province, with the exception of two who were born in Guizhou Province and one, Chongqing City (data not shown). Compared to the drug traffickers we surveyed (see table 4.1), heroin dealers we interviewed in Kunming were better educated. Most of our heroin dealers (80%) reported that they also used heroin, and with the exception of one, the rest all stated that they began to use heroin long before they started to sell heroin. Most of them (72%) said they were not engaged in any type of legitimate work.

Our subjects stressed that not every heroin user can become a heroin dealer. Even after a user begins to sell heroin, there is no guarantee that he or she will be able to do well in the drug business. Mr. Xia, a 35-year-old Han male born in Kunming, recalled why he did poorly in the heroin retail business:

> I came out of a labor camp in 1998, and that is when I began to sell drugs because I did not have any money. However, I wasn't doing very well because I did not have the three requirements of being a good dealer. First, a dealer needs to have a certain amount of investment money, say from \$36 to \$60. Not many heroin users have 15 cents, not to mention

> 40, 50 dollars. Two, he or she needs to know someone who distributes drugs to low-level dealers. Third, he or she needs to know seven or eight drug users who will be the base customers. I wasn't a good dealer because I was lazy (not very diligent in delivering the drug to customers), I did not maintain a good relationship with my customers, and I was smoking most of my drug myself.

Of the three requirements, the second one—connection to a supplier—is probably the most significant. A subject explained the need to be connected to a *real* supplier:

> After I spent all my savings, I began to sell heroin. Of course not every heroin addict who is desperate for money can become a dealer. What is important is that you must have a person whom we low-level dealers called *laobioa*—the supplier. A real supplier, for us, is someone who can obtain drug from the source area and sell the drug to us without diluting it or overcharging us. Many street dealers nowadays get their drug not from a *laobiao*, they get it from a middleperson who buys the drug from a *laobiao*. Very often, a dealer is pushed out of the drug business simply because his or her supplier is arrested.

Reasons for Selling Heroin

We found that, with few exceptions, all heroin retailers were addicts themselves. As expected, the only reason for them to engage in the retail business was to support their own habit. Many of them were in relatively good financial shape when they began to smoke heroin. In fact, the majority of the heroin users in Kunming in the early 1990s were businesspeople who began to use heroin (smoking cigarettes laced with heroin) not only for fun and entertainment but also for status and reputation.[10] At that time, smoking heroin was an indication of a person's wealth, success, and, above all, ability and willingness to come out and "play." After a while, they realized that they could not continue to smoke the drug because it was a huge financial burden; then they began to inject heroin to save money. However, even with injection, it was still a very expensive habit. Their addiction to heroin not only depleted their savings but also interfered with their own legitimate business (if they had one) or their ability to remain in their jobs. As a result, many of them, after years of heroin use, eventually decided to sell it. According to one subject, "I will say almost 90 percent of those who are addicted to heroin also get involved in heroin distribution, even though their length of involvement could be very diverse. The 10 percent who were never involved in dealing are those who are wealthy enough to sustain their habit without having to rely on drug sales."

Ms. He, a 39-year-old Hui woman who had been a relatively well-to-do entrepreneur, told us how she became a heroin dealer after being a user for about eight years:

> I began to use heroin in 1990 when I was 24. At that time, I owned a small clothing store and had savings of about $10,000. By 1995, because of my drug habit, I had depleted my savings and my store was sold. Then, for about three years, I borrowed money from my family and relatives. However, by 1998, my family and relatives stopped giving me money. At that point, I met this man. His financial situation was not good, either. However, he at least owned a small apartment in Kunming. When the two of us realized that we were running out of money to support our drug habit, we decided to sell his apartment and enter the drug retail business. We sold the apartment for $3,400 and used the money to enter the drug business and began selling drug.

Mr. Li, a 40-year-old Han male, also became a dealer, not because he was desperate money-wise, but because he thought he could regain all the money he spent on heroin through selling drug:

> I started to sell in 1995 because, at that time, heroin was very cheap to buy, so the profit from selling was high. Heroin could be bought from the dealer at a wholesale price of $9.50 per gram and it could retail for as much as $23 per gram. At that time, I still had a lot of money (about $7,700), even though I had also wasted a lot of money on drugs. I probably had spent $9,000 on drugs by that time. I was thinking, if I get involved in retail, I can earn back the amount of money I spent on drugs. On my first sale, I spent $950 to buy 100 grams of heroin. I used some of the drugs myself and sold the rest.

Unlike Ms. He and Mr. Li, most of our subjects entered the drug business with only a very small amount of money. Mr. Xu, a 46-year-old Han man born in Kunming, recalled how lucky he was in finding a way to start his heroin business:

> After using heroin for more than ten years, I began to sell it in 2001. After I was released from a detention center in 2000, I finally realized that if I wanted to continue to use drug, I had no choice but to sell it. However, I did not have the money to enter the drug business. One day in December 2000, I was fortunate enough to be able to steal 12 bicycles in a day. I sold the bicycles for $200 and on January 2001 I had a drug-using friend introduce me to a supplier. I bought 5 grams of heroin from the supplier for $120 and paid the intermediary $12. From then on, I've been selling heroin until now.

Mr. Lo, a young man of Hui origin, was able to enter the drug business without start-up money because an uncle, a mid-level dealer, fronted him the drug:

> I was a drug retailer for about two years, between 1998 and 2000, and had been using heroin for a while before I started selling it. At one point, I was using heroin heavily and was running out of money and did not know what to do. My uncle came to my home and when he saw me, he said: "Look at you! You are eating so much 'seafood' [*haichan* or heroin]!"[11] I told my uncle I might have to sell heroin to support my habit. My uncle said: "Look, if you are going to do it, I know a friend from whom I can get ten grams for you. You can sell it and use the money as your seed money to start your own drug retail business. Or you can use up the heroin yourself and forget about the drug business!" So he gave me ten grams for free. At that time, I did not know he was involved in the heroin business. People normally won't tell anybody that they are doing it, including their wives. Why should they? After I got the ten grams, I used one gram and sold the other nine grams to my *duyou* [drug-using friends]. After that, I was in.

Some female subjects picked up prostitution when they were desperate for money to support their drug habit. These women also began to sell heroin after they hooked up with a supplier and found out that they could use their workplaces to sell heroin to female co-workers and male customers. Ms. Gao, a 28-year-old Han woman, explained how she became a heroin user first, and then went on to become a sex worker and a heroin dealer:

> When I was in Daguan County of Zhaotong City, I met a man who was working for the court.[12] My family gave us some money to open a boutique store and we were about to marry. However, my boyfriend ran into a group of drug users and began to use drug and got addicted to it. I tried to get him to quit, but it did not work. Later, I also began to use drugs and we pretty much "smoked" the boutique store away. My family was very upset about all this, so they opposed our marriage. Daguan is a small place; many people knew what had happened to the two of us, so it was tough for us to continue to stay there. That's why I came to Kunming and found a job as a hostess [sex worker] in a nightclub. Later, my boyfriend brought drugs from Daguan to Kunming for me to sell to my colleagues [hostesses in the same nightclub] and customers.

In brief, subjects who were addicted to heroin began to sell the drug after several years of heavy use; eventually, they lost their jobs, homes, and marriages, depleted their savings, and found out that their families, relatives, and friends were not willing to loan them any more money. Most of them had also been arrested several times for heroin use, and after a few trips to rehabilitation centers, repeat offenders usually would be sent to a labor camp. Once a heroin addict has spent a year or so in a labor camp mingling with chronic offenders, including drug dealers, he or she is ready to enter the drug trade upon release. If the addict can come up with some money to buy a small amount of heroin (only a few grams), and meet someone who can supply them the drug, then the person can begin to be a dealer by selling to his or her drug-using friends. For the addict, the main reason for selling heroin was to enable continued heroin use. Making money was not a major concern.

Five of our subjects were nonusers, and the reasons for their engagement in heroin sales were quite different from those of users. Mr. Zhao, a 36-year-old Han man, explained how he became a drug dealer:

> When I was serving time in 2001 for burglary, I met the person who later became my partner in the drug business. The two of us had become very close inside the detention center; he told me that the heroin trade was a lucrative business. I was released in November 2001, and he got out two months later. At that point, I realized that it was better dealing drug than doing anything else (like robbery or theft) because selling drug not only made money quickly but was also less risky. A street-level drug dealer would only need to serve four to five years at the most. However, the money a dealer can make could allow him or her to live a comfortable life. When the man I met in the detention center urged me to sell heroin, I said yes.

Mr. Ting, a 35-year-old handicapped man from Guizhou Province, a very poor area where many drug traffickers or dealers were believed to have originated, admitted that he took advantage of his shortcomings to enter the drug business:

> After living in Kunming for a while, I wasn't getting anywhere. While I was stealing small items just to get by, I saw people from my hometown living a very comfortable life. One day I was having dinner with a person from my hometown and he told me how lucrative the drug business was. I was tempted, but I was also afraid of being arrested. The guy from my hometown, a heroin dealer himself, said: "Look, you are a handicapped, and that means even if you are arrested, the police are not going to know what to do with you. Why don't you give it a try?" I went home and told my mother that I am going to start a small business and asked her to lend me $120. I came back to Kunming, found that friend, and through him hooked up with a supplier, and bought two grams from him to see whether I could do it. My first try, I bought two grams for $30 and sold them for $50.

Mr. Wen, a Yi minority man who was from Silin County, a major tourist attraction not far from Kunming, told us how he became a heroin dealer after he met a woman who was selling drugs:

> I came to Kunming in 1994 because I had been working as a farmer but having a hard time supporting my four children, my wife (now deceased),

> and my mother. After I moved to Kunming from Silin, I had various jobs: selling fried bean on the streets, shining shoes, fixing bicycles, and buying and selling old furniture. By 1998, I had saved about $500. One day I went to a neighbor's place to chat and met a woman in her forties (now my girlfriend and we are living together). We had a long talk, including life, family, and ways to make money. The woman told me that the most lucrative business was selling drug. She said she had a nephew living in Kaiyuan who worked as a truck driver.[13] Whenever he came to Kunming in his truck, he brought a certain number of grams of heroin for her to sell. After she told me repeatedly that the heroin business was an extremely profitable business, I decided to invest $500 in the business; she also invested $700. With the $1,200, we bought 100 grams from the woman's nephew. At that time, I did not use drug or know anyone who used it. As a result, it was she who bought and sold the drug. She was divorced and she had a son working in Kunming. She had been living in Kunming for more than ten years, and had been in the drug business for several years. Later on, she bought me a bicycle and asked me to deliver the drug to the buyers.

Another subject got into the heroin business simply because her husband was using and selling the drug and soon she found herself helping him with his drug business. Eventually, she took an active role in the business. According to Ms. Mao, a 42-year-old Han woman who had never used heroin:

> I came to Kunming from Xundian in 1983 and found a temporary job. I got married in 1998 and my husband began to use drug in 1990. Two years later, he also began to sell drug to support his own drug habit because we were poor. He bought a few grams every now and then and packed the drug into small bags for retail. Occasionally, my husband was not home and regular customers came, and I did the retailing.

Group Characteristics

Of the 25 dealers we interviewed formally, 8 said they were selling heroin alone, 15 said they were dealing drugs with a partner, and 2 said they had three people working with them in the drug business. Most of the 15 subjects who were dealing heroin along with a partner said their partners were their boyfriends/girlfriends or husbands/wives, and both they and their partners were heroin users. Some subjects were very unhappy working with their partners, and others, quite happy. Ms. Lu, a 34-year-old Han woman who claimed to be HIV-positive, explained how she and her boyfriend worked together to sell heroin and how unsatisfied she was with her boyfriend's performance:

> My boyfriend is responsible for purchasing the drug from suppliers and I am responsible for packaging and delivering it to our customers. However, I am afraid that I might get robbed when delivering the drugs at night (it did happen before), so my boyfriend will do the delivering at night. My relationship with my partner/boyfriend in this business is not a happy one. That's because I believe he often gives the drug free to those women he was sleeping with, or he will sell the drug and tell me it was stolen and keep the money himself.

Ms. He, a 39-year-old Hui woman who entered the heroin retail business with the money her boyfriend received after he sold his apartment, complained about how little her boyfriend was contributing to the partnership:

> My main responsibility is to get in touch with the suppliers and make purchases. Maybe because it was my boyfriend who came up with the start-up money, you can say he almost does nothing to help me. My boyfriend does not know as many users and suppliers as I do. At the very beginning, he did help me deliver drugs, but later on, I began to do everything all by myself (purchasing, packaging, and delivering). If something happens, I am the one who will go to jail but he is the one who will pocket the profits. The start-up money was from selling his apartment. I will help him for a certain period of time and after I save enough money, I am going to leave him and do it myself. While I was locked up for two years for selling drug, he did visit me, so I am returning him the favor for now.

Some subjects, on the other hand, were very happy with their partners in the drug business. Ms. Chen, a 40-year-old Naxi woman whose boyfriend was executed for heroin trafficking, recalled how she and her boyfriend used to work together:

> When I began to get involved, I asked my drug-using friends and those retailers from whom I bought drugs in the past if they need stuff. I told them I had a friend who got the stuff. If they said yes, I will go back home right away and ask my boyfriend to pack the right amount of drugs and I will deliver it. After the delivery, I will turn over all the money to my boyfriend and he will give me $25 as allowance. Since he was providing drugs for me to use for free, I really did not care how much allowance he was giving me. I worked along very well with my boyfriend and we never fought over money. I loved him very much, and he also loved me deeply. I was pregnant with his child, but after he was executed for drug trafficking, I had an abortion. I was arrested along with him, but he took the heat and told the authorities I had nothing to do with it. Besides, I was pregnant at that time, so the authorities let me off the hook.

Ms. Zhou, a 34-year-old Hui woman, said she was satisfied with the way she and her boyfriend were working together in the heroin retail business:

> I invest money, I buy drugs, I maintain contacts with buyers, and I weigh and pack the drugs. When buyers call, I ask my boyfriend to deliver the drugs. I do not share the profits with him; just provide him free drugs for his own use and pay for all the living expenses. We work along fine because we've been together for such a long time and we love one another. He is nice to me; he always listen to what I have to say.

If a man and a woman working together in heroin retail are not intimate partners, they are most likely to be brother and sister. Ms. Feng, a 30-year-old user who was working as a prostitute, revealed how she helped her brother to sell heroin bags to her colleagues at a nightclub.

> Ever since I began to take drugs, I have been supporting my habit by working as a *xiaojie* (prostitute). My brother is also a drug user. After my brother got involved in the drug business, I helped him out by selling

> his drugs to my "friends." Every day, after I wake up in the morning, I give myself a shot, and then go back to bed. If someone calls, I will deliver drugs to him or her. I have my lunch at home. Then I usually go to work in a dancing club. I sell drugs to the girls who are working with me. When I get home and finish my dinner, I take another shot. Around eight o'clock I go back to the club to work. After my colleagues get paid for work, they purchase drugs from me. Eventually, I come back home around midnight. I have only one way to get drugs—every day my brother gives some to me. After I sell the drugs, I give all the money to him. He also gives me about $12 to $24 every day. I work very well with my brother. After all, we are brother and sister.

Some low-level heroin dealers may ask their co-workers to help them with their drug business. According to Ms. Gao, a 28-year-old woman working as a hostess in a nightclub: "My roommate (also working as a hostess in the same nightclub) helps me with the business. However, I don't share the profits with her; I just provide her with free heroin every day for her to use."

After a careful examination of the social organization of retail heroin in Kunming, we can say that it is primarily a family business based on the element of mutual trust. However, there were also subjects who were engaged in the drug business with non-family members. As mentioned previously, only two subjects said they were not working alone nor with a boyfriend/girlfriend or husband/wife. They said they had three other people working with them, and their groups should be considered the better organized ones. Mr. Fan, a 37-year-old Han Chinese male, explained how his group was organized:

> My *laoda* (big boss) invests money and purchases the drugs from our suppliers. I am responsible for receiving the drugs here in Kunming and then distributing the drugs to our retailers. My *laoda* takes 80 percent of the profits, and I, 20 percent. I only provide free drugs to our retailers and some living expenses. My boss is 30, does not use drugs but lives a fast life. He is having fun all day long, and has four or five mistresses. We get together once a week to talk about our drug business. We do not get together every day because we do not want to attract attention from the police.

Actually, as that quote demonstrates, Mr. Fan's group was quite different from an individual dealer or a husband/wife or boyfriend/girlfriend team. Mr. Cai, a former heroin dealer cited earlier, went on to describe in detail the fragmented nature of the Kunming heroin retail market:

> I don't think there are well-organized, large heroin-distribution groups that exist among low-level drug dealers of Kunming origin. We Kunming people are selling it alone or with a spouse or a boy/girlfriend. There was once a young Kunming woman who hired two men to work for her in her heroin business. She was a user herself. She stayed in contact with her employees every hour to make sure they were safe. At that time, her business was considered to be the largest and the best organized. Of course, the Xingjiang, the Kangsu, the Chuxiong, and the Tongbei (northeasterners from the three provinces of Heilongjiang, Liaoning, and Jilin) people in Kunming are better organized in heroin distribution. They operate as a group and they dominate the heroin business that caters to sex workers. As you know, sex workers here in Kunming are mostly from out of town, so we Kunming drug dealers are not going to be able to enter the heroin business in the sex industry because the girls are mostly non-Yunnanese. Besides, if you want to do business with sex workers, you have to stay up late because these girls normally buy drugs around midnight after work. We Kunming dealers usually stop selling around ten or eleven o'clock, then we go home, inject the heroin, and go to sleep. We don't want to get up after the injection, deliver the drug, come back and have another injection. It's just not worth it. Some of these (non-Yunnanese) groups are organized gangs, for sure. However, among the Yunnanese drug dealers, none of them can be considered organized gang members. Most Kunming dealers only sell to local users; the out-of-town people have their own customers, so there is no direct competition between them and us.

Heroin retail in Kunming, like many other urban centers in China, is not associated with mafia-style organized crime groups, street gangs, or drug gangs. There are many mafia-style crime groups in China; indeed, one of the main concerns among Chinese authorities and the general public is the existence of the so-called *baohusang* or "protective umbrella." A protective umbrella is a government official who takes bribes from criminals and in turn provides protection to the criminals and their illegal activities.[14] There is a conviction among the Chinese that the existence and prevalence of the protective umbrella is the main reason for the rapid growth of organized crime in China. Chinese government officials and law enforcers are, in general, not particularly concerned about their affiliations with mafia-style gangs as long as these gangs are not engaged in the heroin business or violent crime. As a result, most mafia-style gangs in China refrain from engaging in the drug trade, especially heroin, because the drug is considered to be much more addictive and destructive than any other drug. Many organized gangs did, however, play an important role in the distribution of so-called newly emerging or soft drugs to young drug users in the gangs' own entertainment establishments, such as nightclubs and dance halls.

Heroin retail in Kunming is also much less complicated than in New York. According to drug researchers Bruce Johnson and his associates, in addition to face-to-face transfer of drugs from a seller to buyer, heroin retail in New York also involved many other activities in which people tried to obtain drugs with little or no cash outlay by helping dealers to distribute drugs. Standard drug-distribution roles included steering (steerers direct a potential customer to a dealer), touting (touts locate customers for a particular dealer), copping (cop men transport money and drugs between a dealer and buyer), holding (the dealer makes the sale, takes the money, and directs the customer to the holder who holds drugs for the dealer), testing (evaluating drugs for a dealer to determine the purity of the drug and how many times it can be cut), lending works (to a friend, acquaintance, or paying customer who does not have a needle or syringe), hitting (injecting drugs into veins the user cannot reach), and running a shooting gallery (where others can inject their drugs).[15] None of the drug dealers we interviewed in Kunming mentioned anything about these other roles in heroin retail.

Daily Activity

Most of our subjects used heroin first and then began to sell it after they realized they could no longer support their drug habit through conventional means. Of course, as already mentioned, in order for a retail operation to begin, the addict must have some start-up money and know a supplier. Once they begin to sell drugs, their daily activity becomes a routine. For example, Mr. Ma, a 30-year-old Hui male user and dealer, explained:

> Every day I wake up around noon and inject heroin right away. After that, I eat something. In the afternoon, I sleep, or go out for a walk. The main thing is, if someone calls, I deliver the drug. Last year, I bought a car, and now after my injection and lunch, I will go out and park my "black car" (unlicensed taxi) somewhere, and will drive for fares. But if someone wants drug, I will deliver it by car.

Ms. Hu, a 40-year-old female Han, characterized her daily routine of drug use, drug sale, and drug purchase as follows:

> Every day, I inject heroin first thing in the morning. After that, I will eat something if I am hungry. Then I will clean the house. If I want to eat something special, I will go out to buy something and will then fix my lunch. If a customer calls, I will deliver the drug. In the afternoon, I will contact my supplier and either pick up the drug or he will send it to my house. After I get the drugs, I will pack them into $6 or $12 bags. If someone contacts me, I will deliver the drug. If someone wants one or more grams, I will call my supplier, get the drug, and deliver it to the buyer. After midnight, I will not answer any phone or deliver drug.

Ms. Lu, a 34-year-old HIV-positive Han woman, had this to say when asked about her daily routine:

> I wake up around nine, have a fix, and then go back to sleep. If someone calls for drug, I ask the person to come near to where I live, and then I will deliver the drug. If the order is very small, just a $1.20 or $2.40 bag, I ask the person to call back in the afternoon; I won't be bothered. I wake up around one in the afternoon and will get something, anything, to eat. If the drug is running short, I ask my boyfriend to get more. Then I have another fix, sleep, and wait for buyers to call. At night I go out to buy something or go to a curbside stall to eat. This is how I normally spend my day.

In Kunming, there are many so-called mahjong rooms where people go to play mahjong. Many drug dealers we interviewed said they often played mahjong in these places while waiting for customers to contact them. In a place like China, where waiting for customers on a street corner is too risky, most heroin dealers take advantage of the many mahjong rooms as cover. According to Mr. Wang, a 41-year-old Hui man who preferred to work late into the night:

> Every day, I wake up around noon and eat something. Then I go to a mahjong parlor close to where I live and play mahjong and wait for phone calls. If someone calls, I ask the person to come to the vicinity of the mahjong parlor and there I will sell the drug. At 9 p.m. when the mahjong parlor closes, I will go eat something and go home and get in touch with my supplier. At 2 a.m. I use my motorbike to pick up the drug from the supplier. By 3 a.m. I pack the drug into bags, all ready for tomorrow's business. And then I will have a fix and go to bed.

Some of the subjects who were non-users also utilized mahjong places to facilitate their drug-selling activities. For example, a 33-year-old Han man told us how he often visited mahjong rooms or entertainment establishments during the day:

> Every day I wake up in the morning and watch TV. If we are running out of heroin, the two of us will contact the supplier and go get the drug. I eat lunch outside, and after lunch go to a mahjong parlor to play mahjong. If someone calls for heroin, I will deliver the drug. I eat dinner outside as well, and after dinner will continue to play mahjong. Or I will go to an entertainment establishment to find girls for companionship. At night I go back to the rented room to sleep. I normally do not deliver drug at night.

Some of the non-user sellers, on the other hand, rarely left their homes. Mr. Ting, who was handicapped, said he conducted most of his business transactions in, or near, where he lived.

> I am a handicapped, so I rarely go out. After breakfast, I stay home and wait for buyers to come and buy my drugs. If a buyer calls and says he

or she dare not come to my place to buy, I ask the person to come near where I live and then I will deliver the drug. Some of those who come to my place to buy drug may inject it while still there. When I am running out of drug, I go out to buy it.

Buying and Selling

One of the main challenges for street-level drug dealers in Kunming is finding a supplier who can offer good-quality heroin for a reasonable price and on a regular basis. Some of our subjects had family members or relatives who were mid-level dealers, and they of course relied on their families and relatives for regular drug supplies. Mr. Lo, a Hui man, explained in detail how, after his uncle became a mid-level heroin dealer, he bought heroin from him for resale:

> My uncle is a major drug dealer. In the early 1990s, he was involved in the opium business. One day he was arrested with more than forty *joi* of opium and was sent to prison. In prison he became acquainted with someone from Laukkai, Kokang. After my uncle got out of prison, he traveled to Laukkai and began to get involved in the heroin business. Typically, my uncle traveled to Laukkai, ordered a few kilograms (from two to six kilograms) of heroin and paid a certain amount of money as down payment, about $1,200 to $2,400. Then he came back to Kunming and waited for the heroin to be delivered; once it got here, he sold it immediately to drug dealers. My uncle paid the balance due his contact in Laukkai once he received the drug. At that time, in 1998 and 1999, my uncle paid the seller in Kokang from $6 to $10 per gram, depending on the quality of the drug. He then sold the drug to others for $13 to $16 per gram, making about $5 to $6 per gram. People who bought the drug from my uncle retailed the drug for $17 to $18 per gram, and made $1.20 to $2.40 per gram only.
>
> When I was selling heroin, this was how it worked between us. My uncle would sell me 100 to 200 grams per transaction. Often I had to pay him for the entire drug right away; sometimes he would let me leave with the drug after paying for half of it. After I left my uncle's place with 200 grams of heroin, I went straight home and immediately took 150 grams of

> it and hid it. I then packaged the other 50 grams into one gram or half-a-gram bags. I did not add anything to the drug. Normally, I would sell the 200 grams in seven to ten days. When I was down to 30 grams, I would call my uncle and ask him to get another 200 grams, and he would tell me when to stop by his place. At that time, people had money and it wasn't that hard to distribute 200 grams in a week or so. Now, people are selling one-quarter gram or even one-fifth gram bags. These days, users do not have money like the users in the late 1990s.

According to our subjects, the power dynamic between them (as buyers) and their suppliers (as sellers) was very much one-sided: the sellers decide almost everything, from the price of heroin to the time and location of the transaction. Ms. Lu, the 34-year-old HIV-positive Han woman, characterized a typical buyer-supplier relationship:

> My partner and I have three suppliers. The price is determined by our sellers. We can only bargain with them a little bit over the phone. The meeting place is also picked by the sellers: they tell us where to go and we go. Normally, it is COD, but if we are familiar with a seller, he or she may let us pay them the next time if we are a little short, like $12. Basically, in this relationship, it is the seller who set the tone for everything.

Most dealers maintained a business relationship with two or more suppliers; if one supplier was arrested, they could go to the other supplier. There were two ways to maintain a relationship with two suppliers. The first strategy was to buy from one supplier on a regular basis, and from the other, on occasion. According to Ms. Guan, a 39-year-old woman who was selling heroin along with her husband: "I have two suppliers. I always buy from one supplier and only if that supplier is out of stock, would I call the other supplier. The first, regular supplier delivers the drug to my house because he trusts me. The second supplier just tells us where to pick up the drug."

Some subjects bought from two suppliers at the same time so that they could have both good and average quality heroin to meet the demands of all kinds of customers. When asked why he was doing business with two suppliers simultaneously, Mr. Xu, a 46-year-old Han man, stated: "I have two suppliers. One supplier's heroin is more expensive, but the quality is great. The other supplier's heroin is cheaper, but the quality is so-so. I normally will buy some from each supplier, so that I have both expensive and cheap heroin all the time and can satisfy all types of customers."

Unlike the subjects previously quoted, some of our subjects went outside of Kunming to buy heroin from suppliers closer to the source areas in Burma. For example, Ms. Ren, a 32-year-old woman born in Jinghong and who had engaged in sex work briefly before she began to sell drugs, explained:

> I needed money to support my drug habit. One day a friend of mine told me he had a friend in Xiaguan, a district of Dali, who could supply me with heroin.[16] He and I took a bus to Xiaguan and met the supplier. She was a Han, about my age. I don't think she uses heroin. I bought 20 grams of heroin from her for $500 and paid her cash. My friend and I took a bus back to Kunming. The package of heroin was stuck to the bottom of a seat that was two rows in front of us. I was nervous, my heart was beating. We knew this was a serious crime. I did this six or seven times (20 to 30 grams per trip). The process of meeting that supplier wasn't complicated. We showed up, my friend introduced me to the supplier, we talked for a while, and then she agreed to sell me the drug as long as I pay cash right away. The bottom line was that she had the drug and wanted to sell it.

Regardless of where our subjects bought supplies of heroin, they had to find a way to sell it. None of our subjects said they sold their drugs to strangers on the street (a marked difference from what we had witnessed here in the United States in regard to street-level drug distribution). A small number of drug dealers in Kunming might sell heroin to strangers in the streets of *Xiao Chang Cun* (near the railway station), but this was not what our subjects did. Most of our subjects were selling to a bunch of regular buyers, ranging from several to about 20. These regular customers may occasionally refer new customers to the sellers. While mid-level suppliers dictated the terms of the drug transactions to the low-level dealers, the low-level dealers controlled the interactions between themselves and their addict customers.

Location of Sales

According to our subjects, they sold heroin to mostly regular buyers, and the drug transactions were mostly conducted in a public place of their choosing. Some subjects said they never, ever conducted business where they lived, as exemplified in Mr. Cai's description of his retail heroin business:

> I never let any buyer come to my place to pick up the drug. For me, there is no such thing as "trust" in this business. If you trust people, you are not going to last long. Some dealers not only allow people to come to their places, but also let their customers inject the drug in their places. Sooner or later, you will get yourself into trouble if you trust people. I always conduct the transaction away from where I live, and I always arrive there early to make sure it is not a trap. If I think there is a slight risk, I walk away. Sometimes, we are talking about selling a $3.60 bag, why should we take the risk?

However, if a subject was dealing with regular customers he or she trusted, then the subject would conduct the transaction in his or her place and find a public place to deal with unexpected customers. It is possible that conducting the transaction in the dealer's place is safer than in a public place.

> Usually, it is the buyer who calls me, and I will tell the buyer where to meet me. I only tell a few regular buyers where I live and will let them pick up the drug at my house. (A 40-year-old female dealer)

> We will let those customers whom we trust come to our house to pick up the drug. Otherwise, we will tell the customer to meet us in a place we pick. (A 34-year-old HIV-positive female dealer)

> I have quite a few friends with whom I used to take drugs. I am sure they won't sell me out, so I tell them that they can come to my place anytime if they want to buy drugs. For other clients, I only deal with them between noon and 11:30 p.m. They call me, and then I will deliver the drug to a place I pick. (A 39-year-old Muslim dealer)

A 42-year-old Han woman said she categorized her customers into two groups: one group who is allowed to buy heroin inside her house and the other group, outside her house.

> When customers arrive at my house, only certain ones are allowed to come upstairs. Otherwise, I won't open the door. For those who are not regular customers, I tell them to wait downstairs and then ask my 18-year-old son to take the drug to them. My son began to help me when he was 14. I observe from my window at how the new customer looks; and then make a decision whether or not I allow him upstairs next time he calls.

Some heroin dealers said they owned a mahjong business and were utilizing the premise to buy and sell heroin. A supplier can deliver the drugs there, and buyers come by to pick up the heroin. Because mahjong places are everywhere in Kunming and they are open from morning to night, it is normal to have people coming and going in these rooms at all times.

Time

Most subjects did not sell heroin 24 hours a day. Most of them were drug addicts as well as sellers, so their selling activities were very much restricted by their drug-user lifestyle. As described, they got to bed late and they get up late. And after they get up, most needed to have a fix before they can do anything, and after that, they might go back to sleep. By the time they wake up again and have eaten, it is already around noon. As a result, most of them did not begin to start selling until noontime or later. Our subjects also indicated that they were the ones who decided when a transaction was going to be conducted.

Terms

Our subjects also stressed that the majority of the transactions were cash on delivery. A seller and a buyer met, the buyer gave the seller the money, the seller gave the buyer the drug, and the transaction was completed. However, if a seller was dealing with a valued regular customer, and the amount of the drug was relatively small, the seller might let the customer pay the following day if the customer was out of cash. According to Ms. Hu, a 40-year-old Han Chinese woman, "The norm is they (buyers) pay me first and then I give them the drug. Some may come without money, and if the person is a regular customer who I think will pay later, I will offer him or her small amount of drug." Ms. Lu, a 34-year-old HIV-positive dealer, also said that: "If the buyer is a regular customer who buys from us on a daily basis and doesn't have the money, we will give him or her $1.20 bag to get by."

Mr. Ma, a 30-year-old Hui man who was driving an unlicensed taxi to facilitate his drug-selling activities, said he was sometimes willing to waive immediate payment: "Most of my customers are regular customers. More than 90 percent of the time, it is cash on delivery. However, if a regular customer buys $6 of drug and cannot come up with the money, I will let him or her pay the following day. The person is a regular customer, so it is not polite to refuse his or her request. Besides, if the customer goes to another dealer, I might lose his business forever."

Other dealers said they were willing to front the drug mainly because they did not want to upset their customers. They thought that unhappy customers were more likely to turn them in if arrested by the police.

Risk Management

Even though heroin retail is significantly less serious than cross-border drug trafficking or wholesale distribution, it is still a major crime in China. As a result, risk avoidance or management is a seller's number one priority. Earlier in this chapter, we briefly alluded to risk management tactics adopted by our subjects. In this section, we will focus on the precautions our subjects took to minimize risk.

To protect themselves, some subjects would not tell their buyers that they were selling drugs. For example, Ms. Hu, a 40-year-old female, used this tactic when she began to sell heroin:

> At the beginning, I went to a supplier and bought two grams of heroin. I came home and packed the drugs into $6 bags. I then approached my drug-using friends and told them that I knew a drug pusher from whom

> I can get good-quality drug. After they asked me to get it for them, I walked around the block and went back and handed the drug to them.

This tactic, however, is feasible for only a short period of time. Sooner or later their buyers will catch on. After our subjects could no longer hide that they were selling heroin, they began to screen their customers more carefully. Mr. Wen, a 52-year-old Yi man who was a non-user, noted: "The one thing that concerned me the most was being sold out by a buyer. That's why when someone new calls and asks for drugs, I screen the person over and over again before I tell the person to come and pick up the drug."

One of our subjects, a 42-year-old woman, said she lied to the police about her supposed heroin use:

> When I was arrested in 1997 with some heroin, I did not dare tell the police that I was a non-user. I told them that I was selling to support my addiction. If I told them that I was a non-user selling drug, I would have been definitely sentenced to prison. Since I told them I was a user, they sent me to a drug rehabilitation center for three months.

Zican (self-mutilation) is another tactic heroin dealers might use to pretend to be emotionally disturbed and to avoid punishment after they are arrested. A 39-year-old woman who was arrested and punished numerous times told us how she was able to get away the last time she was arrested:

> I was arrested in 1996 for heroin sale and received a two-year sentence. In 1998 I was arrested for drug use and sent to a drug rehabilitation center for six months. A year later, I was sent to a labor camp for one year for drug dealing. In 2001 I was again arrested for drug dealing but I was only fined. Two years later, I was arrested for illegal possession of drug and sentenced to labor camp for two years. However, because I swallowed several pieces of metal at the time when I was at the police station, the police released me.

To avoid being arrested red-handed with the drugs she was selling, this subject said she did not keep heroin in her home: "When a buyer comes by to buy drug, I go outside my house and enter a back alley. That's where I hide my stuff."

In sum, most drug dealers we interviewed said they were very careful when they were either buying drugs from their suppliers or selling drugs to their customers. According to Mr. Cai, a 46-year-old Hui man, dealers can always tell when something is wrong:

> Normally, sellers get suspicious if a customer buys more than usual or changes the buying time. We know drug addicts have a very fixed schedule: when they go to *gu* (find money by all means) money, when they receive the money, when they call us, how much drug they buy, and when they buy it.
>
> We are also very cautious when we are purchasing. Once I called a supplier of mine, but someone else answered the cell phone. The man who answered the phone said my supplier was away, and that he was now taking care of the business. He asked me how much heroin I wanted. I cut the conversation short, and that's that. I knew the supplier was in trouble.

Punishment, Concerns, and Perceptions

Arrest and Incarceration

Of the 25 subjects we interviewed formally, only one was never arrested—a 33-year-old Han male who did not use heroin. The remainder were arrested two times or more. More than half of the subjects were arrested five times or more. Seventeen (68 percent) of the subjects were incarcerated at least once. Some subjects were able to avoid incarceration after their arrests because they were HIV-positive and the authorities were reluctant to deal with them. Some subjects engaged in self-mutilation behavior to force the authorities to release them. Mr. Zhao, a 36-year-old Han man, said he was once arrested by the police for selling drugs, and after he swallowed metal inside the police station, the police released him with just a fine. The same subject was arrested a month later for the same crime, and again the police let him walk after he told them about the activities of a female dealer. Four months later, the police caught him again for selling drugs, and he was released after he provided information about several heroin users who occasionally bought heroin from him. Obviously, people who are caught selling heroin on a retail level are not punished as harshly as cross-border heroin traffickers or wholesale distributors. We will discuss *maima* (snitching) at the end of this chapter.

Concerns

Of all the concerns associated with selling a small amount of heroin to drug users, being arrested is probably the number one concern for the majority of our subjects. No matter how careful a heroin dealer is, he or she knows that if a buyer is arrested, there is a good chance that the buyer will cooperate with the police by identifying the seller. One way for the police to accomplish this is to have the user call the seller and ask for a drug delivery. When the seller shows up with the drug, the police make the arrest. If the buyer knows where the seller lives, the buyer can simply lead the police there.

Heroin dealers in Kunming are also wary of not being able to purchase heroin when they need to. Most heroin users buy and use heroin on a daily and routine basis: when a buyer calls, the seller must come up with the drug. If not, the buyer most likely will look for another dealer promptly, and it is also likely that the buyer will continue to buy from the new dealer. As Ms. He, a 39-year-old Hui female user, described: "My main concern is that my supplier is out of drug. When that happens and my clients are asking for the drug, I have to find other retailers to loan me some heroin. I must spend a lot of time and energy to find retailers who are willing to help me, and sometimes it doesn't work out."

Perceptions of the Heroin Business

Most heroin dealers we interviewed saw their engagement in selling heroin as something they need to do to survive as a heroin user. Being a heroin user for many years put them in a position to become a dealer because they already know many heroin users and these users can form the base of their clientele. As a seasoned user, they are also quite likely to know someone who can supply them with heroin on a regular basis for retail. Mr. Yuan, a 31-year-old Han male, summed up all the advantages of being a heroin dealer:

> If I rob, the risk is too high. I do not dare to steal either. I do not have the skills to do it. Relatively speaking, drug retail is easier. Plus, dealing heroin allows me to have the drugs anytime I want, so it is very convenient for a drug user like me. Being a dealer means I never have to beg other people for drugs. Instead, drug users would call me and beg for drugs.

Another dealer thought that selling heroin was just a business and that he was entitled to make good money from selling heroin because of the risk involved: "For me, there is no difference between selling heroin and selling cigarettes or alcohol. They are all businesses. I have to take such a huge risk (arrest by the police) doing this, it is only reasonable for me to make a huge profit."

Even so, many heroin dealers who are also users know that their future is bleak and hope that they can stop using and selling heroin one day: "I know I am committing a crime, and people like me (who use and deal drug) either die or go to jail. I want to quit heroin and live a normal life with a man" (a 40-year-old Naxi woman).

Mr. Zhao, a 36-year-old non-user, views his engagement in selling heroin as a way for him to save enough money to marry, though he had ambivalent feelings about the men and women who bought heroin from him: "After I make enough money to marry someone, I will quit. As far as the drug users are concerned, I have mixed feelings about them. Well, they need to maintain their habit, and I need to eat to survive. For me, this is just a business."

Mr. Su, a Han male in his early fifties, described the dynamic relationship between addicts and dealers in the street-level heroin market.

> People in the drug business are all very businesslike when it comes to money. They know they are in possession of a commodity that is indispensable for a large number of heroin addicts. For heroin addicts, the drug is more important than anything else. It is not something you can say, well, I'll do it tomorrow. Once you are addicted, you must use it every day, and if you don't, it will be hell. You can skip doing anything and everything, but not heroin. That's why heroin dealers normally ask what they want, and they know they will get it. There is no such thing as compassion in the world of heroin dealers. The same is true with the world of heroin addicts. They will do whatever they have to get the drug.

Maima

Regardless of how careful a heroin dealer is, he or she is vulnerable to law enforcement authorities simply because of *maima*. *Maima* means someone who is arrested for drug use or sale and who will, in order to save one's skin, turn in someone else who is using or selling drug. Ms. Wu, a 43-year-old Han woman born in Kunming, explained: "*Maima* means someone turns you in to the authorities. This is how the authorities go after the dealers. They will demand a user to turn in three dealers. Then they will force these dealers to turn in three suppliers each. Many users and dealers have no choice but to do as asked by the authorities."

According to our subjects, *maima* was rare in the past, but over the past several years, more and more drug users and dealers have been using this approach to avoid punishment. Mr. Lo, a Hui man who claimed to have many relatives in the drug business, offered this example:

> I have eight relatives who were involved in the drug trade. Right now, there are still three or four who are active in the business. A female cousin of mine was arrested for selling heroin and turned in her suppliers in return for her freedom. She called her supplier in Pingyuan and asked him to deliver more than 2 kilograms of heroin to Kunming. He showed up in Kunming with his wife and the drug. After they were arrested, the couple was executed. That's life in the world of drug dealers. When a dealer is arrested and he wants to walk, he may turn in his suppliers or buyers to the police.

To avoid being betrayed by their customers, some dealers said they tried to be nice to their customers:

> I've been selling since 2000 and my customers never turned me in to the authorities after they got arrested. That's because my heart wasn't so black. I always give my customers a reasonable amount of the drug and I never add anything to the drug. I also would allow some of my customers to pay me later or pay me a little less than the market price. I also never turned in those who used drugs or sold drugs. Nowadays *maima* is very common. This is how the authorities go after users and dealers. After they arrest a user or a dealer, they will ask the arrestee to turn in

> others in exchange for freedom. That doesn't always happen, though. (A 46-year-old Muslim male)

Another subject, a 36-year-old male non-user, also deliberately tried to please his customers solely for the purpose of protecting himself: "During festivals, I will give my clients $1.20 to $3.60 bags of heroin for free. Actually, I am just trying to establish a good relationship. If they go out to make money and get arrested, they will not sell me out to the police." Ms. Ren talked about the prevalence of *maima* nowadays:

> *Maima* is now very common. It rarely happened in the past. Four years ago, I was arrested because one of my customers turned me in to the authorities. He called me for drug and as I was planning to meet him, I was arrested. Luckily, I only had a small amount of drug with me, and I was only charged for illegal possession of drug. I was sentenced to a labor camp for a year.

Some subjects suggested that *maima* is more likely to occur at the lower end of the drug business and is not as prevalent at the higher end. Mr. Su, a Kunming man in his early fifties, explained:

> If you are doing this on a higher level, like providing 20 grams a day to a bunch of low-level dealers, you are relatively safe. If these dealers are arrested, they are not going to turn you in. If they do, they know they are also going to die. The big time dealer will simply tell the authorities that these dealers have been buying 20 grams a day from him for the past two years. With that amount of heroin, these dealers are going to be executed as well. That's why if they get arrested, they will just tell the authorities that they are new in the business and they were arrested the first time they were buying 20 grams of heroin. This way, they would save their lives. This is very different from a drug addict turning in the low-level dealer from whom he or she was buying drug.

Needless to say, we found the retail market of the heroin trade to be a complex one. Drug addicts found a way to establish their own supply chain. These circles of distribution networks overlapped in some territories but remained isolated in others. Multiple players were involved, many of whom were addicts themselves who engaged in *yifanyangxi* (selling drugs to support their own addiction). These addicts often viewed their retail business as an inseparable part of their addiction lifestyle, as one subject stated:

> I don't see *yifanyiangxi* (dealing drugs to support one's addiction) as *fandu* (drug trade). Most addicts have done it or will do it. I would buy the drug for a friend, but take a cut out of it. For instance, I was asked to buy one gram for a drug-using friend. I would then siphon off 0.1 gram. There are times when the police crack down hard on drug dealings and I would ask the friend to reward me an additional 0.1 gram. But you know there are limits to this practice. No one wants to buy drugs for another person without being benefited in the process. At the same time, drug addicts know that they are being ripped off. They still have to buy drugs through the only channels available to them. Because when drug addicts get together, we use drugs and we also talk about the latest development in the market. Sooner or later, we all learn where to find these professional drug dealers. It usually takes about half a year from the first drug use to learn one's way around and find a professional dealer. It is usually safer to buy heroin from the dealers. The quality and quantity can be trusted.

According this subject, it was difficult to be an addict and sell drugs at the same time. Most addicts try to find the direct source to the professional dealer, as all heroin addicts are very sensitive to the quality and quantity of their purchase. But during police crackdowns, which often disrupt the heroin trade, addicts would become desperate and go to anyone who could supply the drug. During peaceful times, as this subject stated, "Any cutting will reduce the quality of your product, and you would lose your client. No one wants his stuff to be diluted. Every addict wants the full dosage to deliver the full effect."

As for the relationship between addicts and the so-called professional dealers, this subject claimed that most addicts would go out of their way to protect them:

> There is a golden rule among the addicts that you never tell the police who sold you the drugs. You can snitch on your drug using friends, but

not the dealer. I mean the professional dealers. First of all these people did not do you any harm. They are business people, like a store owner, who provided you something you were willing to pay for. More importantly, one day you will be released from the prison or drug treatment centers, you will still come back to these people to get drugs.

An Invisible Retail Market

Our data suggest that the heroin retail market in Kunming is very different from the American drug retail market. First of all, drug dealers in Kunming rarely sell drugs in the open-air drug markets. In Kunming, some dealers are selling heroin in the streets of Xiao Chang Cun (Small Factory Village), near the Kunming North Railway Station (Beizhan), but it is not where most heroin users in Kunming go to buy heroin. As mentioned previously, only desperate users who cannot obtain drugs from their usual providers will venture into Xiao Chang Cun to look for it. At one point, the area was a major hot spot for heroin retail in Kunming;[17] however, the Chinese authorities reacted quickly after the public got the impression that the place was getting out of control. In fact, open-air drug markets are rare in most other major urban centers in China, simply because the authorities do not tolerate the presence of any such drug hot spots. Therefore, most drug dealers try to cultivate a clientele as quietly as possible and will go to great lengths to avoid any trouble with either neighboring businesses or their clients.

In the United States, low-level drug distribution is carried out mostly in the streets, as depicted by Bruce Johnson and colleagues in their work on the retail heroin trade in New York City;[18] by Terry Williams on the sale of cocaine in New York City;[19] by Phillipe Bourgois on the sale of crack in Washington Heights in New York City;[20] by George Rengert on the illegal drug markets in Wilmington, Delaware;[21] by Bruce Jacobs on the sale of crack in St. Louis, Missouri;[22] by Ric Curtis and Travis Wendel on the heroin retail markets in New York City;[23] and by Howard Campbell on drug retail in El Paso, Texas.[24] Almost all the heroin dealers in Kunming we interviewed did not push drugs on the streets; they made sales only after their regular customers initiated the interaction by calling them. Most of the actual transactions took place in the sellers' homes or in a public place such as a mahjong room, a restaurant, or a quiet park. In Kunming, a drug transaction in the streets between a first-time buyer and a seller is very rare.

Second, heroin retail in Kunming was not related to street gangs or organized crime. In fact, the heroin retail business is not related to the criminal underworld. Most low-level sellers are themselves drug users and only a small percentage of non-user sellers are in the drug business for money. Although mafia-style gangs are active in Kunming, these gangs are more likely to engage in traditional organized crime activities such as gambling, loan-sharking, debt collection, and the sex business, rather than be involved in the heroin business, whether it be trafficking, wholesale, or retail. However, these mafia-style gangs are reported to be active in the distribution of "newly-emerged drugs" such as ketamine, ecstasy, and MDMA. In the United States, retail-level drug distribution is often dominated by inner-city street gangs.[25]

Third, drug-related violence was almost unheard of in Kunming, whether it was systemic, economic compulsive, or psychopharmacological, as suggested by drug researcher Paul Goldstein in his analysis of the drug/violence nexus. According to Goldstein,

> [T]he psychopharmacological model suggests that some individuals, as a result of short or long term ingestion of specific substances, may become excitable, irrational, and may exhibit violent behavior. . . . The economically compulsive model suggests that some drug users engage in economically oriented violent crime, e.g., robbery, in order to support costly drug use. . . . Systemic violence refers to the traditionally aggressive patterns of interaction within the system of drug distribution and use. Some examples of systemic violence follow below. 1. disputes over territory between rival drug dealers. 2. assaults and homicides committed within dealing hierarchies as a means of enforcing normative codes. 3. robberies of drug dealers and the usually violent retaliation by the dealer or his/her bosses. 4. elimination of informers. 5. punishment for selling adulterated or phony drugs. 6. punishment for failing to pay one's debts. 7. disputes over drugs or drug paraphernalia 8. robbery violence related to the social ecology of copping areas.[26]

Psychopharmacological drug-related violence is rare among heroin users in Kunming because heroin is a sedative drug. Most heroin users we talked to told us that once they have their fix, the only thing they want to do is to lie down and do nothing. Most heroin addicts in Kunming turn to drug sale instead of other criminal activities such as robbery to support their drug habits because, in China, robbery is a much more serious crime than selling a small amount of drugs. Besides, predatory crimes such as robbery are not an option for female heroin users. As a result, economically compulsive, drug-related violence is almost nonexistent within the context of the Chinese heroin market.

Most heroin dealers we interviewed also said they had never engaged in, or had been subjected to, systemic violence, even though some of them had participated in certain activities that could have resulted in violent confrontation. For example, Mr. Lo, a 28-year-old Hui male, told us a story about one of his friends:

> There is not much drug-related violence. When there is rivalry, it is more likely that one party will report the other party's activity to the police. Killing the rival is never an option. One of my friends was involved in a drug deal with buyers from Nanning (Guangxi) a few months ago. The buyers showed up in Kunming with $1,800 to buy 100 grams of heroin. My friend said he could get the drug for them. My friend showed them some samples, and the buyers paid for the drug. My friend later told the buyers that someone took the money and fled. As a result, the Nanning buyers vowed that they will come back and kill my friend. My friend said the hell with their threat, but as a precautionary measure, he enrolled himself in a drug rehabilitation center.

Disputes over territories between rival drug dealers are uncommon because low-level heroin sale in Kunming is not territory-based. Even though some of the blocks near the railway station are well-known areas for copping heroin, no individual or group is strong enough to claim exclusive rights to the area. As one 34-year-old addict in Kunming observed:

> You hear drug traffickers get killed by one another. You don't see violence at the local level. Drug users don't cause troubles to drug dealers. Drug dealers also don't like trouble makers to get close to their store. These dealers may set up stores that don't sell anything, as a front. They deal

> drugs to a set of customers. Anytime they notice a drug addict who is causing trouble, they will stop doing business with him. No one wants any trouble on his turf. It is business.

This is not to say the street-level heroin trade was a collaborative and peaceful one in China. We also encountered subjects who claimed that some street vendors were quite adept at using the police to eliminate rival dealers. When there was competition, some dealers would report to the police of their observed "drug dealing" activities. According to two dealers:

> Violence is rare in this business. If there is competition among the dealers, we will try to eliminate the competition by telling the police who is selling drug. Of course, to do so, you must have a good relationship with the police. (A 46-year-old Muslim male)

> There's not much violence in the retail business. If we want to eliminate competition, we tip the police about our competitor. (A 36-year-old man from Guangdong Province)

In sum, street-level retail of heroin in Kunming is carried out predominantly by heroin addicts who must rely on drug sales to support their drug habits. Heroin retail in Kunming is fragmented, and there is no coordination among individual dealers. There is no evidence to suggest that violence and corruption are associated with heroin retail in the city. The retail drug market in Kunming has all the characteristics of a drug market located within a strict enforcement country.

British criminologist Ross Coomber conducted a study on drug pushers and he concluded that, contrary to the popular belief that drug markets are the worst kinds of criminal market (due to its violent and unforgiving nature) and drug dealers, the worst kind of criminal (who spread drug use indiscriminately): "Drug use (particularly dependent drug use) is often mundane and so is much that takes place in the drug market."[27] Our research on heroin retail in Kunming supports his conclusion.

7

Women in the Heroin Trade

During our time in the field, we encountered numerous women who were involved in either wholesale drug transportation or street-level dealings. Although we expected female drug addicts to engage in the retail business as a means to support their addiction, we were impressed by their active roles in this illicit enterprise. We do not believe women are playing a dominant role in the drug trade in China, but the high frequency of their appearance in the news stories on official drug seizures and arrests as well as in our field activities requires some explanation and conceptualization on the role of gender in a business that remains largely male-dominated elsewhere in the world.

Women and paid labor have long been studied by social scientists, but women's participation in illicit enterprises (i.e., organized crime) has not received much empirical attention. Unlike the legal economy, where deliberate efforts by the Chinese government have improved women's participation and altered certain gendered stratifications, their active presence in criminal enterprises must be explained by the contextual characteristics of the specific illicit market. In this chapter, we examine women's participation in drug trafficking and street drug dealings in Yunnan, China, to understand how women have played a role in gaining and maintaining market positions in this illicit business. Drawing on data from a survey of 297 convicted female inmates and in-depth interviews with more than a dozen active female drug dealers in the community, we will propose a niche market perspective for understanding women's participation in this illicit enterprise.

Compared to their male counterparts in terms of demographic backgrounds, market entry methods, and roles, we believe that (1) the unique sociolegal context in China, and (2) the importance of interpersonal networks in facilitating drug dealings, have created a more meaningful niche for women in the drug trade than is found in traditional organized criminal enterprises. We argue that the market conditions within the Chinese political environment become important constructs to explain gendered participation in this illicit enterprise.

Gender and Organized Crime

Women are not often studied by mainstream criminologists in the contexts of drug trafficking or organized crime in general. The paucity of empirical data on female participation in drug trafficking or any other organized illicit enterprising activities is mostly because women are traditionally and historically excluded from such activities. They are not easily found in traditional racketeering activities. Of the few studies that focus on the issue of gender in organized crime, women are mostly relegated to auxiliary roles such as the family members or accomplices of their male relatives or partners. In her analysis of women and the mafia, sociology professor Renate Siebert described female members of the mafia family often as the target of exploitation and subordination, excluded from this men-only world.[1] Although these women were portrayed as playing the important role of a "virtuous" mother or wife, which was central to the maintenance of the mafia's territorial sovereignty, their contacts with or entry into the mafia were mostly via their complicity.

A few studies, however, have begun to recognize the active roles that women play in criminal organizations. For example, sociologist Alessandro Dino (1998) synthesizes research on the female world in the mafia, beginning with observations of how mafia families communicate with the outside world.[2] She found that women often played central roles in maintaining organized crime groups, as they substituted for their fathers, husbands, and brothers in the management of the clan's affairs. These women, like their male counterparts, took on the mentality of defending the family honor. However, it should be noted that these women were already members of an existing family business, thus requiring no effort in entering the illicit market.

Rosalva Resendiz, a criminal justice scholar, found significant variations along the gender line in professional auto theft along the U.S./Mexico border.[3] Males were introduced via friends, while for females, introduction took place via intimate sexual relationships and family ties. Although women tended to occupy relatively low-risk and low-paid positions in the auto theft rings, they were nonetheless active participants in the enterprise.

More recently, in their analysis of women's participation in transnational human smuggling, criminologists Sheldon Zhang and his associates turned their attention to the organizational context and market demands that might have shaped the extent and nature of women's participation in the illicit enterprise.[4] Drawing from interviews with 129 human smugglers, Zhang and his colleagues found that the market contexts within which criminal enterprises exist provide the main explanation for these women's entry.

The organizational structure of traditional organized crime has been compared to that of modern corporations. It is characterized as hierarchical, centralized, and bureaucratic in structure, with women nearly absent.[5] However, we argue that an enterprise model may be better suited in explaining most contemporary Chinese organized crime, particularly those that are transnational in nature.[6] The enterprise model does not assume a hierarchical structure and instead envisages adaptive and flexible networks that easily expand and contract to deal with the uncertainties inherent in illicit marketplaces. While such networks may have a small core of organizers, they are best characterized as transitory alliances, with participants organizing only to the extent necessary to effectively carry out the illicit activities.[7] Although some mafia groups, such as the *Camorra* of the Naples region, have occasionally accepted women into the leadership of a mafia organization, female mafia bosses are rare and they are always the spouses or sisters of incarcerated male mafia bosses. Sicilian women are rarely part of the effective force of a mafia organization.[8] As organized crime scholars Alan Block and William Chambliss observed a few decades ago, women may have been involved in the "enterprise syndicate" but not the "power syndicate."[9]

Stratification by gender in the labor force is often explained from an occupational perspective[10] or with historical conditions.[11] Researchers who study illicit labor markets emphasize either human capital or situational exclusionary practices to explain women's limited involvement in criminal enterprises, rather than seeking explanations in the organizational contexts within an illicit enterprise.[12]

Much research on women and crime has emphasized supply-side explanatory factors, including human capital and women's gendered preferences. For instance, women's limited participation in criminal networks is often attributed to its deviation from traditional gender expectations. Women may be deterred from involvement in crime, or particular types of crime, because such actions are "doubly deviant": not just a violation of broad social norms against offending, but also specific violations of appropriate behavior for women *as women.*[13] Moreover, some authors argue that it is not simply the deterrent effects of being labeled "unfeminine," but women's adoption of more relational social values, that makes crimes, and especially those that require physical violence, undesirable.[14] These aspects of gender ideology have featured prominently in both human capital and demand-side explanations of women's limited participation in criminal enterprises. Women have less exposure to opportunities for the display and use of violence and the mastery of weapons. Thus, they are less able to bring such human capital to illicit enterprises and also are perceived, categorically, to lack physical capacity for success within criminal networks.[15]

Darrell Steffensmeier, a professor at Pennsylvania State University, also argued that there is "*variability* of sex segregation across the spectrum of organized crime activities."[16] Like scholars who examine gendering within the formal labor market, he suggested that the organizational context of criminal groups affects the extent to which homosocial reproduction and sex-typing take place, and thus the degree and nature of women's exclusion. Specifically, he hypothesized that sex segregation would be more marked in illicit groups that require physical strength or violence, face competition or threat from other groups, have exclusively economic goals (rather than in combination with social and/or political goals), and exhibit greater organizational complexity and professionalization.

Research on a variety of criminal enterprises—including drug sales,[17] burglary networks,[18] professional thieves,[19] robbery crews,[20] street gangs,[21] and traditional organized crime[22]—has offered support for Steffensmeier's propositions. These researchers generally found the male-dominated practices within these criminal organizations; and within these contexts, women are routinely defined by men as physically and emotionally weak. While women can occasionally overcome these labels[23] or encounter circumstances that allow for their temporary inclusion,[24] most research is clear in documenting the rigid sexism within criminal enterprises.

While researchers have documented the existence of homosocial reproduction and sex-typing in illicit economic enterprises, they have paid less attention to Steffensmeier's contention that organizational context is fundamental to understanding women's place in criminal networks. While our study was not designed for theory testing, we have found many cases through our prison survey and conversations with active female street-level drug dealers that lend empirical credence to Steffensmeier's argument. The illicit economy of drug trafficking and retailing in China possesses unique features likely to shape the nature of women's involvement.

The relationship between gender ideologies about women and work may also contribute to women's participation in the drug trade. An integral part of the communist state's agenda under Mao Zedong was a set of progressive policies toward women, including equal pay for equal work, marriage rights, maternity provisions in the workplace, and the promotion of gender equality in educational settings. While "few societies in history have prescribed a lower status for women than traditional Confucian China,"[25] the result of these policies was not just dramatic improvements in women's educational achievements and economic participation, but also changing ideologies and attitudes in favor of gender egalitarianism, particularly among younger generations in urban areas.[26] More than 90 percent of urban women were part of the paid labor force during the Mao era,[27] and the majority of married women shared nearly equal economic resources with their husbands—a rate higher than that found in some economically more advanced countries.[28] Of equal importance, work has become central to urban women's identities.[29]

The egalitarian principles under Mao suggest fewer ideological barriers to gender inclusion among contemporary generations of Chinese, and these may translate to the interstitial enterprise of drug trafficking and retailing. When there are no direct requirements for physical violence, women may find themselves working side by side with their male counterparts in licit as well as illicit enterprises. The heroin trade perhaps presents a special case study of a gendered labor market in illicit economies.

Gendered Differences among Incarcerated Drug Traffickers

As described in chapter 4, we conducted a survey of 578 convicted drug traffickers in a major prison inside China. These respondents, although based on convenience sampling, represented more than 10 percent of the prison population at the time. We oversampled women to allow meaningful statistical comparisons. The actual prison gender ratio was about 3 to 1 in favor of males. Because drug offenses were capital crimes in China with no known preferential treatment to either gender, we can only assume the observed gender ratio in the prison was reflective of the drug trafficker population in the real world. Although there is no way to verify this observation empirically, we are fairly confident that women's participation in the drug trade was not a rare phenomenon.

Demographic Profiles

As shown in table 7.1, there were notable variations between men and women in several key demographic measures, suggesting some gendered differences in the circumstances that precipitated their involvement in the illicit business. The women in our sample were significantly older than their male counterparts, on average by 3.74 years ($t = 5.0$, $p < 0.0001$). As one may have guessed, such an age gap pointed to the increased likelihood that the female smugglers were either married or had their own families. A significant number of the male inmates in our prison survey sample, 45 percent, were single, compared to only 16 percent of the females. Our female subjects were also far less educated than their male counterparts. Women without any formal education accounted for more than one-quarter of the sample, which outnumbered their male counterparts by more than 2 to 1. By combining these two characteristics, it is not difficult to see the limited opportunities for these women in any formal economies. Moreover, being married also implies that these women's participation in the labor force was part of a family economic strategy in which "women are expected . . . to earn wages in ways that do not conflict with their family obligations."[30]

When we asked about their employment status prior to the most recent arrest, there were interesting differences between the two sexes. As shown in table 7.1, women were far more likely to have been

Table 7.1. Demographics of Incarcerated Drug Traffickers by Gender

	Male		Female	
	N	%	*N*	%
Marital status				
Single	125	45	44	16
Married	99	36	145	52
Separated/divorced/widowed	50	19	88	32
Total*	274	100	277	100
Education				
No formal education	31	11	76	26
Grade school	106	38	111	38
Middle school	100	36	80	27
High school	30	11	19	7
College	12	4	6	2
Total*	279	100	292	100
Occupation prior to arrest				
Self-employed	22	18	54	39
Commercial driver	24	19	1	1
Peasant	28	22	50	36
Factory workers	30	24	17	12
Public-sector employee	10	8	7	5
Private-sector employee	11	9	10	7
Total*	125	100	139	100

*Effective sample size.

self-employed (39 percent) than their male counterparts (18 percent), running their own small businesses. The figure alone seemed to suggest that these women were no strangers to entrepreneurial activities. Their enterprising experiences perhaps propelled them to seek additional money-making activities. However, most of these female entrepreneurs appeared to occupy the low-end commerce jobs, such as retail produce stands or street food carts. We inquired about their monthly income. Of those who disclosed their pre-incarceration income (97 men and 75 women), women on average earned $85 a month, compared to $115 for men.

Our instrument was not precise enough to capture many subjects who were peasants, as farm laborers in China typically do not consider farming an occupation. Therefore, a large number of both men and women in our survey claimed to be unemployed at the time of their arrest. We did not probe about their means of subsistence to differentiate farming from true unemployment. However, of those who identified themselves as peasants, women outnumbered men by more than 2 to 1.

Men, on the other hand, were more likely to have worked in factories. More interestingly, we found that close to one-fifth of the males (19.2 percent) were commercial drivers, an occupation that could easily lend to opportunities in drug trafficking.

In sum, based on our prison sample, there were a few demographic profiles associated with women in the drug trafficking business. They were low on educational attainment, married with families, no stable jobs, and they had prior experience as entrepreneurs. Although women's participation in the labor force is high in contemporary China, there are clear patterns of discrimination in career opportunities. The educational disparities found in our sample may reflect economic choices made in this context. Coupled with the limited opportunities for women in border regions in formal economies, our data suggest a specific economic incentive for these women to consider drug trafficking a viable enterprise. Few of our surveyed subjects—male or female—held regular salaried jobs. Most had irregular employment histories, thus probably were familiar with more entrepreneurial activities. Entrepreneurialism offers an important avenue for upward mobility in border economies, albeit an illicit one.

The demographic information presented here suggests that women's entry into the drug trade may be shaped by gendered life circumstances related to economic opportunities, such as education, marital status, and family finances. To examine these issues further, we begin with a discussion of women's entry into drug trafficking, and compare their experiences to those of men. We then move on to describe the roles these women play. Finally, we offer a gendered market perspective as a means of understanding the place of women in the drug trade, as compared to other types of organized crime.

Drug Trafficking Offenses

There were no differences between the two sexes with regard to the types of drugs that were trafficked. Also, as expected for a region bordering Burma, the vast majority of our subjects were involved in heroin trafficking (98 percent for men and 92 percent for women). A few of both sexes were trafficking opium or other opiate products. Only a handful (two men and eight women) were involved in trafficking methamphetamine.

Table 7.2. Trafficking Offenses by Gender

	Male		Female	
	N	%	*N*	%
Arrest locations				
Hotel	42	16	35	15
Street	84	33	87	38
Home	12	5	22	10
Checkpoint	41	16	18	8
Public transportation	74	29	59	26
Other	2	1	7	3
Self-report role in trafficking				
Manufacturing	3	1	2	1
Domestic transportation	123	53	95	43
Domestic sales	47	20	43	19
Cross-border trafficking	41	18	73	33
Other	19	8	9	4
Convicted offenses				
Transborder trafficking	95	37	98	41
Domestic transportation	126	50	97	40
Distribution or sales	33	13	45	19
Weight of drugs trafficked	Mean: 3,149 grams Std. deviation: 8,963 (*N* = 262)		Mean: 1,351 Std. deviation: 3,709 (*N* = 266)	
Prior arrest				
No arrest	244	90	283	98
Arrest	28	10	7	2
Total*^	272	100	290	100
Prior drug use				
No	211	78	260	89
Yes	61	22	32	11
Total*^^	272	100	292	100
Sentences				
< 14 years	0	0	50	18
14–21 years	21	8	82	29
Life in prison	83	30	89	31
Suspended death sentence	172	62	62	22
Total*	276	100	283	100

* Effective sample size; ^ $p < .003$; ^^ $p < .0001$.

As shown in table 7.2, few differences exist between men and women in terms of the locations where they were arrested and the charges against them. Our survey instrument lacked the ability to probe the details of their most current arrest, but this finding suggests that both men and women, at least in this sample, were probably following similar modus operandi, and their enterprising activities appeared to overlap in similar territories or through similar routes.

Although both men and women may be similar in their modus operandi, there were marked differences in other aspects of their trafficking activities. Men in our sample (52.8 percent) appeared more likely to report involvement in domestic transportation than women (42.8 percent). Women (32.9 percent) were more likely to report involvement in cross-border trafficking activities than their male counterparts (17.6 percent), while both groups were equally involved in drug sales. It is unclear to us why women were disproportionately involved in cross-border transportation compared to men. As reported in chapter 4, our sample did include a large number of ethnic minorities and women from Burma who lived in the border region for a long time. In addition, cross-border commerce was a common practice among these peoples on both sides of the border. However, both men and women living in the border regions are engaged in cross-border enterprising activities. The gendered difference in cross-border drug trafficking is worth future exploration.

On the measure of convicted offenses, both men and women were quite similar. However, on the severity of the offense, men were caught carrying significantly more heroin than their female counterparts. As shown in the standard deviations in table 7.2, men in general carried about 1,800 grams more on average than their female counterparts. There were also greater variations among male traffickers in the amount of drugs they carried. Perhaps due to their physical limitations, lack of access to heavier consignments, or simply lesser roles in the transactions, women were found to be at a clear disadvantage in the earning potential in this illicit enterprise. However, such a disadvantage may have inadvertently played in their favor when it came to punishment. As shown in table 7.2, women in general received far less serious sentences than their male counterparts. Not a single man in the sample received less than 14 years compared to about 18 percent of the women. On the other hand, 62 percent of the men were given suspended death sentences compared to 22 percent of the women. We were unable to interview anyone who was awaiting execution, but it would be safe to say that the majority of those sentenced to death were men. Harsh punishment for drug trafficking offenses is standard in China. Regardless of whether gender plays a role in judicial decision-making, findings shown here suggest that some of the variations in sentencing severity can be explained by the gravity of the offense. The heavier the drug consignment found on the offender, the harsher the punishment.

Entry into the Drug Trade

Our survey data suggest that these incarcerated women followed a rather gendered pathway into the drug trade. For many of them, close social networks, including relatives, families, and friends, provided the most common route to the trafficking business. Research shows that the social networks that provide women entrée into criminal enterprises are disproportionately intimate partners. When the romantic connection is broken, so is the woman's access to the criminal networks.[31]

This was in contrast to their male counterparts' entry into the business, as shown in table 7.3. Men, on the other hand, were far more likely to enter the drug trade on their own, alone. Friends were also a major point for males to enter the drug trade, 69.4 percent compared

Table 7.3. Others Involved in Initial Drug Deal by Gender

	Male		Female	
	N	%	*N*	%
Number of people involved in first drug deal				
One other person	57	22	30	11
Two or more people	198	78	238	89
Total*^^	255	100	268	100
Relatives involved in first drug deal				
No	171	92	170	83
Yes	15	8	34	16
Total*^	186	100	204	100
Family member involved in first drug deal				
No	179	96	183	90
Yes	7	4	21	10
Total*^	186	100	204	100
Friends involved in first drug deal				
No	57	31	102	50
Yes	129	69	102	50
Total*^^	186	100	204	100

* Effective sample size; ^ $p < .01$; ^^ $p < 0.0001$.

to 50 percent of women. In any case, friends, far more than relatives and family members, became the most important route into the trafficking business.

Another way to examine the social networks of the respondents is to find out who was also arrested in the most recent incident that got them into the prison. Again, women (69 percent) were more likely to be arrested together with others, while more men were arrested alone (38.5 percent). It appeared that a greater number of men preferred to carry out the business on their own, while women's trafficking activities involved other parties. Moreover, women were far more likely to be arrested together with their relatives and family members than their male counterparts, as shown in table 7.4.

As for their experiences in the drug trade, there were marked differences along the gender line. Judging from where men and women obtained their drug consignments, as shown in table 7.5, it appears that women in this sample were more likely to be transporters who received their package and attempted to deliver to the next transaction point. About two-thirds of the women in the sample claimed that the drugs

Table 7.4. Most Recent Arrest by Gender

	Male		Female	
	N	%	*N*	%
Number of people arrested the last time				
Self (no one else)	99	39	87	31
Others involved also arrested	158	61	194	69
Total*^	257	100	281	100
Relatives involved in last arrest				
No	128	91	125	78
Yes	12	9	35	22
Total*^^	140	100	160	100
Family member involved in last arrest				
No	133	95	143	90
Yes	7	5	16	10
Total*	140	100	204	100
Friends involved in last arrest				
No	46	33	74	47
Yes	94	67	85	53
Total*^^	140	100	159	100

* Effective sample size; ^ $p < .05$; ^^ $p < 0.01$.

Table 7.5. Experiences in Drug Trade by Gender

	Male		Female	
	N	%	*N*	%
Where to obtain drugs				
Outside China	69	38	39	21
Inside China	41	22	26	14
Delivered to me	72	40	120	65
Total*^^^	182	100	185	100
Decide on drug price				
Cannot	171	80	200	86
Can	42	20	34	14
Total*	213	100	212	100
Decide on trafficking route				
Cannot	144	70	172	81
Can	62	30	40	19
Total*^^	206	100	212	100
Decide on distribution of money				
Cannot	140	77	167	87
Can	41	23	24	13
Total*^^	181	100	191	100
Decide on organization or partner tasks				
Cannot	159	88	180	96
Can	22	12	8	4
Total*^^	181	100	188	100
Other business aside from drug trade				
No	123	49	93	33
Yes	126	51	186	67
Total*^^^	249	100	279	100
Perceptions of other drug traffickers				
Honest businesspeople	33	18	58	28
Unscrupulous	25	13	26	13
Hard to say—a mixed bag	128	69	120	59
Total*^	186	100	204	100

* Effective sample size; ^ $p < 0.05$; ^^ $p < 0.01$; ^^^ $p < 0.0001$.

were delivered to them, compared to about 40 percent of their male counterparts. While the number of men who waited for the drugs to be delivered to them was also sizeable, the majority of women were most likely couriers or mules. In comparison, men were more proactive in approaching their sources, either from outside China or within the country.

We further probed the extent to which men and women could play any decision-making roles or dictated the direction of an operation. While in most cases, neither men nor women were able to call the shots in a trafficking operation, there were noticeable gender differences. For instance, when it came to the pricing of their drug consignments, neither group seemed capable of charging a price of their own choice. This makes sense, since the price of heroin was mostly dictated by the prevailing market conditions. The margins that each successive traffickers or wholesale dealers could add were limited. However, as for the trafficking route, men (30.1 percent) seemed to have much more control than their female counterparts (14.5 percent). The difference was quite significant. Again, as shown in table 7.5, men appeared to have more control than women over how the drug money was to be distributed and how tasks were to be divided among partners, although in both cases, those who were able to make decisions in money matters and task delegation were among the minority of their respective gender group. Nevertheless, the gender differences were quite noticeable.

Perhaps in line with their cultural expectations for women's participation in paid labor, women were far more likely to operate other businesses on the side. More than two-thirds of the women in our sample claimed to do business aside from the drug trade, compared to only half of the men. On the other hand, women were also more likely to hold a benign view of people involved in the drug trade than their male partners. Far more men considered drug traffickers to be a mixed bag of both good and bad people, while slightly more women preferred to think drug traffickers were honest businesspeople who were just trying to make a living.

Gendered Pathway into the Drug Trade

Our questionnaire was constructed with the prisoners in mind, all straightforward questions with structured choices. There was, however, one open-ended question, inquiring about the circumstances under which the respondent took the initial step into the drug business. The initial entry was of great importance to us in understanding how people of various backgrounds became involved, thus allowing us to explore the different pathways as well as mechanisms that respondents took to enter the business. However, this question was often left blank by the respondents. Perhaps the question was better suited for face-to-face interviews in which adequate time and rapport may yield useful information.

Open-ended questions often are not filled out even under the best survey circumstances because they require effort on the part of respondents to think and compose on the spot. Ours was a voluntary and uncompensated survey inside a prison, and the vast majority of the respondents had only limited education. Despite these methodological challenges, a few respondents left brief remarks describing how they first got involved. By comparing their statements, we found gendered as well as common themes among both male and female respondents.

As expected, the lure of quick money and financial returns far superior to what these respondents' existing circumstances could offer were the most common theme in the few written explanations on the initial entry into the drug trade. Although personal circumstances may vary, many of our subjects were simply "lured" into the business because they were desperate for money and happened to be in a social network with direct access to the illicit trade. There were also similar themes that both men and women seemed to share when they recounted their initial journey into the drug trade. As mentioned in chapter 4, gambling debts and drug addiction were some of the recurrent themes that pulled both men and women in. Some of our respondents got involved in the drug trade as a result of a series of unfortunate events that culminated in a desperate situation.

The money-making motive is a common albeit simplistic explanation to the varied circumstances in which our subjects found themselves involved in the drug trafficking business. A close examination of the circumstances revealed that women's personal networks were often tied to their initial entry into the drug trade. As shown in table 7.3, women were more likely than men to venture into the illicit enterprise with multiple partners such as family members and relatives. A 33-year-old woman from Yunnan Province, who received a suspended death sentence for transporting 229 grams of heroin, said she became deranged after a big argument with her husband. Soon she found herself in need of money desperately: "When I was hopeless, my husband's sister asked me to help her move some heroin. At that point, I was completely lost and did not think any consequences could be associated with illicit drugs. I had lost my mind when I was arrested."

Another woman, 37 years old, who received a suspended death sentence for transporting 3,500 grams of heroin, said she was recruited by her own sister into the business at a time when she was leaving her husband:

> I was recruited into this business by my own sister in 1991. At that time, I was having problems with my husband. I wanted to make a lot of money and then would be able to leave my husband and raise my daughter by myself. Because my husband was not from my hometown, I did not know him very much before our marriage. Only after we got married did I find out that he had someone else in his heart that could not be replaced by me. That made me very unhappy and I decided to get into the drug business with my sister. I made up to $3,500 a year.

There was also a story of trafficking drugs for love. A 30-year-old woman from Guizhou Province recalled that she was running a beauty shop, earning $240 a month, when she met her boyfriend. She claimed that he deceived her: "He was really nice to me. He asked me to divorce my husband, and I did. He then told me that it would cost a lot of money for him to leave his wife, and then we would be able to get married. He then got in touch with a friend in Yunnan who was in the drug business and brought me to Ruili to involve in a drug deal." For about a month, she was helping her boyfriend transport heroin. When she was arrested, she was carrying 277 grams and later received a suspended death sentence. For that consignment, her boyfriend promised her $60.

The familial and group orientation became more pronounced when women were the primary providers for the family and were under severe financial pressure on the home front. Unlike those described earlier, who were desperate to find money due to personal predicaments, clear gendered differences were also observed in our subjects' descriptions that seemed to corroborate their demographic profiles. Women were far more likely to cite financial pressure from their families and the need to support their children and sick family members as a recurrent theme in their explanations of how they got into the trafficking business in the first place. Their response to the mention of familial responsibilities clearly suggested gendered disparities in their entry into the illicit enterprise. A 31-year-old woman from Sichuan Province, who received a suspended death sentence for transporting 1,600 grams of heroin, told her story:

> In the year 2002, I was in Beijing. A friend of mine who was in Guangdong asked me to go visit her after she learned that my business in Beijing was not going well. At that time, my son was still young and his father had passed away. Everything fell on my shoulders. I need to make money to pay for my son's education and our living expenses. There's no way you can live a life without money. When my friend in Guangdong asked me to get involved in the drug business, it really scared me to death at first. To be honest, I had never ever thought of doing anything illegal. But in this world, how many people can really escape the seduction of money?

As shown in the demographic profiles in table 7.1, the vast majority of the female respondents (84 percent) were married at least once, compared to 54 percent of men in similar situations. Therefore, it was no surprise that these women were often caught in financial difficulties. Another woman from Yunnan Province, who was serving a life sentence, told her story:

> At that time, we were very poor. There were seven people in our family and they all depended on me to provide. My husband could not see due to eye ailments, and he was unemployed. And I needed money to pay for a surgery for my oldest son. But I did not have a penny. So I borrowed $120 from a loan shark and used the money to buy 10 grams of heroin to start the business. Later, I went back to get another 40 grams. That was when I was arrested. All my drugs and earnings were seized by the police.

Not all women entered into the drug business for altruistic reasons. A few subjects were simply tired of their life circumstances, either due to divorce or unhappy marriages, and wanted to strike out on their own. Both men and women can be driven by a desire to change their life through unconventional venues. We found both men and women in the group of entrepreneurs who were striving to pursue their material dreams. A 29-year-old man from rural Yunnan Province, who received a life sentence for transporting heroin, wrote: "Have you ever been to the farm villages, to the mountainous areas? Do you know how it feels when you don't have any money to pay for school? When I was physically and mentally young, I did not do anything wrong. After I left home to work and got cheated and robbed, after I spent many nights sleeping in the dark, cold, dirty street corners, I see myself as garbage who had been discarded by our society."

Such a strong desire to change one's life through whatever means possible was also shared by another inmate, 38-year-old man from Hunan Province who received a suspended death sentence for trafficking 10,520 grams of heroin: "I lost one leg after a car accident. However, I had strong will, and I want to make a lot of money quickly through the drug business and then I will invest my money in legitimate businesses and become a person with high social status."

A Gendered Market Perspective

Despite extensive sociological research on gender and organizations, criminologists have paid insufficient attention to how market conditions may shape the extent and nature of women's participation in illicit enterprises. Findings from the survey and our field interviews carry some theoretical implications. The presence of a sizeable number of women in the marketplace demands explanations on whether gender plays a role in the drug trade.

Unlike traditional criminal rackets, such as gambling and extortion, that are typically exclusive to men, women seem able to carve out a meaningful niche in the drug trafficking and retailing markets in China. This is particularly the case when abusing or selling illicit drugs are socially stigmatized and prosecuted by the government. For women to deviate from their traditional gender roles and engage in buying and selling heroin in China, the market must have a set of requisites that accommodate their entry. It is our view that the unique social context—the absence of open street drug dealing—makes open competition practically impossible. In China, buying and selling illicit drugs rely almost exclusively on personal connections and occur within highly restricted social networks. As a result, the lack of competition among potential rivals doing business in the same neighborhood prevents any possibility of interpersonal violence. When physical violence is not necessary to ensure success in drug dealings, any segregation by gender does not appear to serve a viable purpose in a criminal enterprise.

Therefore, we are proposing a theoretical framework, which we call "a gendered market perspective," to explain how it is that opportunities emerge for women in the drug trafficking and street retailing business in the Chinese context. This paradigm is predicated on three prerequisites for entry into the drug business and a set of market conditions that we believe have reduced—though in no way eliminated—the traditional gender barriers commonly found in organized criminal activities.

Prerequisites for Market Entry

The transportation and sale of illicit drugs require few special skills, aside from those who are charged with constructing and concealing compartments in vehicles for hiding the contraband. No particular training or knowledge is needed, thus making it accessible to anyone. However, there are two general prerequisites—proper social connections (i.e., resources and opportunities) and sufficient entrepreneurial spirit. Both qualities must be present for any men or women to participate in the business, and neither alone is sufficient. Access to the source of illicit drugs provides the opportunity or entry point into the trade, and the risk-taking spirit encourages one to venture into unconventional business activities.

Traditionally, opportunities to be involved in criminal enterprising opportunities are limited to women. As found in our prison survey and field activities, men were far more prevalent in the drug trade than women. Because drug manufacturing sources and addict populations are hidden, one must be placed in a social network where the connections either already exist or will emerge. Data from our prison survey appear to support this observation. As shown in table 7.3, men were far more likely to enter the drug trade via their friends than women, suggesting drug trade opportunities are more likely to be found among one's social friends or acquaintances than his or her family members or relatives. The prerequisite of entrepreneurial spirit is easily understood, but difficult to define. It is more than one's desire to take risks and make money but also a willingness to break with traditional gendered expectations—those more in line with looking after the welfare of the young and the old of a family. We have described some of the situations that draw women into the drug trade, such as the need for financial independence, and the desire to provide for the family. These women were aware of the illicit nature of the contraband that they were transporting or selling. As shown by the long sentences they received as a result of the harsh social environment, these women had to have enough risk-taking spirit to outweigh the potential costs in association with the violation of their gendered social roles.

A Market without a Turf

In the few studies on women's involvement in the drug economy, they are mostly confined to the margins.[32] This may in fact also be the case in the Chinese context. However, there were enough women in the drug trade to lead us to believe that certain market conditions must have given rise to women's limited but meaningful roles in this illicit economy. The prerequisites discussed previously are necessary but insufficient to explain how women manage to enter and remain in the drug trade. Certain market conditions that have traditionally excluded women from other criminal networks—such as ruthlessness and the ability to utilize violence—can be somewhat tempered. It is our belief that two key market conditions appear to make women's participation possible.

Drug transportation and sales at the street level in China is a business with few discernible territorial boundaries. Unlike gambling and prostitution, where clients and business activities are tied to specific neighborhoods, drug transportation and sales mostly involve transient and highly concealed transactions. Although we were aware of a few neighborhoods in Kunming where there were frequent sightings of drug addicts and drug sales activities, to our knowledge the vast majority of drug transactions were carried out in unrevealed street corners, nightclubs, and parks. The clandestine nature of the business and harsh law enforcement environment prevent the drug trade from forming well-defined territories in China. In other words, transactions are only possible through negotiations between the traffickers or vendors and their clients with few observers, thus limiting opportunities for anyone to intervene. A drug deal involves secretive and idiosyncratic arrangements known only to those directly involved. Such one-to-one transactions are essential in reducing exposure to law enforcement.

During our stay in the field, we found no evidence of any drug traffickers or street vendors attempting to drive away potential competitors. Competition among traffickers—male or female—to control wholesale or distribution networks or gain market shares was unheard of. Without a clearly defined turf and with most transactions based on one-to-one interactions, the drug trade seems to garner two essential attributes that render traditional gender barriers found in other forms of illicit enterprises somewhat less salient.

First, as long as the patron-client relationships remain one-on-one and the transactions are clandestine, both parties in a drug trade can retain control of their own business activities, which by the very nature of these business practices will make competition unlikely. Although a buyer could potentially talk to other dealers or peers in search of additional sources of drugs for better prices or quality, our field data suggest that few were able to cultivate such alternatives easily in any short period of time. With little possibility for competition, violence is of little use.

Second, without a turf to defend or rivalry to fend off, monopoly is difficult to achieve. Thus, the construction of the basic masculine identity around interpersonal violence found in other criminal enterprises is less material. The ability to use violence to control and manage volatile situations is probably the most salient element that relegates women to the margins of most illicit markets, and it is their perceived lack of such qualities that is used to exclude them from all but peripheral involvement.[33] The drug trade, at least at the lower level, is a business that relies heavily on personal connections rather than violence, thus providing women an avenue for participation, whether it be in partnership with husbands, lovers, or family members, or, independently.

An Illicit Enterprise Built on Social Networks

In many traditional Chinese organized crimes, such as extortion, prostitution, and gambling, the ability and willingness to use violence for instrumental purposes is a prerequisite as well as a hallmark for successful and sustained operations. As Ko-lin illustrated in his study on Chinatown gangs, multiple strategies—ranging from shootouts to unruly disruptive behaviors—may be used either to drive out rival gangs or to subdue unwilling store owners.[34] However, given the lack of territorial conflicts between addicts and dealers, most facets of the drug trade, at least inside China and on the street, do not require physical dominance or muscle power. Instead, most transactions consist of interpersonal exchanges.

Our sense was that while violence did erupt between some traffickers during their border crossing, we believe it was mainly used to fight off police to escape the inevitable death penalty as opposed to eliminating competitors. It was not clear to us if women would ever find themselves in need of muscle power to settle scores with unscrupulous partners or addicts. One thing was clear—violence attracts attention. Since risk management is of supreme priority to all drug traffickers and dealers, the less of it the better, even when it means a loss of investment.

Conclusion

Findings in this study suggest that there are several market-oriented prerequisites within the organizational context that support systematic involvement by women in drug trafficking and street dealing activities in China. It should be noted that drug trafficking and retailing are still predominantly male enterprises. Nonetheless, unlike other traditional enterprises, these women were not simply relegated to invisible margins, but instead were present in many levels of the drug trade. In most cases, women worked for or with male partners, but they occasionally participated independently.

The use of informal social networks for recruitment and hiring leads to discretionary practices that reproduce gender segregation and women's exclusion.[35] This is a constant in illicit organizations, which are neither bound by nor able to adhere to legal guidelines in hiring practices. Women's entry into the drug trade was significantly tied to their personal networks. Within the drug trade, we believe women were in general limited to lower-level trafficking and sales activities, but they were not blocked from entering the market in sizeable numbers.

Perhaps the most important feature of the drug trade along the border between Yunnan and Burma that shapes women's participation is the absence of violence. It is not common in most facets of drug trafficking operations; therefore, a primary hurdle for women's participation in organized crime is minimized. Women often lack the opportunities to master the use of violence and are widely perceived as incapable combatants.[36] This obstacle appears to be mitigated in the Chinese context, where organized crime, violence, or illicit drugs attract nothing but the harshest response from the justice system.

An important question emerging from our research is the extent to which these patterns are limited to the drug trade in China. We have found little empirical evidence to suggest that women in other parts of the world are as active in drug trafficking and street dealing as the Chinese.

Our research also suggests that cultural influences are significant. Ideologies about the importance of economic participation for women may be more meaningful in the Chinese context, with the Communist government advocating principles of gender egalitarianism.[37] Immigration experts Richard Wright and Mark Ellis found much greater gender segregation in the labor market experiences of U.S. immigrants from Mexico and Central America than those from China and other East Asian countries.[38]

Future research should mind Steffensmeier's early call for attention to these facets of criminal networks and organized crime.[39] As he hypothesized, our research does suggest that there is variability in the extent and nature of gender stratification in illicit enterprises. Female participation in the heroin trade or some other racketeering activities will likely increase as their usefulness becomes greater for partnerships and organizations with men. In a male-only or heavily male-dominated underworld, these women must prove their usefulness for entry as well as mobility within the crime networks.

Our study in China suggests that the market environment is as important for understanding gender stratification within illicit enterprises as it is for understanding the same features in the formal economy. It is our belief that, in general, women are playing a secondary role in this illicit enterprise, and gender stratification was abundantly clear, judging from the differences in the weights of the drugs seized and the severity of sentences between men and women in our prison survey. Nonetheless, we believe that the nature of the enterprise and the social context mitigate the obstacles that traditionally exclude women from criminal enterprises.

8

Drug Treatment with a Chinese Characteristic

Beginning in the seventeenth century through the early decades of the twentieth century, opium consumption was a considerable social problem in China, which brought disastrous consequences to the nation's wealth as well as on its population's health.[1] The fall of the Qing Dynasty was blamed mainly on the opium trade, for which China fought and lost two wars (1839–1842 and 1856–1860) to the British-led foreign powers. The secession of Hong Kong to England, indemnities paid to the victorious countries, and the loss of national pride seared deep scars into the Chinese psyche. All governments since, regardless of political persuasions, have established strict rules against the illicit drug trade. Drug addiction has since become highly stigmatized in the Chinese culture, symbolizing personal as well as familial failure worthy of nothing but disgrace.

Soon after the Communist government was established in 1949, a nationwide campaign was launched to eradicate this century-long addiction; opium dens were shut down, opium manufacturing facilities closed, drug traffickers were summarily executed or imprisoned, and addicts were sent to labor camps en masse. The massive drug prohibition campaign, coupled with draconian penal sanctions, was so effective that in less than three years the Communist government declared China a drug-free country.[2]

Drug abuse returned to China in the 1980s as the country once again opened its door to the outside world, its commerce and goods, licit and illicit.[3] Drug addiction soon spread across the country. Drug-related crimes and addiction-induced problems such as the spread of HIV have now become a major challenge to the Chinese government. For instance, at the turn of the millennium, 72.1 percent of all confirmed HIV cases were attributed to intravenous heroin injection.[4] Needle sharing was a common practice among heroin users. Even after years of public campaigns and a few needle exchange programs, intravenous heroin injection continues to be a major contributor to the spread of HIV virus, accounting for 24.3 percent of all newly reported cases.[5]

Although attempting to stamp out the problem quietly in the early years of its economic reform, the Chinese government in the past two decades has openly acknowledged in its official documents that illicit drug consumption has infested every province, with users mostly concentrated in urban centers. The central government has been issuing an annual report since 1998, through its National Narcotics Control Commission, providing information on trends, law enforcement activities, and treatment and intervention accomplishments.[6] China is no longer just a transit country favored by transnational drug traffickers, but a major market demanding a growing amount of illicit drugs.

One unique practice in China's attempt to control illicit drug use is its extensive use of the criminal justice system, from police to court and to correctional agencies. Official efforts are not limited to the application of criminal law to control drug traffickers or retail vendors but also to the addict populations. Law enforcement agencies across the country are required to register active drug users they have come into contact with. A national registry has been established wherein all local police agencies routinely submit statistics on their drug enforcement activities, including arrests, seizures, investigations, and contacts with drug addicts. Although rather inconsistent in its format as well as content, official drug enforcement data are regularly published in the Annual Report on Drug Control in China. To provide some glimpses of the extent and nature of drug abuse in China, table 8.1 is constructed using the data published in the official annual reports for the decade of 2001–2010.

Ever since the drug user registration system was established in the 1990s, the official figures have been on a continuous climb, some years more rapidly than others. As shown in table 8.1, the vast majority of drug addicts are heroin users, although their proportion has been on a steady, albeit slow, decline over the ten years. In a recent report delivered by the Minister of Public Security, China's registered heroin users increased to 1.19 million, making up 63 percent of all officially known drug addicts.[7] It appears that the total number of heroin addicts was on a continuous rise in recent years, albeit accounting for a declining portion of the total registered addicts.

Table 8.1. Officially Registered Drug Addicts in China

	Total registered addicts	Total heroin addicts	Heroin addicts (%)	Users ≤ 35 years old (%)
2001	901,000	745,000	83	77
2002	1,000,000	876,000	88	75
2003	1,050,000	740,000	71	72
2004	1,140,400	924,864	81	70
2005	1,160,000	700,000	78	68
2006	*	*	*	*
2007	957,000	746,460	78	62
2008	1,126,700	877,736	78	60
2009	1,335,000	978,000	73	58
2010	1,545,000	1,065,000	69	*

* Figures not reported.

In recent years, the official reports showed an increasing number of registered users who were abusing synthetic drugs, including methamphetamine (commonly known in China as *bingdu* or "ice drug"), ketamine, and ecstasy (commonly known in China as *yaotouwan* or "head-shaking pills"). These amphetamine-type stimulants mostly appeal to urban youths and are often found in nightclubs and KTVs (karaoke lounges).

One other interesting trend in the annual reports is the percentage of registered users under the age of 35. As table 8.1 indicates, drug addicts appear to be aging. At the beginning of the decade, the vast majority of registered users were under the age of 35. By 2009, the proportion decreased to 58.1 percent. No official explanation can be found as to why there has been such an aging trend among drug users. For many years the Chinese government pointed to its youth population as the main demographic category for drug abuse. In 2011, the annual report stopped reporting this figure. It remains to be seen whether such an aging trend continues. More interestingly, one may ask why a growing number of mature adults (over 35 years of age) would use illicit drugs and get in trouble with the law at an age when most people should have passed their prime delinquent or rebellious years.

Our sources in China claim that the Chinese authorities have great confidence in their counts of active drug users who have come into contact with the police, more so for heroin users than users of other psychedelic drugs. One high-ranking official at the Narcotics Control Bureau of China's Ministry of Public Security stated:

> I can tell you the registration of heroin users is highly reliable because of our local police work. Community-oriented policing is far more efficient than that of the United States because of our existing residential registration system. We comb through the neighborhoods of the entire country and knock on doors to interview residents to find out who the drug users are. Neighbors and even family members also tell us who the heroin users are. It is hard for them to escape the police attention.
>
> However, the same can't be said of other psychoactive drug users—those taking head-shaking pills, crystal meth, or ketamine, because these drugs are often consumed in entertainment facilities, at bars, karaoke clubs, or restaurants. Even when family members suspect their children are using drugs, they are never sure because these children often only tell their parents that they are going out with friends. For heroin users, their physical signs and living conditions easily give away their addiction problems. But psychedelic drug users are often in good spirits and leave few physical traces. Therefore, we have great confidence on the number of heroin users in China. I would venture to say the accuracy is greater than 90 percent. But we don't have an accurate count of stimulant drug users.

The official reports also disclose the number of new addicts discovered by local police agencies, although the format and the associate contents tend to vary from year to year. Also, there are few explanations for major changes in these annual reports. For instance, in 2001, there were a total of 25,900 newly registered active users in the national registry.[8] In 2005, the figure increased to 101,000; and in 2010, the total number of newly registered drug users jumped to 214,000.[9] Regardless of whether the rapid rise in the number of new drug users was due to increased drug enforcement efforts, hence more records of police activities, or actual worsening of the abuse, these figures suggest that China is fighting an uphill battle with its drug problems.

Empirical studies on Chinese drug addicts remain scarce. However, published survey studies appear to corroborate the official reports in terms of the prevalence of use and main characteristics of the addict populations. According to a national survey conducted in six high-prevalence areas in China, 1.17 percent (male 1.80 percent, female 0.48 percent) of survey participants reported use of illicit drugs in the year prior to the interview, with the number of new drug users steadily rising since 1986.[10] Other researchers found that the majority of addicts in China were male, relatively young to middle aged (20–40 years old), unemployed, and had a middle school education or less.[11] Heroin was the predominant drug used by addicts, with regular use rates ranging from 83.7 percent to 87.5 percent depending on the study.[12]

In a recent survey of drug addicts in compulsory drug treatment centers, Chinese criminologist Huang Kaicheng and his colleagues found that addicts were mostly young, male adults, unemployed, and with less than a high school education.[13] These findings are consistent with those found among U.S. drug users.[14] Huang et al. also found that Chinese drug users were likely to be single and come from poor families. Heroin was the most commonly consumed drug, followed by methamphetamine. In comparison, in the United States, the most commonly used drugs reported by prison inmates and the general population are marijuana, followed by cocaine (crack and powder).[15] Such differences in the choice of drugs may be due to geographical differences in the source of production and supplies. While Southeast Asia has a long history of opium poppy cultivation, which provides the raw material for heroin production, coca leaves are mostly cultivated in the American continent. Synthetic drugs (e.g., methamphetamine and ketamine), however, are made with chemical precursors widely available in legitimate products, which are less constrained via illicit global trades.

Factors Contributing to the Rise of Drug Addiction

Two macro-level factors may have contributed to the rapid return of drug abuse in China, both of which are intricately linked to the economic development and concomitant social changes in the country since the 1980s. First, the ever-expanding drug trafficking business from the source countries into China, a transit country favored by transnational drug traffickers, has made illicit drugs widely available and in turn has also stimulated the growth of domestic consumption.[16] The shift from a command economy toward one that relies on the entrepreneurial initiatives of private citizens awakened a massive population eager to seek opportunities to enrich themselves. Enterprising individuals mostly organized in small groups have found ways to collaborate with relatives or business contacts at home and abroad, transporting illicit drugs from the border areas through China.[17] Events taking place in the Golden Triangle have created a market ripe for cross-border drug trade when major confrontations erupted between the Burmese and Thai border forces, and the Burmese authorities shut down all the border posts in retaliation, which prompted drug traffickers to cultivate their China route in earnest.[18] The expansion of the China route was met with tens of thousands of individuals from around the country in search of money-making opportunities.[19] Increased cross-border drug trade has made access to illicit drugs much easier than ever before.[20]

In addition to the increased availability of illicit drugs, rapid economic development has also brought about profound changes in social and interpersonal relationships. The weight of economic development forced the government to loosen its residential control, which in turn unleashed massive internal as well as international migration (or the so-called floating population). The country is now too porous to keep the "evil invasion outside its gate."[21] Riding along with this floating population are drug dealers, traffickers, as well as addicts who are spreading not only illicit drugs but also subcultural practices and values. A United Nations assessment of drug demand in South Central China found a significant linkage between heroin trafficking routes and areas of rapid economic development.[22]

Further influencing the anomic social environment, immense disparities in wealth resulting from uneven economic development also pose serious challenges to the political and social systems in China. The most obvious result is the wealth gap between urban and rural areas. With average urban real incomes now four times that of rural real incomes, China's levels of inequality surpass those of Eastern European economies, Western European industrialized nations, and other Asian developing nations such as India, Pakistan, and Indonesia.[23] The collapse of many state-owned enterprises uprooted large numbers of workers from previously safe government-funded jobs.[24] Persistent unemployment among the urban population has turned many into economic losers. The immense income disparities have been cited as one of the most important causes for migrants from the rural areas and the urban poor alike to engage in drug trafficking and retailing.[25]

Another contributing factor to the resurgence of drug abuse is the rapid spread of cultural influence from the West. For instance, rave parties and designer drugs (such as ecstasy) have quickly become a youth theme in most urban cultures. Ecstasy has soared in popularity as the party drug of choice since it was introduced by party-goers from Hong Kong.[26] Large seizures of ecstasy are regularly reported in China's National Narcotics Control Commission annual reports. For instance, in 2010, police agencies seized more than one million ecstasy pills nationwide.[27] Synthetic drugs are rapidly gaining acceptance among urban youths; some scholars argue this phenomenon indicates a breakdown of social norms, as a generation of youth reared on promises of a workers' paradise face a complicated reality of unemployment, broken homes, and corruption.[28]

Although few empirical studies directly examine the effect of the anomic social environment on the vast populace in China, it is fair to speculate that many disenfranchised individuals may be seeking mental insulation, thus contributing to the rising problem of drug abuse. In a recent study of 240 drug addicts, "spiritual emptiness" (which loosely translates to "feel bored and a lack of purpose in life") was ranked third among the causes of initial entry into the drug world, following "curiosity" and "peer pressure."[29] In two separate anonymous surveys conducted in one compulsory drug rehabilitation center in Xi'an, capital city of Shanxi Province, researchers reported significant increases in the percentage of addicts who had been previously unemployed, accounting for 58 percent of the center's population.[30] A culture of retreatism, as described in Robert Merton's theory of social adaptation, has thus emerged where marginalized individuals seek support from like-minded peers and comfort from drugs.[31] At the same time, unsympathetic and even hostile attitudes toward drug addicts by the general public hinder the development of effective treatment policies and strategies, which practically push addicts into the outer margins of society. Many studies in China have found that the majority of drug retailers are addicts themselves who must push drugs and develop new addicts, often among their close social circles including their own family members and relatives, to support their own drug habits.[32] One study estimated that an addict on average requires six additional users (i.e., customers) to support his/her addiction, thus creating a fast snowball effect.[33]

These macro-level factors combined with personal difficulties have thus contributed to the rapid increase of the addict population in China. It is this appreciation of the socio-structural as well as interpersonal intricacies that we review, and also assess current addiction treatment and rehabilitation strategies in China.

Compulsory Treatment or Rehabilitation through Labor

In China, two outcomes are inevitable for most heroin addicts—either they die of an overdose or other infectious diseases due to needle sharing and unsanitary living conditions, or they are caught by the police and sent to compulsory drug treatment. Even for those with financial wherewithal, addiction can quickly ruin one's fortune. During this project, we met a heroin addict at a compulsory treatment center in Fujian Province. This addict, in his thirties, recalled how he made his fortune and lost it all to heroin:

> In late 1990s, I owned an aquaculture farm raising eels for export. The business was so good that I made a lot of money. People in my hometown admired my success and I became a millionaire in my 20s. My eel farm was very successful but I also worked very hard and felt a lot of pressure. Then one day a group of friends and I were eating and drinking. One of them started introducing this white powdery stuff for us to smoke. I was told that the stuff would help reduce my stress. We rolled a little into our cigarettes. I didn't feel much at first, just dizzy and sleepy. After a few times, I was hooked. Soon all I could think about each day was how to smoke some of the stuff. I soon became derelict in my responsibilities and my business went downhill. I didn't care anymore. I used whatever money I had to buy heroin. Before long I started injecting heroin because I could no longer afford smoking it.

The entry into drug addiction in China was rather uniform, with friends as the most immediate access and parties at private residences as the most common venue for the initiation.[34] As one 34-year-old addict in Kunming told us: "It was after work one day, in the evening, at a friend's place for a party. There were many people in my social circle who did drugs. Many of my co-workers were also using. When we got together at this party, my friends ask me to give it a try. I don't think they were deliberately setting up a trap to get me addicted. It was just a party, and I was curious."

Although private facilities are beginning to appear in major urban areas, drug treatment remains mostly under the control of the criminal justice system. Use of illicit drugs is considered an administrative offense, and police frequently detain anyone identified as a drug user. Once confirmed by the police as an active drug user, all arrestees are checked against the existing roster (i.e., the national drug user registry), and enrolled in some form of compulsory drug rehabilitation program run by local justice agencies. Individuals detained during police activities, especially involving property crimes, are routinely interrogated for possible drug use. A female heroin addict and dealer in Yunnan Province, who served time in a compulsory treatment facility, described how the police identified drug users: "In the old time, police just asked you to roll up your sleeve and they looked for injection marks on your arm. So I learned to inject in the veins in my thighs. The police don't check there. Now they use urine tests all the time if they suspect you are using drugs."

Aside from drug raids and detaining property crime suspects, police also employ other strategies to screen for and rope in drug addicts. A Kunming addict who had been sent to compulsory drug treatment and rehabilitation facilities four times, spending anywhere between 40 days to 12 months each, told us how he was busted the last time:

> The first two times someone snitched on me. My drug friends. In Kunming, anti-narcotics police have to fulfill certain quotas. When they are under pressure to produce the numbers, they would ask an identified drug user to lead them to other users. Once the police knock on your door, you know why they are there. You have physical signs that give away your drug use. In this last time, I was approaching a professional drug dealer. This guy was what we addicts call "the licensed drug dealer." He is licensed to deal because the police cannot touch him. He is HIV-positive and has nothing to lose. If the police arrest him, they will have to give him special treatment and take care of him inside

> the jail or treatment facility. So they just let him deal drugs from his residence. But police closely monitor the people who approach his residence. So when I showed up this last time, my clothes were dirty and I looked like an addict. My appearance gave away my identity. The police took me away.

There are two main strategies for treating addiction in China: (1) enrollment in compulsory drug detoxification/rehabilitation centers, and (2) sentencing to "rehabilitation through labor" camps. Both involve lock-up residential stays, but the former typically lasts one to six months and the latter for one to three years. According to one official count, there were a total of 583 compulsory drug treatment centers and 151 labor rehabilitation camps in China in 2003.[35] Hundreds of thousands of drug addicts are compelled to enter treatment each year in these facilities.

The main difference between these two types of facilities is whether the drug user is arrested for the first time. First-timers are typically sent to compulsory treatment centers, whereas repeat offenders must enter labor camps for a longer "treatment," regardless of how they are brought to the attention of law enforcement agencies (e.g., arrested for crimes, turned in by relatives). These treatment facilities are typically isolated from the outside world. "Patient" movement is restricted and daily schedules are highly regimented. All treatment facilities impose a military-style routine, along with manual labor, physical exercise, and education.

Addicts brought to the compulsory treatment center are kept in isolation for the initial 7 to 10 days to "cleanse" their system. Basic medical services are available at the better-financed facilities. Addicts going through withdrawal are supervised by medical staff and receive doctor's visits and medications. In economically deprived regions, however, addicts are forced to go through the so-called "dry" detoxification (without any medication to alleviate physical pains associated with the withdrawal). After detoxification, addicts undergo rehabilitation, which mainly involves physical labor, education, and group discussions featuring mostly self-criticism. Medications used for detoxification are discontinued during the rehabilitation phase. Treatment usually lasts about 3–6 months at these centers.

With one or two exceptions, few compulsory treatment facilities offer psychosocial counseling or behavioral-oriented therapy. In our interactions with public health officials as well as those operating the rehabilitation centers, the need for psychosocial treatment was consistently expressed. However, psychotherapy is still in its infancy in China, and its future depends heavily on the degree of acceptance or change in the traditional culture. For instance, we inquired about any systematic measurement of the severity of addiction for client assessment purposes in many of our visits to these facilities. There were none. Clinical assessment tools that are commonly used in the United States such as the Addiction Severity Index and Hopkins Symptom Check were unheard of in these government run facilities. Considering how widely available these instruments are in the literature, one would expect someone could have adopted them for use in the Chinese population. In all government-run facilities, physical labor remains the most common treatment protocol. Addicts are required to participate in various production activities (e.g., growing crops, raising livestock, and manufacturing electronics) to distract themselves from yearning for drugs as well as to serve as a means to support the facility financially.

For repeat addicts, compulsory rehabilitation centers are regarded as too lenient and therefore no longer appropriate. The only option available is a one- to three-year sentence in a labor camp, usually located away from the cities. Most labor camps involve some form of farming activity, and are controlled by correctional agencies (as opposed to the police) that are in charge of running the local jails and prisons. Information on rehabilitation activities at these labor camps is scarce but is believed to be similar to that found at compulsory treatment centers.

All incarcerated people in China, whether in prison for a criminal offense or in compulsory treatment centers, must work to support themselves and their facilities. The prison system is a booming industry because of its cheap labor. In one of our visits in Yunnan we saw hundreds of drug addicts sitting or squatting in an open field under the hot sun, sorting chili peppers into different piles according their color and size. We were told that some of the chili peppers were produced in the prison farms while others were brought in by contractors. Once sorted, the chili peppers were sent out to food processing factories. We were told that the "patients" were not paid individually, and the "collective" income was used to pay for their food and other amenities such as exercise equipment. In another compulsory treatment facility we saw dozens of drug addicts polishing gemstones in a workshop. We were told the vendor was from Hong Kong who imported rough stones from Burma and Thailand and had them delivered to different facilities in mainland China to be polished into marketable shapes. This treatment facility was one of those where the "patients" underwent "treatment" by spending long hours grinding and polishing the stones according to the merchant's specifications. We were told that the Hong Kong vendor paid the facility roughly 20 cents in Chinese yuan (roughly three U.S. pennies at the time) for each finished stone. It took a half hour to polish one. Depending on the resourcefulness of the treatment officials, some drug treatment facilities have more money-making opportunities than others, and the standard of living and equipment in the dorms thus vary enormously. Treatment facilities at less developed regions leave much to be desired.

Fig. 8.1. A nursery tended by drug addicts.

Fig. 8.2. A hog farm tended by drug addicts.

During our fieldwork in China, we visited many compulsory treatment centers in different provinces and observed the daily treatment activities. These centers varied enormously in their treatment activities and support services. For instance, at the time of our visit, the Fuzhou Municipal Compulsory Drug Rehabilitation Center housed about 500 addicts (about 30 percent female). With a staff of 50, this facility was located on the outskirts of the city. Of all the sites we visited in China, the Fuzhou facility had the most diverse addict population in terms of their abused drugs, although heroin was the predominant drug of choice. A sizeable number of the addicts at this facility abused

Fig. 8.3. Polishing gemstones for export to Hong Kong.

methamphetamine, ketamine, and ecstasy. Fuzhou is the capital city of coastal Fujian Province, which is a wealthy and economically progressive region in the country. The market reform in recent decades has brought about unprecedented economic development as well as drug use problems. Ocean-based commerce, manufacturing, and transportation are among the main industries in the province. Because of its proximity to Taiwan, across the strait, Fujian was among the few provinces in China with an early exposure to synthetic drugs.

The best equipped and probably most professionalized treatment facility we visited was the Kunming Municipal Compulsory Drug Rehabilitation Center. It is also among the largest in China. The facility has a daily average population of 2,500 (about 20 percent female) with a staff of close to 300. The vast majority of the patients are heroin users. During the first two weeks at the center, program participants are closely supervised by medical staff. Medications are prescribed to alleviate withdrawal discomfort. Upon leaving the detoxification ward, addicts are assigned to different quarters according to their job experiences and educational backgrounds. Most participate in manual activities, such as tending livestock, performing janitorial duties, growing vegetables, and processing food products.

Kunming is the capital city of Yunnan Province, which shares borders with the infamous Golden Triangle that has placed the region well ahead of the rest of China on issues of drug trafficking and abuse treatment.[36] As a result, Yunnan law enforcement agencies were the first in the nation to establish drug treatment facilities. The province is generally considered the most sophisticated in China in its ability to treat drug addiction.

The effectiveness of these compulsory treatment facilities and labor farms has not been examined either by the government or independent researchers, although the government frequently acknowledges the difficulty of preventing relapse in its annual drug report. No systematic follow-ups of participants in the compulsory treatment programs have been reported anywhere in the government's annual report, suggesting a lack of attention to outcome assessment by the authorities. We are not aware of any national depository for data related to substance abuse treatment or addiction research. However, in 2010 and 2011, the National Narcotics Control Commission began to report the number of addicts who had stopped using drugs in the past three years.[37] Only a total figure of those who "stopped using in the past three years" was provided, without any contextual information as to how many others of the same cohort were still using. The figure is nonetheless a step forward in the gradual improvement of the national report on drug treatment outcome assessment.

Community Reentry and Medical Treatment

Upon completing the compulsory treatment or the labor camp, addicts are released back into the community. Aftercare support or reentry services in most communities range from inadequate to nonexistent, although the Chinese government has been campaigning to establish "drug-free communities" (also called drug-free counties, drug-free cities, or drug-free districts) by implementing surveillance of released addicts, organizing support groups, and sponsoring various anti-drug education campaigns.

Community-based organizations that are not affiliated with government agencies have begun to appear in urban areas to assist addiction recovery and coordinate "self-help" groups. For instance, we visited one such facility in Kunming during our field activities. The organization, called the Rainbow Community Care Center, relied on donations and client fees. It followed the peer counseling and self-help model started by the Daytop program in the United States. The organization operated an outreach center in the city and a farming community in a rural area. We saw recovering addicts reaching out to other addicts and paid staff members who were conducting drug education classes. Posters and flyers lined the walls and corridors of the modest office outfit, with scores of addicts participating in various activities.

Recognizing the increased drug abuse and related problems, Chinese authorities are seeking treatment alternatives. For example, in 2002, China announced a new policy allowing a wider use of methadone.[38] The methadone maintenance treatment has been expanded more aggressively in recent years by the Chinese public health agencies

Fig. 8.4. Rainbow Community Care Center.

Fig. 8.5. Rainbow office entryway.

in an effort to curtail the spread of HIV infection. Methadone supply and clinical use are under tight government control with multiple screening criteria, such as individuals who repeatedly failed compulsory treatment or labor camps and those already infected with HIV.[39] It is unclear how well these methadone clinics are integrated into the larger community-based reentry effort, but they are indeed growing at a fast pace. According to the latest official report, there were a total of 700 such clinics across the country by the end of 2010, with an active clientele of 130,000.[40]

Needle exchange programs began to appear in limited regions for many years to prevent the spread of HIV infection among intravenous drug users. However, the practice has been controversial. During our fieldwork in Kunming, we visited one such needle exchange program. Although limited in scale, this organization obtained a license to purchase bulk needles and syringes. Community outreach workers from this community organization would put out the word in neighborhoods where addicts congregated about their upcoming outreach events. On the designated day, program staff and volunteers (mostly recovering addicts) would come to pass out educational pamphlets, hand out clean needles and syringes, as well as collect used ones from addicts. The relationship between this organization and the police had been awkward at best. Using HIV prevention as the front, this community organization was pushing for greater access for injecting users to obtain clean syringes and needles at no or low cost. However, drug use is considered an administrative offense, and addicts caught carrying any heroin use paraphernalia can be detained and sent to the compulsory treatment centers. From our conversations with the program staff, we learned that they must walk a tight line. Each time the community organization planned to conduct an outreach it was required to notify the local police station so that drug users could come out without fearing arrest. On the other hand, staff at the organization also told us that some addicts took advantage of their knowledge of the outreach activities and claimed they were with this organization for recovery services whenever they were questioned by police for drug use.

Despite wide availability of amphetamine-type stimulants (ATS), most addicts we met in the treatment facilities were abusing heroin and other opiate-based substances. Demand for heroin continues to surpass that for all other illicit drugs. Medical researchers suspect such predominant preference for heroin and other opiate analgesics over other types of substances is perhaps linked to genetic predispositions, particularly among the Han Chinese. For instance, when exploring the potential association between heroin dependence and different serotoninergic receptors thought to modulate mood and emotion, Gao et al. found that compared to controls, a group of Han Chinese heroin addicts had significantly higher amounts of a particular type of serotoninergic carrier—the HTR1B.[41] These researchers believe that such a high rate of preference for heroin among Han Chinese drug users may have a genetic explanation that deserves greater attention in future neurobiological studies on heroin dependence.

Medical treatment for heroin addicts remains available, but mostly for those of ample means. The expense often makes the treatment out of reach for many street addicts. The research community has made advances in medical interventions in recent years, although methadone maintenance remains the main choice of medical intervention.[42] The use of opiate antagonists such as Naltrexone, which block the effects of opioid substances, is not common.

Multiple substance use is common among heroin users in Western countries, and the same is true in China. However, the substances vary tremendously. For instance, cocaine and marijuana are the most common substance combination among Western heroin users. However, such combination is rare in China.[43] For heroin addicts, other opioid analgesics such as tramadol, and benzodiazepines such as triazolam and diazepam, are often reported in China.[44] In a study of heroin addicts attending methadone maintenance treatment (MMT) clinics in Yunnan, China, Li et al. found alcohol and tobacco were the most common combination for poly-drug users.[45]

Formal studies using rigorous methods to assess the effectiveness of these community-based recovery efforts are rare, although there have been sporadic attempts by foreign researchers and Chinese researchers affiliated with medical institutions. These researchers found that the relapse rate following departure from official treatment centers was high, 80 percent to 95 percent within a year.[46] Some of the main reasons for relapses included wide availability of illicit drugs, lack of will to fight physiological addiction, lack of reintegration support, social rejection (stigma), and lack of employment.[47] In a recent study of methadone maintenance treatment, a group of researchers in Yunnan found that, although the proportion of injecting users was reduced, ephedrine (i.e., amphetamine-type stimulant) use actually increased.[48] Furthermore, many program participants continued to use heroin and benzodiazepines during the treatment in this study.

The cost of delivering treatment will remain a key factor in the development of effective substance abuse treatment in China, as drug addiction does not receive much sympathy from the public, thus lacks the urgency in government's policy making. With limited funding, the chronically anemic treatment community struggles to cope with the throngs of drug addicts who are mostly destitute and looked down upon by the society as well as their own families.

Social Stigma and Drug Treatment

The loss of face due to the stigma associated with drug addiction is probably the most salient factor among the Chinese; tremendous obstacles remain for community-based organizations working toward de-stigmatizing or de-labeling.[49] Drug addicts we met expressed pervasive pessimism about their future prospects. One female addict told us:

> People like me are human garbage. No one will hire us. We are looked down upon. I have no future. The only way I can make a living is to import heroin and sell it to my customers to sustain myself. I have no other options. I try to be careful so I don't get arrested. But even if I get arrested, I will spend a few months in a compulsory treatment center. Then I will go back to doing it again. There is no cure. I don't know anyone who actually quit using. I know I will die of overdose one day.

In China, the family is the fundamental unit of one's social position and supersedes the individual in the construction of one's social identity.[50] Because of the cultural emphasis on interconnections, individual behavior to a large extent reflects the family and kinship network to which one belongs. Unlike Western culture, which emphasizes self-sufficiency and mastery of one's own destiny, Chinese culture views individuals as the product of their relationship to the family, especially their parents.[51] Social control is accomplished through the teaching of "face" at a young age. Social and legal transgressions are considered a disgrace to one's parents and to the family and detrimental to one's social standing within the community.[52] Drug addiction is therefore considered a personal as well as family failure. Shame (or losing "face") is most often used to reinforce the adherence to shared social expectations and norms of acceptable behavior because the consequence of a transgression will lead to the withdrawal of the family's confidence and support. In a culture where interdependence is important, the actual or threatened renouncement by others, especially one's own parents, is a serious punishment.

Much of current reliance on the justice system to deal with drug addicts has been a relic of the old system that emphasizes "thought correction," which may only intensify the social stigma of substance abuse. For instance, a common theme that runs through most compulsory drug rehabilitation programs in China is that addicts must attend regular "study" sessions to reflect on their past and recognize the emotional pains and financial distress their "filthy" and "loathsome" habits have brought onto themselves, and more importantly, their families and society. Upon attending these guilt- and shame-inducing study sessions, self-criticism is often expected; and addicts are often required to write essays about these reflections. We have not encountered any treatment facilities (either run by the criminal justice system or community agencies) that seem concerned about possible labeling effects of these "thought correction" activities.

When drug addiction is viewed as a disgrace to the family and its social network, drug addicts are shunned in public and looked down upon by community members. In a culture where drug addiction is highly stigmatized, addicts released from any treatment and rehabilitation facilities encounter great difficulties in reintegrating into the mainstream society. Opportunities for employment are limited. One can predict that such strong social stigma can easily become internalized expectation of rejection on the part of the addict. As a result, to cope with the devaluing and discriminatory attitudes of the society, addicts can only choose secrecy and withdrawal from social interaction.[53] Drug subculture thus becomes a refuge for addicts to escape social pressure. Isolation from social interaction, particularly one's family, absence of re-entry opportunities, and retreat into drug-using peer networks can only lead to greater likelihood of relapse.[54] Such a self-defeating cycle has long been examined in the U.S. literature on drug treatment and recovery, which finds that aftercare and social support are critical for sustaining drug abstinence.[55] Drug treatment programs in China, particularly those run by the government, perhaps should explore different treatment approaches and carefully assess the outcomes.

Research and Professionalization of Drug Treatment

Much needs to be done to develop a treatment framework that not only is culturally sensitive but can also withstand rigorous empirical assessment. It is our belief that a community of research and treatment professionals that specialize in drug treatment and recovery is needed to augment the police-led compulsory and labor camp approach. A more systematic and rigorous research is of vital importance to understanding the process of sustained recovery from drug dependence and developing effective intervention strategies that are humane and oriented toward harm reduction.

There are two major shortcomings in current drug treatment in China—(1) a lack of venues for practitioners and researchers to share and exchange ideas and experiences; (2) a general lack of capacity in conducting rigorous clinical tests and assessment of treatment protocols in practice. To our knowledge there were few data collection activities in any of the treatment facilities that we visited, such as staff surveys or even basic qualitative analysis on existing treatment, so that better understanding of any clinical practices may be obtained.

Based on our personal contacts, we learned that repeated efforts have been initiated by the U.S.-based treatment clinicians and researchers attempting to initiate clinical trials of medical and psychosocial treatment programs in China. These efforts are often embraced by community-based and other nongovernment entities; however, they are generally viewed with suspicion by Chinese authorities and receive a lukewarm response at best. Although we are in no way claiming that Western countries have found bullet-proof treatment methods or even have been effective in dealing with drug addictions, we must acknowledge the greater social awareness of the problem and its social costs as well as collective efforts in finding ways to deal with substance abuse. In contrast, drug treatment in China remains either a fringe enterprise endeavored by a few do-gooders in the community or by the criminal justice system that believes in the simple method of manual labor and deprivation of personal freedom.

Conclusion

After three decades of economic expansion at a speed that is the envy of the world, China faces a host of social problems, including widespread drug use. The increased number of drug addicts also exacerbates the spread of HIV and criminal activities. Recognition of these problems can help concerned government officials to consider alternatives other than punishment-based responses, including various forms of drug treatment. Most of the drug abuse problems in China involve opiates, predominantly heroin. While the rates of illicit drug use and associated adverse consequences have continued to escalate across many areas in China, options for effective treatment have remained largely unchanged.

Examples such as the Daytop program in Kunming suggest that a small but growing community of treatment professionals and researchers has begun to examine psychosocial factors and macro-level factors related to treatment interventions for them to be effective for Chinese addicts. Greater international collaboration between treatment and research professionals can facilitate the development of effective intervention strategies. In this vein, China can benefit greatly from a wealth of knowledge already accumulated in Western literature.

9

Combating Drug Trafficking

In China, the government has a firm hand on every aspect of anti-narcotic activities. Drug enforcement activities are mainly led and coordinated through the Narcotics Control Bureau (NCB) of the Ministry of Public Security, the equivalent of the Drug Enforcement Agency (DEA) of the U.S. Department of Justice. However, compared to their counterpart in the United States, which has close to 10,000 in staff and a budget that exceeds $2.2 billion, the Chinese anti-narcotic bureaucracy is small. NCB in Beijing has a staff of 50, divided into seven divisions: (1) narcotics control, (2) propaganda/drug education, (3) intelligence, (4) chemical precursors, (5) treatment/rehabilitation, (6) international cooperation, and (7) psychedelic drugs. Nationwide, police officers assigned specifically to anti-narcotics details numbered about 17,000 in a country with a population of 1.3 billion.

The Chinese government takes drug enforcement policies seriously and sets it as a national priority in its overall scheme of social control. National strategies in combating drug trafficking in China can be broadly grouped into two categories—(1) harsh punishment to deter participation in drug trafficking and dealing, and (2) mass education campaigns aimed at raising awareness among the populace. Under these two broad themes are a set of specific priorities, which the Chinese government calls the "comprehensive" counternarcotics strategy. One senior official in China's Ministry of Public Security elaborated on this all-encompassing drug policy:

> We have adopted a comprehensive counternarcotics strategy that includes: (1) stop the flow of drugs, meaning that we are striving to prevent drugs from entering the country and to intercept them along trafficking routes; (2) rehabilitate addicts, meaning we treat our drug addicts humanely, not as criminals but as people in need of service and

treatment, and (3) reinforce any progress made in our counternarcotic efforts through establishing drug-free communities with local governments. We are also in active collaborations with our neighboring countries in investigations of and crackdowns on drug trafficking and manufacturing activities.

Slogans aside, these national strategies represent the agenda of the Chinese government to get a handle on its ever worsening drug problem. Both official statistics and stories we heard during our field activities suggest that China is fighting an uphill battle because the supplies of illicit drugs are cheap and abundant from nearby countries full of enterprising agents eager to do business.

China—The Emerging Illicit Drug Supermarket in Asia

Sources in both the public and private sectors have informed us that the proportion of heroin addicts in the total substance abuse population is declining in China, but the overall population is still growing. While heroin addicts are struggling with relapses and hustling for money, the so-called new drugs (i.e., methamphetamine, ecstasy, and ketamine) are gaining in popularity among young people in urban areas. These drugs are thought to be non-habit-forming and "fun" to use, particularly in nightclubs, KTV establishments, and private parties.

In our interactions with ordinary people in the streets as well as law enforcement representatives, we get the impression that heroin is losing its luster and often considered a thing of the past, or is viewed as a drug for the older addicts, or burned-out junkies and losers. In contrast, the use of synthetic (ATS) drugs rises at an alarming rate. As shown in the table in chapter 8, the proportion of registered drug addicts who are primarily abusing amphetamine-type stimulants (ATS) is on a steady upward trend. Among police-seized drug consignments, crystal methamphetamine (i.e., ice), ecstasy, and ketamine are now making up the majority, as shown in table 9.1. Since 2005, seizures of ATS surpassed heroin in total weight. By 2010, there were three times as many synthetic drugs seized as heroin and opium combined. Although official records are not necessarily an accurate reflection of the actual volumes of the illicit drug trade, these figures nonetheless suggest some

Table 9.1. Annual Drug Seizures in China (in Metric Tons)

	Heroin	Opium	Methamphetamine	Ketamine
2001	13.20	2.82	4.82	*
2002	9.29	1.22	3.19	*
2003	9.53	0.91	5.83	1.76
2004	10.84	0.89	2.75	0.61
2005	6.90	2.30	5.50	2.60
2006	5.79	1.69	5.95	1.79
2007	4.59	1.18	6.62	6.00
2008	4.33	1.38	6.15	5.27
2009	5.80	1.30	6.60	5.30
2010	5.30	1.00	9.90	4.90
2011	7.08	*	14.32	*

Sources: Annual Report on Drug Control in China, 2001 through 2010.
* Total figures not reported.

fundamental shifts in the types of drugs abused and the composition of the addict populations.

Although the majority of drug users continue to abuse heroin in China, it is the rapid increase in the number of individuals identified for abusing ATS and related seizures that has alarmed police agencies across the country, even in Yunnan Province where heroin had historically been the drug of choice. One ranking intelligence official in Beijing attributed the increase of ATS abuse to greater global exchange in commerce and exposure to outside cultures:

> In the 1980s and 1990s, I would say 90 percent or more drug users abused heroin. Now the percentage has decreased to about 70 percent. The rest uses "Shaking Head Pills" (or ecstasy) or ketamine. I think this shift in the type of drugs is inevitable as our exchange with outside world increases and the sources of synthetic drugs become more available.

Intelligence officials and drug analysts in China told us that since the 1980s, China has changed from mainly a transit country to mainly a destination for drug traffickers. China is adjacent to two major drug sources in the world (i.e., the Golden Triangle and the Golden Crescent), and to a host of countries with weak drug control. Therefore, the supply side eagerly awaits the demand side to grow. And grow it did. Economic development, expanding personal wealth, and increased exposure to the outside world have afforded Chinese people greater opportunities to experiment with things that are new and "fun." Officials in Beijing as well as in the frontline in border provinces have realized for years the shift in the direction of drug consignments that entered the country.

People's War

Much in line with the political tradition of the Communist Party, propaganda campaigns are regularly launched in China as the main venue to indoctrinate and mobilize the masses to combat illicit drugs. The government has always portrayed its fight against illicit drugs as a people's war, stirring up public sentiment and enlisting participation from the masses. While in recent years some political topics may be met with skepticism and lukewarm participation, anti-narcotic activities appear to be well received in China because of the cultural taboo toward drug addiction and the fact that Chinese people, young and old, have long been taught about the national humiliation brought about by the two Opium Wars.

The Chinese government launches these campaigns on national scales, particularly around June 26 each year, the International Day against Drug Abuse and Illicit Trafficking, to showcase the government's resolve to combat this growing social problem. On these occasions, mass events are held across the country, featuring visits by high-level government officials to drug treatment facilities and drug enforcement police units, public display and destruction of seized drugs, public gatherings, a media blitz of major drug raids, presentations by former addicts, and public trials of drug traffickers.[1]

For instance, on July 4, 2011, Zhou Yongkang, then a member of China's Central Politburo who oversees China's internal security apparatus, went to Shanghai and inspected local drug treatment facilities; and Meng Jianzhu, then minister of Public Security, visited a compulsory drug rehabilitation center in Shenzhen, Southern China on June 26, 2011.[2] It was also reported that major government leaders of most provinces (26 out of 31 provinces and municipalities) across China participated in counternarcotic campaign events; 129 counties in Hunan

Province (located in central China) formed Mothers United against Drugs; Beijing organized counternarcotic summer camps; Yunnan Province launched major anti-narcotic campaigns along main transportation routes through the province; and Sichuan and Fujian held public speeches on drug control.[3]

Each year one or more features of the central government's drug policy gets announced and promoted, while a few other themes are reiterated. The main feature of the 2011 anti-narcotics campaign was the promulgation of the newly published Regulations on Drug Rehabilitation, which delineates the roles and responsibilities of all stakeholders in the identification and treatment of drug-abusing individuals. Other regularly occurring themes include: establishing and strengthening drug-free communities and community-based drug treatment facilities. Most of the anti-narcotic slogans remain the same from year to year, casting the government in a paternalistic position that asks the society in general to save the drug addicts and then urges drug abusers to treasure their lives and strive to become productive citizens.

On and about June 26 is also the time when China's National Narcotics Control Commission releases its Annual Report on Drug Control, summarizing major accomplishments such as drug seizures, number of suspects arrested and prosecuted, addicts registered, and treatment facilities established. These annual reports and other accompanying announcements are typically delivered by ranking officials in the Ministry of Public Security in Beijing and carried by all major news media outlets in China.

For instance, on June 26, 2012, minister of Public Security, Meng Jianzhu, gave a speech on the main accomplishments by the Chinese government in its fight against illicit drugs, while acknowledging continued challenges from increased production in both heroin and synthetic drugs in neighboring countries, and pointing to the Golden Triangle as the most serious threat of illicit drugs.[4] As reported in his speech, the vast majority of all drugs seized continued to enter from the Golden Triangle region. Police seized 5.1 tons of heroin and 7.9 tons of methamphetamine that were produced in and smuggled from the Golden Triangle in 2011, accounting for 72 percent and 55 percent of total nationwide seizures of heroin and methamphetamine respectively.[5] Meanwhile, the Chinese government also recognized the increasing threat from the

Golden Crescent (referring to Afghanistan, Pakistan, and central Asia) where cases of drug seizures increased significantly in recent years. Furthermore, the report recognized that more cocaine arrived from South America and methamphetamine from Northeast Asia.

Because of the increased influx of synthetic drugs, in recent years, the Chinese government cranked up its propaganda machine at youths who abuse these party drugs, and directed educational institutions and local communities to increase their counternarcotic efforts. In 2011, the Ministry of Public Security and Ministry of Education jointly launched the 2011 Operation Staying Away From Drugs in schools and communities across the country. Major news media put on shows depicting how well-known stars fell into disgrace because of drug addiction. Web-based games were held for youths to compete on the extent of their knowledge of drug control issues. The entertainment industry is also enlisted to participate with famous entertainers hired as anti-drug spokespersons.

School-aged populations aside, governments in different parts of the country also design and organize anti-narcotic campaigns targeting specific segments of the populace and neighborhoods, such as villagers in rural areas and migrant laborers in the cities. It was estimated that in 2011, these mass-based outreach activities distributed more than 30 million copies of campaign materials such as pamphlets, and reached more than 110 million people.[6]

Deterrence through Harsh Punishment

Drug trafficking is among the few criminal offenses that qualify for the death penalty in China, and the threshold for capital punishment is relatively low. According to Chinese criminal law, people who smuggle, sell, transport, or manufacture heroin or methamphetamine in the amount greater than 50 grams can be sentenced to 15 years in prison, life imprisonment, or death. Aside from the weight factor, other circumstances such as being the head of a trafficking organization, using armed protection during transportation, or engaging in violent resistance against police inspection or search will also qualify one for the death penalty.

In the past, the death penalty was typically carried out in an open field as a public spectacle, where the condemned was forced to kneel and then shot at close range with a rifle.[7] Lethal injection is now the standard procedure and the execution is held away from public view. Prior to the execution, the condemned is allowed to have a final face-to-face meeting with his immediate family. On the final day, the inmate is allowed to order his favorite meal and pick out his favorite clothes before being sent away. A 45-year-old inmate we interviewed in a city in southern China, who was sentenced to death with a reprieve for his role in trafficking 60 kilograms of heroin from Burma to Yunnan, described the final hours he spent with his brother-in-law, the leader of the trafficking ring:

> On the day of the execution, my sister, her two children and I went to meet with my brother-in-law. There were four families in a visiting room and we had breakfast together. None of us were interested in eating. My brother-in-law was calm. He talked to his family as if he was leaving on a long trip, asking his children to listen to his mother, to look after each other, and to never ever touch drugs. I think most of them on the death row would tell their families never to get involved in the drug business before they were executed. My brother-in-law was put to death by lethal injection.

Nobody knows how many are put to death each year for drug trafficking offenses. Jonathan Watts, a reporter with the *Guardian*, claimed that China executes 1,700 to 10,000 people each year, which account for seven out of every ten executions in the world.[8] China never publishes its annual number of executions. The last time China mentioned executing drug traffickers was in the 2000 Annual Report on Drug Control in China issued by the National Narcotics Control Commission, in which brief statements were made on 54 executions in different parts of the country. The National Narcotics Control Commission, a gathering of representatives from all major central government ministries, has since stopped publishing any statistics on the executions of convicted drug traffickers in its annual reports.

However, one can frequently find local newspapers in China that carry stories of drug traffickers being sentenced to death. From time to time, stories of executions for drug offenses are also reported in official news outlets in foreign languages. For instance, a recent report, issued by the official Xinhua News Agency, provided a glimpse of the serious consequences resulting from drug trafficking. The story was a summary of a few high-profile drug trafficking cases from around the country, involving a total of 117 people in four provinces:

> In central coastal province of Zhejiang, 16 traffickers were convicted; two were sentenced to death; six received the death sentence with a reprieve; four sentenced to life in prison, and four were given prison terms of 7 to 15 years. These 16 individuals were convicted of trafficking more than 6 kilograms of methamphetamine. In central China's Hunan province, 15 members of a trafficking ring were sentenced for trafficking 210 kilograms of *magu* (a derivative of methamphetamine). Four of them were sentenced to death and three were sentenced to death with a reprieve. Four were sentenced to life in prison, while the other four were given prison terms of seven to 15 years. In northeast China's Jilin province, a drug trafficker was executed by lethal injection for trafficking about 4 kilograms of ice (crystal meth). In Fujian province, three men from Taiwan were executed after being convicted of smuggling a popular club drug across the Taiwan Strait.[9]

Although rare, foreigners caught smuggling drugs into China are not exempt from the death penalty. For instance, in the highly publicized case of Akmal Shaikh, a British citizen from north London, was sentenced to death for trafficking 4 kilograms of heroin from Kyrgyzstan via Tajikistan into China's Xinjiang Autonomous Region in 2009.[10] China did not waver in the face of international pressure from human rights groups, family members, and prominent political figures including British Prime Minister Gordon Brown. However, Chinese officials claim that when it comes to putting foreigners to death, additional reviews and greater procedural care are in place. One high-ranking official in Beijing told us that, whenever possible, extraditions of convicted foreigners are preferred to get rid of the problem:

> Extraditions with foreign countries can sometimes be tricky, but we have strict laws and procedures on how to handle foreign nationals caught dealing drugs in China. Although they are also subject to our legal punishment, their death penalty must be reviewed by the Supreme Court.

In other words, death penalty for foreigners is handled with far greater scrutiny than that for Chinese citizens.

It is unclear how much deterrence effect such harsh penal response has produced, as there appears to be no shortage of risk takers, judging from the ever-increasing number of addicts on the official registry and the growing amount of drugs seized each year. Not a single inmate we talked to did not regret their involvement in the drug business, particularly those who came close to being executed or who saw their partners being put to death. However, the temptation is simply too great to resist for many. A former county-level government official who entered the drug trafficking business through his brother-in-law recalled how he got involved:

> I was actually trying to convince my brother-in-law to quit many years ago. I told him to quit while he was ahead. I told him that this was a high-risk business and sooner or later you would be caught and at your level, death sentence would be the only outcome. But he said the money was really easy and much faster than any other businesses he ever involved. It is ironic that I was the one who joined him. This was the same case with my partner. His brother-in-law was also in the drug trafficking business, and for many years, this partner of mine was trying to convince him to quit.

Another 50-year-old inmate, who was sentenced to death with a reprieve, commented on the mind-set of people like him who came from a small rural village: "It was natural for people to get into the drug trafficking business. My hometown was a rather isolated place and with little land to grow crop and there were so many people. For us peasants, our mentality is simple. We seek fast returns, just like when one blows away the husk, rice should appear (or *chuikangjianmi*). We want to see profits right away. There is no talk of long-term investment or doing things the right way. It takes too long."

Faced with a large addict population, which ensures a strong demand for illicit drugs, China is likely to see an ample supply of enterprising individuals willing to take the risk in search of quick money. Even police officials admit that most executed drug traffickers are probably mules or low-level organizers, individuals who are paid to transport consignments of drugs from one location to another. As one ranking official in China stated, "These mules are young and jobless. . . . The real organizers, like Tan Xiaolin (arguably the best known drug trafficker in the early 2000s), only plan behind the scene and coordinate the overall operation."

Drug Enforcement in China

Based on our interviews with police officials, we learned that anti-drug trafficking strategies at the tactical level largely revolve around three major lines of defense, which one provincial official called the "three circles of barriers." The frontline is along the borders, where border patrols and customs attempt to stop traffickers from entering the country. Second, the police attempt to set up barriers along major highways extending from the borders to all other provinces, such as Guangxi, Guangdong, and Guizhou. Around-the-clock checkpoints and random mobile inspections are strategically positioned to prevent drugs from getting any farther along major transportation highways. Finally, the police establish inspections at all major ports of exits to other provinces and countries—including airports and train stations. One provincial official described that at these barriers: "We rely on a host of measures to catch drug traffickers—human inspectors, machines, drug sniffing dogs, and intelligence."

However, like all illicit enterprises, drug trafficking contracts and expands according to market demand and law enforcement activities. As police step up enforcement in one area, drug traffickers will retreat and find alternatives, as a ranking Chinese police official confided:

> The vast majority of heroin is now being smuggled to Guangdong because of its largest number of drug users in China. The trafficking route is not necessarily through Yunnan and Guangxi. There are multiple routes. Wherever the crackdowns become serious, traffickers would pick less restrictive routes. Traffickers are always looking for routes of the least resistance to transport drugs.

Professionalizing Drug Enforcement

China started its professionalization of drug enforcement fairly late. The first police force in China specifically trained and assigned to drug details started in 1982 in Yunnan Province. This was mostly due to the rampant influx of heroin because of Yunnan's geographical vicinity to the Golden Triangle. As a result, drug enforcement police are probably the most advanced and well organized in Yunnan Province, as one senior provincial police official noted:

> Yunnan provincial government has always taken anti-drug tasks seriously because of its location. We have a special responsibility in this field. Since the 1980s till now, we have had 20 to 23 years of experience. In comparison, most other provinces started a lot later. We were the first to have a special anti-narcotics police force; many other provinces didn't even have such specialized police forces until very recently.

Because of the severity of the drug trafficking and addiction problems, the Yunnan provincial government has placed greater emphasis on its drug enforcement development and professionalization, as well as drug treatment, than most other parts of the country. Such an advantage in early development of a professionalized drug enforcement police force is evident today. As one provincial police official stated:

> Yunnan has the most developed system of anti-drug trafficking and treatment efforts. We have done it for decades and we were the first to begin systematic counternarcotic programs; and our system has matured over the years. In China, about 80 percent of all heroin seizures occur in Yunnan, which means we have done a successful job in stopping the trafficking activities. Furthermore, if you compare all the surrounding countries in the Golden Triangle, China probably seized the most heroin. Within China, Yunnan is number one. What we really have is a highly efficient system, with very few people but a high success rate.

However, in the early years, frontline police officials frequently voiced complaints about the poor equipment and inadequate firepower. Because of their early and frequent encounters with transborder drug traffickers, drug enforcement police in Yunnan have arguably engaged in the most firefights and also suffered the most relative to police agencies in other parts of the country. According to one news source, since the force's establishment in 1982, more than 360 police officers have been injured and 40 died on drug enforcement duties.[11]

Equipment is now much better for the police force in China in general. SWAT teams and masked snipers are frequently seen at drug raids broadcast live over the news media. However, such highly equipped police are typically concentrated around major urban centers, while most cross-border trafficking activities occur in rural areas. Relative to their Western counterparts, China's drug enforcement is still underfunded and ill-equipped. For instance, despite decades of anti-narcotic efforts, China was only able to establish a fully operational lab in 2010 to conduct chemical assays of seized drugs; and the current analysis is limited to major drug ingredients such as opioids and amphetamine-type stimulants.[12] As one senior police official in Beijing observed:

> We have about 50 staff members at the Headquarters, and about 17,000 police officers nationwide assigned to drug details. We are of course not as well equipped as the U.S. DEA agents. They have far better equipment. Our budget is minuscule compared to the U.S. drug enforcement budget. This is not because our government does not pay attention to drug enforcement issues. Our budget and drug enforcement forces are increasing steadily. Yes, it is true that our workload and the number of people involved are far inadequate to the societal needs. Our investment in the drug enforcement, education, and treatment is also inadequate compared to our needs. But we are such a huge country and the government has so many places to spend money. It would be unrealistic to ask the government to spend all its money on drug enforcement activities.

It would be unfair to compare the resources China and the United States devote to drug control issues because of the differences in their national wealth as well as severity of the drug problem. The United States also started building specialized drug enforcement forces much earlier at both the federal and local levels. However, what China lacks in financial resources, it attempts to make up with efficiency and hard work. As the ranking police official in Beijing stated:

> We have far fewer people than our partners in the United States and our workload is extremely heavy. I don't know of any superiors who do not work overtime on a regular basis, which is why I work overtime all the time, and which is also why I expect my subordinates to work overtime. Usually the higher the rank, the more overtime you are expected to work. I never work my regular 8-hour day. Free weekends are rare for me. Technically this kind of work life is against the labor law, but we are the police. Working overtime is to be expected. Our overtime is never expected to be compensated. If the government has some extra money, we may get a small bonus, which we take with great appreciation. If there is no bonus, we still have to work overtime. On the other hand, we have a highly efficient work force; and I can proudly say our productivity is far greater than our U.S. counterparts.

Relentless Pursuit of Big Players

With all the drug enforcement strategies in China, nothing occupies higher priority than identifying and breaking up criminal organizations involved in drug trafficking. As a totalitarian society, nothing poses a greater threat to the political establishment than extralegal organizations, let alone ones that engage in the sale and distribution of illicit drugs. Almost without exception, crackdowns of major drug trafficking organizations are announced around June 26 each year to coincide with the rollout of the annual counternarcotic campaign. For instance, in 2011, China broke up a 52-member criminal gang that organized HIV-positive people and juveniles to transport drugs. The group leader, Liu Fucheng, was sentenced to death.[13] The government's priority on catching the leader of a trafficking organization is so great and the consequences so dire that every drug trafficker arrested is desperate to find someone else to take the blame. An inmate who received a stayed death sentence told us:

> In the trafficking business, you can't hide for long. If you have developed a reputation or any reputation for trafficking drugs, the police will immediately find you. A person should avoid being noted, just like a pig should avoid gaining fat. There are all kinds of people involved in this business. Many are arrested and begin to *maima*.

While many low-level traffickers are more than eager to turn in their conspirators or anyone they can identify as their "up-line" (the one who supplied them the drugs), such practices are rare among major traffickers when the amount of consignment well exceeds the threshold for the death penalty. As we ascertained from the stories told by the convicted traffickers we interviewed, those who were put to death were often the ones who would acknowledge that they were the leader of the trafficking ring. One inmate told us how he was caught with his brother-in-law in their last consignment:

> The police did not want to arrest us right at the airport because there were many passengers and it would make a big scene. Also, who knows, we may have carried weapons. They waited until we were cleared the security and entered the waiting area. It was so ironic. The trap was right there. One policeman was sitting on one end of the bench and another sat on the other end. My brother-in-law and I chose the center to sit down. They immediately came up and asked us to follow them to another place. Soon the director of the police department and his people arrived. Television people also showed up. It was a big case. We were all over the press.
>
> My brother-in-law took the responsibility immediately. I think he knew for such a quantity the outcome was obvious. Besides, he had been arrested before and served time in prison for drug charges. He told the police that I was simply traveling with him for personal reasons. I told the police I was supposed to go to Guangzhou to seek medical treatment for an ailment in my leg. I was going there anyway and had nothing to do with the consignment. I claimed total innocence. But it didn't matter to the police. I was sentenced to death, later I appealed and the sentence was changed to death sentence with a reprieve. Till this day, in the police records, my statements remain that I was innocent and I had no idea what my brother-in-law was doing.

Extensive Use of Confidential Informants

Most drug enforcement officials in China will be quick to admit that they operate an extensive network of informants, many of whom are developed from the arrested traffickers. These informants provide vital information about the flow of drugs and names of major players in the region. All officials we interviewed in this study agreed that without intelligence development and maintenance of a large network of informants, drug enforcement will not likely make any progress. One senior official in Guangdong put it bluntly:

> Random inspections and checkpoints on major highways are basically useless. Even in the United States after the September 11 attacks, less than 5 percent of shipping containers are inspected. In Guangdong, which relies on export and import businesses, we have neither the manpower nor the equipment to inspect the millions of containers. Here is an example. A few years back, the Guangdong provincial government spent about $145,000 to set up checkpoints on all major trans-provincial highways to inspect passengers and cargo vehicles in an effort to stop the flow of drugs. Guess what the result was by the end of the yearly campaign? A total of about 500 grams of heroin was found on only two occasions. And in both incidents, we received concrete intelligence pinpointing the specific vehicles. In other words, without intelligence, nothing would have come out of this massive inspection campaign.

This observation seems to be a perfect match with what we found in our conversations with the convicted traffickers in prison. In all cases, someone had informed the police of their plans, and a trap was set up for them to enter. Information-sharing and joint investigations are considered the backbone of drug enforcement in China. Officials interviewed for this study were clear about how their tasks differed from those of their colleagues in regular criminal investigations. One senior police official in Beijing commented:

> Unlike street crimes where you have victims, there are no "victims" in the drug trade who will call on the police for help. Even when drug dealers or traffickers have defrauded each other, you will be lucky to have one case out of every 100 cases where you will get a call from the involved party. They simply don't report. Without active intelligence development, there will be no cases. Drug enforcement police must be proactive and work hard to develop cases, or they will have nothing to do. As a result, a serious challenge that we all face is to constantly improve ourselves because drug traffickers change constantly.

Drug Enforcement and International Collaborations

China has for years worked to increase collaborations with its neighboring countries to combat cross-border trafficking activities, such as training drug enforcement police officers and providing financial incentives to convince farmers to grow cash crops in place of opium poppy. China also pressures its neighboring countries to be more forceful in eliminating opium cultivation and the trafficking of heroin and other drugs across their borders into China. According to ranking officials we interviewed, each year China conducts multiple joint investigations on major drug traffickers who have escaped China, seeking protection in remote areas in the Golden Triangle. For instance, during his heyday, Tan Xiaolin, who had evaded the Chinese authorities for years by hiding in northern Burma, was captured with assistance from the Burmese authorities.[14] Through collaboration with the Burmese government alone, more than 60 Chinese suspects involved in drug dealing have been caught and transferred back to China since 2009.[15]

Despite China's eagerness to seek cooperation from neighboring countries to help reduce the influx of illicit drugs, its relationship with countries around the Golden Triangle remains sensitive at times, because of its political and economic dominance. Many neighboring countries have long been wary of China's growing influence in the region. However, China's outreach to its neighboring countries may also be viewed as a necessity in the global fight against illicit drugs. Many law enforcement agencies in Southeast Asia have come to realize that ethnic Chinese have long played a dominant role in transborder drug smuggling activities in the region. The rise of mainland China as a major drug consumption market will only reinforce the prominence of ethnic Chinese in the region for their roles in the drug trade. Trafficking groups made up of ethnic Chinese rely on their extensive contacts within the Chinese enclaves to purchase and transport drugs to places where profits can be made.[16]

As a result, international collaboration has been an important aspect of police work in China's effort to combat drug trafficking. Every provincial police agency has a foreign affairs office assigned to coordinate and assist with investigations involving international matters. All law enforcement subjects in Beijing and other parts of China appear to have had varying degrees of contact with foreign police agencies. China hosts regular drug enforcement seminars and training workshops for neighboring countries in Southeast Asia, and also sends its own police officials to other countries to receive training.

The importance of international collaboration was difficult to miss in our conversations with police officials. One top-ranked police official in Beijing stated that China emphasizes three things in international collaborations: (1) maintain open communication, (2) develop pragmatic strategies, and (3) strive for efficiency. He commented on the increasing international exchange of police work in recent years:

> Drug enforcement is one of the few areas where the exchange of intelligence and collaborative investigations are the easiest to carry out. Because all nations share the same goals and objectives in combating drug trafficking and reducing its demand, police agencies tend to have far fewer political obstacles to overcome than many other areas of government affairs.

It was noted that during the interviews in this study that most officials were highly appreciative of the collaborative spirits that most foreign police agencies have shown in their exchanges. One top drug enforcement official in Beijing observed: "We rarely encountered any resistance from a foreign country. We have made great strides in multilateral and bilateral collaborations in our intelligence sharing and cooperative investigations with many countries. Most countries, including the U.S. DEA, have been quite impressed with our productivity and efficiency. Honestly, I have not encountered any problems I cannot solve in our international collaborations. Maybe this is because of my confidence."

According to his accounts, international collaborations between China and neighboring countries have expanded at an even greater pace since 2000. He claimed that at any given time there are 20–30 joint investigations or inquiries involving foreign partners:

> Most major drug cases that we have solved thus far involved some foreign assistance. For instance, we worked with the Burmese government

> on Tan Xiaolin's case. Tan thought that by living in Myanmar and never crossing into China he would be safe. He was wrong. Through joint investigations with the Burmese police, we were able to trace 2,000 to 3,000 kilograms of heroin directly to him, and implicate his involvement in another 6,000 to 7,000 kilograms of heroin. We have bilateral, multilateral relationships with some 30 to 40 countries. Our collaborations are all-encompassing, from investigation to intelligence sharing. I can say our efficiency has impressed most of our foreign partners.

Sino-U.S. Collaboration

China has long enjoyed a cooperative agreement with the United States, in its effort to counter drug trafficking and substance abuse. In the late 1990s, China and the United States formed the Joint Liaison Group to bring together police agencies on each side to develop closer working relationships; this was further strengthened by recent high-level discussions and meetings between China's minister of Public Security, Meng Jianzhu, and U.S. attorney general, Eric Holder, who visited Beijing in October 2010.[17]

High-ranking Chinese law enforcement officials claimed that although there are many sensitive topics between Sino-American exchanges, such as intellectual property and trade agreements, anti-narcotic cooperation is not one of them. As one high-ranking police official stated:

> China has signed many multilateral and bilateral anti-narcotic laws, agreements, and memorandum of understandings with many countries. We have maintained a very open channel with these countries and share our intelligence. Our collaboration with the U.S. DEA has also been pleasant. Honestly, they rely on us to get their job done here because no other countries have a worse drug problem than the United States.

For many years, the United States blacklisted China as one of the world's major drug-producing and -trafficking countries, which provoked ire from the China site.[18] A ranking official in Beijing countered this assessment by the U.S. drug intelligence community:

> Drug trafficking in China is mainly for domestic consumption. This has changed from the early 1980s when most drugs were transported through Guangdong Province to reach Hong Kong and Southeast Asia. A very small percentage of heroin from the Golden Triangle was being transported through China to the U.S. market. You have to look at the market economy of drug trafficking. The vast distance between China and the United States is the main obstacle. It is just too far to profit from the small quantities such as 30 or 50 grams. You will have to transport large quantities, which would require significant finance and organization. I would venture to say less than 5 percent of heroin in the United States came from the Golden Triangle.

The distance between the United States and China does appear to be an obstacle for any large-scale heroin trafficking, when easier routes are available through other countries and South America. However, there were a few exceptions, one of which was Kin Cheung Wong and his so-called 125 Organization accused of running a massive heroin-trafficking scheme that smuggled more than $100 million worth of Southeast Asian heroin into the United States in the early 2000s.[19] Sources close to the investigation revealed that such cases were rare because the head of the organization had previously been convicted of drug trafficking in the United States and was familiar with the business; he had used his existing social network from Southeast Asia through mainland China to reach his contacts in Chinatown in New York City. Nonetheless, the case was frequently used as a successful example of mutual legal aid between the two countries and was warmly received by drug enforcement officials on both sides.

According to our contacts in Chinese governments, the most important factor in determining whether a country is a major drug-producing or -trafficking country is predicated upon the profit calculation. One high-ranking police official in Beijing even claimed that drugs going through mainland China to other places are simply unlikely because of the pricing differentials, even for Taiwan:

> I don't even think there is a viable trafficking route from Fujian Province to Taiwan. There might be some small quantities passed through local fishermen, but these transactions would not create any substantial

> market. Look at the political reality. Pricing is crucial in the drug trafficking business. There is just not enough money to be made by transporting heroin to Taiwan through Fujian or from China to the United States. On the contrary, many Taiwanese drug traffickers came to Fujian and the interior of China to establish drug (meth) manufacturing facilities. These Taiwanese, usually members of dark societies, came to China to manufacture drugs because there is a great market.

Drug Enforcement Collaboration with Burma

China is among the few countries in the region that maintain a close relationship with the Burmese government, although tensions arise from time to time because the restive ethnic minorities and warlords in the north are closely intertwined with their ethnic compatriots on the Chinese side. Over the past few decades, China relied on Burmese authorities to seize numerous high-profile drug traffickers.

In contrast, the United States has in recent decades kept a distant relationship with the Burmese government, withholding any direct aid or involvement as leverage for pressuring the Burmese authorities into political reform and democracy. However, most U.S. agents in the field were critical of the U.S. disengagement policy on drug enforcement activities. As one U.S. agent reported:

> Our Burma policy should be improved. Similar collaborations such as those with the Thai authorities should be implemented in Burma also. While we should continue to press for human rights issues and the overall improvement of the political climate in that country, heroin control serves direct U.S. interests. It would be a lot more effective to get into Burma and work with the local and military authorities. We don't have to abandon the whole anti-narcotic efforts and wait for the political situation to improve, meanwhile losing opportunities to prevent and reduce drug supplies.

The role of Burma in Southeast Asia's anti-narcotics efforts cannot be overstated, according to many local government officials and the U.S. officials stationed in the region. Police liaisons we spoke with in the region all agreed that heroin production was on its way down, or at least had stabilized. Even by U.S. assessments, the military junta in Burma made significant progress in recent years (before it was disbanded in 2011) in reducing opium poppy cultivation and opium production, in part because of its cooperation with the United Nations and other regional allies (particularly China and Thailand).[20] Burma has also been recognized for its efforts to collaborate with its neighbors in jointly controlling the transportation of precursor chemicals, in an effort to reduce narcotics production and trafficking in the highlands of Southeast Asia.

However, the political situation in Burma has for many years been discouraging to donor nations that could have been helpful to its law enforcement efforts. This is a pertinent issue because continued opium poppy eradication drives farmers into deeper destitution. Without viable alternative sources of income, it is only a matter of time before the farmers either revert back to growing opium poppies or participate in producing synthetic drugs. Burma has already ascended to prominence in the region for supplying its drug consumers with vast amounts of ATS, including ketamine, ice, and ecstasy. As shown in table 9.1, China has already seized more ATS than traditional heroin or opium since 2006, and the majority of the ATS came through Yunnan Province.

Even though the United States suspended all direct counternarcotics assistance to Burma in 1988, when the military junta crushed the prodemocracy movement led by Aung San Suu Kyi, the U.S. Department of Justice has maintained a regular liaison post in Yangon, and shares intelligence with the Burmese authorities and provides limited assistance in investigations. For instance, the DEA conducted opium yield surveys in Burmese border regions in 1993 and 1995, and annually from 1997 through 2004, which monitored the changing geographic distribution and scope of the opium crop. Such collaboration in intelligence-sharing and mutual assistance led to significant seizures, arrests, and convictions of drug traffickers and producers in 2005.[21] For years, the United States provided limited funding through United Nations programs that benefited drug eradication projects in Burma, particularly in the warlord-controlled Wa State. However, in January 2005, the U.S. federal court in New York indicted several leaders of the United Wa State Army, the de facto warlord government in the Wa State, which brought about a complete halt to any U.S. assistance to Burma's counternarcotics programs.

The military junta is fully aware of the corruption problems among its officials and recently has shown efforts to reform among its ranks. In 2005, Burma joined the UN Convention against Corruption, and launched a series of programs aimed at curbing official corruption, including increasing government employee salaries tenfold, firing officials on corruption charges, and closing businesses suspected of drug trafficking or money laundering. In a 2005 investigation assisted by the U.S. DEA and Australian Federal Police, the Burmese authorities closed the Myanmar Universal Bank and its 38 branch offices throughout the country, and seized assets of more than $18 million.[22] The bank's chairman and his associates were arrested and charged with money laundering and drug trafficking offenses. The military junta government also revoked operating licenses for two other banks suspected of money laundering.

During our field visits in Burma, we learned about the closing down of businesses such as a hotel and a trading company in Mandalay (the country's second largest city), because their owners were either collaborating with or assisting in drug smuggling activities. Whereas such charges would have been easily swept under the rug in the past through briberies, we were told by our community informants that such backdoor dealings were of limited use when illicit drugs were involved.

Similar to Southeast Asian countries weary of China's growing power in the region, Burma is particularly aware of its historical dependence on China for much of its military and commercial interests and its isolation from the U.S.-led Western coalition against its human rights issues. Before handing power over to a civilian government in 2011, Burma's military government made conscious efforts to improve its relationship with the West, which culminated in the release of opposition leader Aung San Suu Kyi after 15 years of house arrest; she was then permitted to run for a seat in the parliament. The United States responded with favorable gestures including a promise to re-open its embassy and exchanges of high-level government and commercial delegations. As mentioned in chapter 2, with the political reform in Burma gaining momentum, it is anticipated that there will be closer ties between the United States and Burma in drug enforcement in the very near future.

On the other hand, the warlords in the opium cultivation regions in Northern Burma continue to maintain a delicate relationship with

China because their economic survival depends more on their commerce along the border than on the Burmese government. These warlords cannot afford a direct confrontation with China on drug issues. The warlords in Northern Burma, who traditionally answer to nobody but their own coffers, have come to terms with the reality that manufacturing and selling drugs will only serve to undermine their own regime. It is perhaps more lucrative to sell natural resources and engage in commerce than to sell drugs, which only invites attention and attack. In fact, for many years, warlords along Burma's border regions signed agreements with authorities in Yunnan promising not to allow any sales or transportation of drugs into China.

Although illicit drugs continue to flow into China, supposedly through unofficial and clandestine channels, these warlords have generally stayed away from any overt involvement in the drug trade, thus avoiding direct accusations from the Chinese authorities. More recently, the warlords have shown even greater willingness to cooperate, as the Burmese government is warming up to the West. The warlords understand that once the Burmese government becomes stronger and more resourceful, it will reclaim its authority over the northern territories. Recent armed clashes between the government forces and warlords' militia in Kachin, a northern state, reflect the ongoing tensions. As a result, warlords in northern Burma are mostly interested in improving their economy and strengthening their military forces. To appease the international community and mostly its powerful neighbor across the border, warlord governments have vowed publicly to eradicate opium cultivation and to ban production of synthetic drugs. Some claim to have achieved the overall goal, while others claim to have set a definitive timeline for doing so. According to one high-level official in Wa State in northern Burma, the Wa government is determined to eradicate all opium poppy cultivation, and international officials and law enforcement agents are invited each year to inspect their counter-narcotic programs.

Collaboration with Hong Kong

Hong Kong's vibrant commerce and its port facilities have long made it an ideal location for transporting drugs from Southeast Asia to the international market. For many years, drug traffickers from Hong Kong were active in planning and financing trafficking operations on the mainland as well as in the surrounding nations. According to U.S. intelligence sources, Hong Kong is no longer a major transshipment hub in Southeast Asia and Oceania. The drug addict population in Hong Kong has been on a steady decline for the past few years, according to the official Central Registry of Drug Abuse (CRDA).[23] Although Hong Kong imports ATS from China to meet the increasing demand among the youth population, both law enforcement officials and government prosecutors claim that there are far fewer heroin users these days.

Both U.S. and Hong Kong authorities attribute this change to Hong Kong's effective intervention efforts and public campaigns, as well as to the availability of alternate trafficking routes in coastal China.[24] Most drugs in Hong Kong are believed to come from China or Southeast Asia. According to local police, there are very few cases of drug manufacturing in Hong Kong territories. Opium poppy cultivation is impossible in this crowded urban setting. One senior prosecutor explained why it was also difficult to set up labs to manufacture drugs in Hong Kong:

> Unlike the 1970s where there were still rural and remote areas in Hong Kong where you could possibly hide small labs for small batches of chemicals, it is very hard to manufacture drugs in Hong Kong these days. Hong Kong is a small place with a dense population. People live in small apartments literally on top of each other. There is a well-developed network of community intelligence. Why risk being caught here in a densely populated place when you can pay someone in China to produce the drugs?

Another senior prosecutor agreed with this explanation on the disappearance of drug manufacturing in Hong Kong. Having worked in Hong Kong's judicial system for 30 years, he recalled that drug manufacturing was common in the 1970s. He noted:

> I rarely see drug manufacturing cases now. The majority of drug cases these days involve street-level dealers, typically psychedelics and cannabis that are sold and used in dance clubs and karaoke bars. It is simply too difficult to produce drugs in Hong Kong. One simple but major obstacle

> is the smell. You have to have very good ventilation. The fumes can easily offend your neighbors who would then complain to the authorities. Also, these people tend to cover up their windows. Any time you cover your windows for a long period of time, and with strange odors coming out of your vents, you will attract attention. The police will raid the place. Besides, if you produce any illicit substance, there will be traces in your ventilation ducts, a great piece of evidence for prosecution purposes.

Another factor contributing to the drop in drug trafficking activities is the succession of laws with harsher punishments for drug offenses. Although Hong Kong abolished the death penalty in the early 1990s, penalties for drug-related offenses are still severe by Western standards. A high-ranking government prosecutor explained: "Compared to other developed countries, Hong Kong has severe punishments for drug offenses. If you shoot a police officer, you get 17 to 20 years in prison. But if you are caught carrying one or two kilograms of heroin, you can get 20 years or more in prison."

However, both U.S. and Hong Kong law enforcement agencies believe Hong Kong still plays an important but limited role in the international drug trafficking business by serving as the coordinating and financial base of operations. Many officials in mainland China tend to agree with this assessment and believe most expertise in financing trafficking operations and laundering drug money still comes from Hong Kong. Because of its large container shipment business, Hong Kong also continues to serve as a convenient transshipment hub for traffickers moving drug consignments through its myriad shipping businesses. Local drug traffickers are also developing routes through adjacent townships in Guangdong and renting warehouses to store large consignments for delivery to Hong Kong or other markets.

The collaboration between drug enforcement agencies in mainland China and Hong Kong was often used as an example of cooperation in police work because of the two different political and thus law enforcement systems. Because of the unique relationship between mainland China and Hong Kong, Beijing is never hesitant to demonstrate its political leadership in dealing with its administrative subordinates. Moreover, a totalitarian regime also makes its police work more efficient. One top-ranked police official in Beijing observed:

> We have a great relationship with Hong Kong in intelligence sharing and joint investigations. In fact, we are doing a lot of law enforcement for Hong Kong authorities. We give each other a lot of valuable information that helps our mutual investigations. We want to catch drug traffickers, and they want to stop the drugs from entering Hong Kong. The more intelligence they share with us, the more we can do on this side of the border and that means less work for them. We have responsibilities to take care of them. But the exchange is not always equal. Because of our different legal systems, we have greater latitude to assist them than the other way around. For instance, if they ask us to assist in arresting fugitives, we will catch them and turn them over. But if we ask Hong Kong authorities to do the same, they often cannot comply. There is no extradition agreement. To put it simply, without mainland police, social stability in Hong Kong will be greatly weakened.

His enthusiasm over collaboration with Hong Kong authorities in regional as well as international drug enforcement work was shared by police liaisons from other countries. U.S. officials in the region were also positive in their experiences working with regional host nations, despite the fact that not all countries are able to accommodate U.S. requests. One U.S. official in Hong Kong commented: "We are fortunate to be in Hong Kong. We have great cooperation with Hong Kong authorities, which are very capable. We have asset sharing, extradition, information sharing protocols with Hong Kong authorities. This is lacking from many other countries. Any investigations we do here in Hong Kong, we always coordinate with our counterparts."

However, this international collaboration is not without its problems. For instance, intelligence sharing in the region is often narrowly defined. Although U.S. law enforcement officials expect a free flow of information between them and their host agencies, they wish at times that they could receive a bit more material on particular cases. One official said:

> At times, we would like to see more detailed information on cases. Occasionally, local authorities take the position that we are merely liaisons working for foreign agencies, therefore only information specifically pertaining to the United States is shared. They don't understand that we

want to get the big picture, from a regional and global point of view. We realize that no one country can do this job alone. However, we have been successful in pushing our collaborating authorities to analyze cases from a regional and global perspective.

Conclusion

To understand drug enforcement policies and activities in China, we traveled to different parts of China, from the capital city to the far corners of the country, interviewing officials and frontline police officers. Our overall impression is that, despite meager budgets and poor equipment, Chinese law enforcement agencies have been striving to gain an upper hand in their war against drugs.

By most indicators, China has managed to somewhat slow down the rapid increases observed in the 1980s in the number of drug users through many measures—compulsory drug treatment of all officially identified drug users and harsh punishment for possession and trafficking offenses. But recent statistics in the number of new drug addicts and seizures forebode more troubles ahead. The control of illicit drugs commands special attention in China's political psyche because of its experiences in the two wars more than a century ago with foreign countries over the influx of opium.[25]

Chinese authorities have launched many campaigns aimed at reducing the demand as well as stopping the flow of drugs in China.[26] Chinese officials in recent years have become increasingly open about the challenges in drug control, regularly publishing statistics on drug use surveys and warnings of emerging patterns in new drugs. Considering the growing wealth and urbanization, and adding to the mix with poor neighboring countries with a long history of opium cultivation and a weak government, China's struggle against illicit drugs will remain an uphill battle in the foreseeable future. China will have few choices but to increase its investment in building drug enforcement infrastructure and training its police forces.

10

Conclusion

By all accounts, China has been relentless in its efforts to gain an upper hand with the drug problem, although some of its measures seem draconian by Western standards, such as its extensive use of the death penalty on drug traffickers and compulsory rehabilitation facilities and labor camps for addicts. However, considering the large numbers of seizures and ever-growing official registry of drug addicts, China's drug problem does not seem to have subsided much. After a few years of progress in the mid-2000s, the Chinese government is now acknowledging that the country has a long way to go in controlling illicit drugs and faces increasing challenges from transborder drug traffickers because of its geographical proximity to the two most significant drug-producing regions in the world—the Golden Triangle and the Golden Crescent. In short, China is surrounded by ample supplies of heroin and ATS drugs.

After a few years of decline in total acreage of opium poppy cultivation in northern Burma in the mid-2000s, Chinese authorities again claimed that production rebounded in the last couple of years, particularly in the most recent survey, from 31,700 hectares in 2011 to 44,866 hectares in 2012, a 41 percent jump.[1] Because China remains the largest drug consumption market in Asia, any increase in heroin production in the Golden Triangle will likely be in direct response to the demand from the Chinese market. Meanwhile, drug traffickers also explore and develop smuggling routes through Central Asia from Afghanistan, the center of global heroin production. According to estimates issued by the United Nations, Afghanistan alone has in recent years produced more heroin than the global market could consume, averaging 380–400 tons a year.[2] It is no wonder that police in China's northwest corner Xinjiang Uygur Autonomous Region seized 20 times more drugs in 2011 than a year ago.[3] However, as discussed in chapter 2, China's immediate threat of cross-border drug trafficking is still primarily through its porous borders with Burma.

The Rise of Consumption in Amphetamine-Type Stimulants

Amphetamine-Type Stimulants (ATS) such as ice and ecstasy have been around for several decades. During our fieldwork in Yunnan and Southeast Asia in the mid- and late 2000s, we encountered numerous reports on the shift in the drug trade and consumption demands. Clearly two divergent markets are gaining a foothold in China's drug trafficking business, one with older traffickers primarily concentrating in the heroin trade, and the other with younger traffickers specializing in ATS.

While the aging addicts are hustling for drug money and struggling with relapses, fewer young people are joining their ranks. Instead, the so-called new drugs (i.e., methamphetamine, ecstasy, and ketamine) are becoming popular among urban youth. These drugs are thought to be non-habit-forming and more "fun" to use, particularly at karaoke and nightclubs. Although there are poly-drug users, ATS use is typically associated with dance clubs and KTV salons where urban youths hang out and party. Heroin addiction, on the other hand, draws an aging crowd and users are generally considered junkies by ATS users. Years of public education and cultural taboo associated with heroin use appear to have gained some momentum in China. Sources in both public and private sectors have informed us that the size of the heroin addict population in China is steadily declining relative to their counterparts in other drug use. As shown in table 8.1, the proportion of heroin addicts on the official addiction registry was on a steady decline over the past decade. The Chinese government has also acknowledged this trend. In his speech to China's legislature, the People's Congress, the minister of Public Security Meng Jianzhu reported that China has about 1.19 million registered heroin addicts, or 63 percent of the country's total drug users, and another 655,000 Chinese were abusing synthetic drugs.[4]

The future of drug trafficking in China is juxtaposed between two conflicting forces. On the one hand, China's booming economy and the frenzy among the populace to become rich will undoubtedly encourage entrepreneurship in all types of commercial trade, licit or illicit. Drug trafficking, with its tremendous profits, will continue to draw risk takers who are limited in conventional opportunities for any substantial material prosperity. On the other hand, the strong social stigma surrounding illicit drugs and related drug trafficking activities, coupled with an unforgiving penal system and totalitarian government, will likely constrain the growth of the addict population and the number of daring entrepreneurs. Unlike other social ills, particularly the so-called victimless crimes (gambling, prostitution, and financial malfeasance), there is little moral ambiguity about illicit drugs. However, because of China's large population, the sheer number of drug users will continue to create a marketplace for drug trafficking and distribution.

As for the speculation that large quantities of illicit drugs only pass through China on their way to other Asian or Pacific Rim countries, there are many obstacles to this prognosis. Aside from China's draconian penal system and stigmatizing cultural environment, the remaining addict population will likely absorb any drugs that manage to enter the domestic market. Despite high-profit potentials for overseas drug orders, the fundamentals of illicit enterprises remain the same. That is, drug traffickers will most likely choose the shortest distance and least risky venue to unload their cargoes and realize profits. China's role as a transit country for the international market, particularly from such remote regions as Yunnan to coastal provinces, will most likely remain limited. It is our belief that most drugs transported from the Golden Triangle are still destined for China's domestic market.

Policy Implications

It is our belief that China and Burma are crucial in the region as well as in the world in curtailing the production and transportation of heroin and ATS drugs. Although Afghanistan has replaced Burma as the major supplier of opium and heroin in the world, the warlord-controlled regions in northern Burma continue to exert influence in the world drug market.[5] The rapid increase in ATS production and distribution in this region since the mid-1990s deserves serious attention from regional governments as well as Western countries. In its 2010 annual anti-narcotics report, the Chinese government claimed that for the first time in history the total seizures of amphetamine-type stimulants surpassed that of heroin, suggesting the shifting balance between the demands for these two types of drugs.

Several major developments are shaping the drug trafficking, distribution, and consumption in the region, which we believe will have far-reaching effects on Western countries. First, rapid economic development in Southeast Asia and China has brought about unprecedented commercial exchanges of goods and services, which break down trade barriers and travel restrictions among countries that historically viewed each other with suspicion and even hostility (such as between China and India, and between Burma and Thailand). Second, there is a general lack of sophistication in regional government's control and regulation of chemical precursors required to produce ATS. Most countries in the region do not have adequate systems of inspection and registration that are commonly found in the United States or other Western countries to monitor and track the production and movement of chemicals likely to be used in producing ATS. Third, because precursors such as ephedrine can be easily obtained and the production of ATS is relatively easy, a greater number of entrepreneurs are starting cottage laboratories producing methamphetamines, a drastic departure from the way heroin is produced in the Golden Triangle (which is still tightly controlled by local warlords). Fourth, shifts in the addict population in recent years have also brought about changing demands for illicit drugs. For instance, because of the years of public campaigns, heroin addiction has become highly stigmatized. ATS, however, is often consumed in KTV clubs and dance clubs, drawing large numbers of young people who just want to party.

All intelligence that we gathered from the region seems to agree with what other researchers have found, that is, the shift toward greater production and distribution of amphetamine-type stimulants in Southeast Asia and China has already taken place and may even become an alternative supply source to North America and other parts of the world.[6] High-ranking officials in Beijing acknowledged the large number of ATS users has created ample opportunities for entrepreneurs to manufacture and transport synthetic drugs. While the production of ATS drugs seems to draw entrepreneurs with different techniques and extensive international travel experience, heroin production in the Golden Triangle has remained concentrated in warlord-controlled territories.

These developments highlight the importance of international collaboration in developing and sharing intelligence, and conducting investigations. More importantly, it serves the United States's interests to collaborate with Southeast Asian countries by leveraging their different legal and political systems against drug production and trafficking activities. For instance, China has relied heavily on draconian penal measures to curtail the spread of drug use and production. As shown in table 4.3, the sentences of the surveyed subjects revealed the severity of punishment for drug offenses in China. A large number of the sample, 42 percent, received the so-called death sentence with a reprieve (or stayed death sentence). Thirty-one percent of the subjects were sentenced to life in prison for their drug offenses, while 22 percent received a sentence of more than 10 years. Only a small number of the subjects, 5 percent, received sentences of less than 10 years. The high concentration of severe penalties in the sample was not a selection bias, because regional officials told us that drug offenders in other provinces typically receive more severe punishments than their counterparts in Yunnan, which has grown accustomed to traffickers of greater quantities due to its proximity to the Golden Triangle.

China's firm stand against illicit drugs, together with its growing status in the world, can provide an ideal platform for the United States to garner support and solicit assistance in promoting its drug policies in the region. Unfortunately, many anti-drug efforts have either been halted or disrupted because of Burma's political situation. Most notably, since 2000, the United States has practically ceased to provide any financial support to assist the Rangoon government or other international organizations working in the country in reducing opium poppy cultivation and heroin production. The U.S. cessation of involvement in Burma's anti-narcotics efforts should be reexamined, especially now that the United States and other Western countries are beginning to engage Burma in political and economic reforms. As one senior DEA official in Southeast Asia commented during one of our interviews:

> Burma policy should be improved . . . similar collaborations as those with Thai authorities should be implemented in Burma also. While we should continue to press for human rights issues and improvement of political climate, heroin control serves more direct U.S. interests. It would be a lot more effective to get into Burma and with local and military authorities. We don't have to abandon the whole anti-narcotic efforts and wait for the political situation to improve, meanwhile losing the opportunities.

> If we take care of Burma, the whole heroin business will collapse in S.E. Asia. This is why we should work directly inside Burma. We have worked effectively with warlords and totalitarian societies in other parts of the world, we certainly can figure out a way to work with the Burmese authorities or at least explore ways to work with them. By ignoring Burma, the problems originated in that country actually make work more difficult and challenging for us.

In comparison, Thailand enjoys much greater assistance (in terms of money, technology, and manpower) in its anti-narcotics efforts from the United States, when in reality the country's drugs are almost exclusively imported from Burma. Such an approach may hurt U.S. interests in the long run, because it neither accelerates the downfall of the *tatmadaw* (the Burmese army) nor helps control drug production and trafficking activities. The absence of any involvement in Burma's anti-narcotic efforts only tarnishes the U.S. image as playing politics at the expense of legitimate law enforcement cooperation, which only further diminishes American influence in the region. While the United States works well with its partners in Thailand, the relationship is probably more utilitarian than anything else, as the senior DEA official cited previously commented, "Thai police are our trusted partners. They have gone through training and background checks and all are polygraphed. They can be trusted and work effectively with us, although their loyalty is probably more to the money than ideology or government."

We believe a distinction should be made by U.S. political leaders as well as policy makers between legitimate mutual assistance among law enforcement agencies and ongoing political contentions. Now that Burma is becoming more open, direct engagement and financial assistance to Burma's anti-drug efforts should be explored and even encouraged. Additionally, the United States should greatly increase its technical support to regional governments in monitoring opium poppy production, which can be seen easily by satellite surveillance, and in analyzing and tracking chemical signatures (or traces) of seized drugs from the region.

After all the field activities and interviews with scores of law enforcement and government representatives in the Golden Triangle region, we believe that the current U.S. role in combating transnational drug trafficking in this region is negligible or marginal at best. Some may argue against our recommendation for greater U.S. involvement in regional anti-narcotics efforts. After all, we do not believe that most heroin and ATS produced in the Golden Triangle region or even the larger Southeast Asia are destined for the United States, and we have not found evidence to suggest any systematic involvement in the drug trafficking business by terrorist organizations. But we do believe that it will not be long before Asia becomes the main supplier of ATS for the rest of the world. The greater influx of consumer products from China and other Asian countries to North America will inevitably increase the flow of illicit goods and services. The global economy and increasingly fragmented drug production and trafficking systems will ensure a convergence of drug distribution networks between Western countries and Asia. It behooves the United States not only to remain engaged but also to play an active leadership role in bringing together regional efforts in combating the production and trafficking of illicit drugs in Southeast Asia.

As for recommendations for the U.S. political leaders with regard to involvement in anti-narcotics efforts in China and Southeast Asia, there are two choices. The first is that the United States maintains its current policy, with minimal involvement other than stationing drug enforcement officials in regional embassies. The second is that the United States becomes more proactive in forging greater collaborations with regional law enforcement agencies and including the Burmese government. Needless to say, the United States is most threatened by the influx of illicit drugs from south of the border and will remain so for many years to come. However, it will be shortsighted for the U.S. authorities to remain on the sidelines just because most drug trafficking activities do not have direct bearing on the U.S. domestic market. In an increasingly global environment, the merging of drug manufacturers, traffickers, and distributors is only a matter of time.

Research and Comparative Analysis

To our knowledge, this is the first study of its kind and certainly it has left many questions for other researchers to continue to explore. One important area that warrants continued effort is to accumulate empirical data on different aspects of drug traffickers and their organizations. As stated earlier, any empirical endeavor of this nature invariably suffers from access limitations. We have made assertions and speculations about the organizational and operational characteristics of Chinese drug traffickers in the Golden Triangle region, based on the data we were able to collect. These data are skewed by our entry point into the secretive underworld, which is undoubtedly far more complex than what we were able to observe. Therefore, it is important for researchers to gain different entry points (either by approaching different subject populations or by employing different research methods) to study drug manufacturing, trafficking, and distribution activities in Southeast Asia.

An extension of the need for additional empirical data is to explore the development and evolution of the organizational structures of transnational drug traffickers. We found most traffickers to be entrepreneurs, loosely affiliated with other like-minded people who are committed to no organizational goals or subcultures. Aside from a few stories about family members willing to sacrifice themselves for each other, most traffickers, once caught, are ready to sell out their partners.

The shift toward more fragmented markets in drug manufacturing and trafficking is likely caused by greater involvement of entrepreneurs in recent decades. Although vulnerable at the individual level, entrepreneurial dominance proves far more resistant to law enforcement interventions than any formal criminal organizations, because of its collective ingenuity. The learning ability develops not within any specific organization, but rather in the growing process whereby surviving traffickers learn from those who are caught. Gradually, drug traffickers become more sophisticated. Understanding a criminal enterprise group's organizational structure is critical in developing effective response strategies. Such knowledge allows law enforcement agencies opportunities to identify weakness and vulnerabilities that provide better application of investigative strategies.

Another important issue for future research effort is to systematically compare how drug traffickers from Colombia and Mexico differ from those in the Golden Triangle. There have been numerous stories in the news media about the exploits of the Colombian or Mexican drug cartels, but little systematic research has been done on drug trafficking in

South America. The same can be said about drug trafficking in China and Southeast Asia.

Because the social and political conditions in Colombia and Mexico are different from those in the Golden Triangle, a comparative approach will enhance our attention to the different strategies and practices that drug traffickers employ in their businesses. For instance, we can examine how drug traffickers along the Burma-China border differ from their counterparts in Latin America in building and maintaining their smuggling routes, and how different requisites in the marketplace make different demands on the formation of trafficking organizations.

Recent studies on drug trafficking organizations in Latin America have produced compelling explanations that illustrate the complexity of this research topic. For instance, the Medellin cartel and the subsequent Cali cartel in Colombia, and the Arellano-Felix brothers in Mexico, have long been known for their large-scale international operations, their ability to influence major social institutions (such as elected offices, law enforcement agencies, and even the military), and their extensive use of violence to accomplish organizational goals.[7] For years, the exploits of such drug kingpins as Pablo Escobar, the Ochoa brothers, Jose Gonzalo Rodriguez Gacha, and the Arellano-Felix brothers in corrupting government officials through bribery or neutralizing state power through assassinations have created an image of large, multinational corporations, made invincible through ruthless tactics.[8] The widespread violence in Mexico has brought about a generation of narco culture and folklore wherein deaths have become an almost inescapable topic of the country.[9] Shadowed in a sense of fatalism, former Mexican foreign minister Jorge Castaneda likened the current counternarcotics policies of both countries to wishing fruits and flowers flourishing in the desert "if only it rained."[10]

In his ethnographic study of Colombian drug traffickers in the Netherlands, sociologist Damian Zaitch found that members of the drug cartels interacted with flexible and even chaotic networks of underground and international criminals.[11] He challenged the mythical image of fixed "cartels" with homogenous, corporate-like organizations and argued that social and business networks in the cocaine enterprises were heterogeneous and flexible, and formed by relations between criminal and legal actors, settings, and businesses. The reality, as Zaitch described, was essentially an enterprise model, which contrasts significantly with what we have known about Colombian or Mexican drug trafficking organizations.

Although few empirical studies on drug trafficking have sought to advance theories on organized crime, these recent studies nonetheless have offered tantalizing evidence of interesting theoretical implications. Since all drug trafficking organizations respond to varied market constraints, it is important to explore how members of a group collectively alter organizational behavior and structural patterns to accomplish the adaptation process. In other words, we need to explore the "learning capacity" of a trafficking organization in adapting to changes in the environment.

As Michael Kenney, a professor at Pennsylvania State University, pointed out, in the face of persistent government efforts to eliminate them, Colombian drug trafficking organizations have proven to be innovative and highly adaptable.[12] Kenney argued that these trafficking organizations essentially "learn" from their experience and can select response strategies based on stored knowledge, thus becoming difficult to eliminate over time. Zaitch explored the subjective perceptions of Colombian traffickers in Rotterdam, and found that economic factors and human resources had a central impact on their key decisions, while law enforcement risks tended to be secondary.[13]

A comparative analysis regarding how these different traffickers operate may help law enforcement agencies to better devise response strategies. By looking at the organizational structure and the political, economic, and social influences in different drug-producing regions, such a comparative analysis can produce empirical guidance that either validates current law enforcement strategies or recommends alternative ones. Furthermore, a comparative approach can produce more nuanced understanding on regional and cultural differences that will enhance our attention to the different strategies and practices that drug traffickers employ in their business.

Finally, from an academic point of view, by comparing drug traffickers as well as street-level distribution networks in Southeast Asia to their counterparts in Latin America, we will develop a much better understanding of how different requisites in the marketplace make different demands on the social organizations and economic transactions of an enterprise that appears to have survived quite well in a hostile environment. Different organizational and operational arrangements emerge in response to different market demands and characteristics of the addict culture. These differences must be carefully examined through comparative analysis to produce coherent and nuanced conceptual frameworks that in turn can explain or even predict these patterns. Here are a few examples of such paired observations:

> Whereas grotesque killings are a common strategy employed by the Mexican drug cartels to control market shares or reduce competition, violence is rarely observed among drug dealers or traffickers in China.
>
> Whereas well-known Mexican drug cartels dare to launch assaults on Mexican authorities, killing police and military personnel engaged in anti-trafficking campaigns, such deliberate attacks by drug traffickers are unheard of in China. Violence only erupts when drug traffickers are cornered by police, and when their capture foretells the death penalty.
>
> Whereas some Mexican drug cartels seem able to remain active for years in spite of government crackdowns and even become celebrated in drug ballads (i.e., narcocorridor), fame and publicity are the last things any Chinese drug traffickers dare to seek. In other words, if Chinese authorities set their scope on a target, there is no escape.
>
> Whereas the deaths of famed drug traffickers have been written in songs and serenaded in nightclubs and on the radio, formulating a unique narco culture and folklores in Mexico, such glorification of drug lords does not exist in China or anywhere in Southeast Asia.

At the beginning of this book, we examined the work of Paoli, Greenfield, and Reuter on the impact of variations in effective illegality on the world opiate market.[14] Our findings support most of what Paoli et al. had predicted about the relationship between strict enforcement and the size, organization, and operating methods of an opiate market. In a strict enforcement country like China, the heroin market can be characterized as nonhierarchical, small, not vertically integrated, and dependent on preexisting social relationships. The operating methods of the heroin market in China can be depicted as having modest inventories, less open violence, incorruptible state officials, and no monopolies or oligopolies. Finally, the drug market is a negligible component of the economy of China mainly because the heroin trade exists on the margins of society. As a result, the unique cultural and political contexts in China have largely determined the characteristics of the drug trade and its prospect as an illicit enterprise. As long as the Communists are in firm control of the country's political and judicial systems, we expect the drug trade to remain dominated by entrepreneurs, and any large, powerful drug cartels, such as those found in Mexico, are unlikely to emerge.

NOTES

NOTES TO CHAPTER 1

1. We use the name "Burma" throughout this book, even though the official name of the country is now "Union of Myanmar" or "Myanmar."
2. McCoy, 1992; United Nations International Drug Control Program, 1997.
3. Chin, 2009; Lintner, 1994; McCoy, 1972.
4. Chalk, 2000.
5. Southeast Asian Information Network, 1998.
6. Chin, 2009; Chouvy and Meissonnier, 2004; Jelsma, Kramer, and Vervest, 2005; Lintner and Black, 2009; Phongpaichit, Piriyarangsan, and Teerat, 1998; United Nations Office on Drugs and Crime, 2010; U.S. Department of State, 2003.
7. McCoy, 1972; Renard, 1996; M. Smith, 1999.
8. Lintner, 1990.
9. Steinberg, 2001.
10. Albor, 1992; Lintner, 1991; Takano, 2002.
11. Zhao and Ke, 2003.
12. Lintner, 1998.
13. Chalk, 2000.
14. National Narcotics Control Commission, 2011.
15. Belanger, 1989; Chalk, 2000; Dobinson, 1993; McCoy, 1999.
16. Gaylord, 1997.
17. Kuah, 2000.
18. M. Ma, 1999.
19. National Narcotics Control Commission, 1999.
20. Gao, 2011; Ting, 2004.
21. Ministry of Public Security, 2011.
22. Central Committee for Drug Abuse Control, 1999; Maung Pho Shoke, 1999.
23. Wang and Liang, 1999.
24. National Narcotics Control Commission, 2003.
25. Huang et al., 2010, p. 140.
26. National Narcotics Control Commission, 2010.
27. Pearson and Hobbs, 2001.
28. McIllwain, 2003.
29. Zhang and Chin, 2002.
30. Cressey, 1969.
31. Block and Scarpitti, 1986.

32. Finckenauer and Waring, 1998; Jennings, 1993; Marotta, 1997; Nikiforov, 1993.
33. Black, 1992; Booth, 1999.
34. Chu, 2000.
35. Booth, 1997, 1999; Posner, 1988.
36. Block and Chambliss, 1981; Passas and Nelken, 1993; Reuter, 1983; D. Smith, 1994; Van-Duyne, 1997.
37. Reuter, 1983; Savona, 1990.
38. Chin, 1999; Myers, 1996.
39. Dobinson, 1993; Yawnghwe, 1993.
40. Potter, 1994.
41. Fijnaut and Paoli, 2004.
42. Chin, 1999; Zhang, 2008; Zhang and Chin, 2002.
43. Bruinsma and Bernasco, 2004.
44. Morselli and Roy, 2008.
45. Burt, 2005.
46. Burt, 1992.
47. Morselli and Roy, 2008.
48. Campana and Varese, 2012; Malm and Bichler, 2011; Morselli 2005.
49. Cornish and Clarke, 1986; Gottschalk, 2008, 2010.
50. Paoli et al., 2009.
51. Ibid., p. 213.
52. Ibid., p. 223.
53. Ibid.
54. Ibid., p. 228.
55. Hu and Li, 2005.
56. Amnesty International, 2009. Since 2009, Amnesty International has not published specific figures on executions in China.
57. Paoli et al., 2009, p. 238.
58. Gao, 2011; Mansfield, 2001; Thant Myint-U, 2011.
59. Liu and Yuan, 1999.
60. In China, drug-related crimes are categorized into trafficking, sales, transportation, and manufacturing. The difference between trafficking and transportation is that the former involves the movement of drugs across borders and the latter, within China. Anyone convicted for trafficking, sale, transportation, or manufacturing of more than 1,000 grams of opium or 50 grams of heroin would receive at least a 15-year sentence, and possibly a death sentence. Drug use is not a crime in China, even though the authorities can detain a drug user for 15 days, and can order drug addicts to enroll in a mandatory drug rehabilitation center or send them to a labor camp for up to three years (Ting, 2004; Zhu, 2004). To maintain confidentiality, we cannot reveal the name or the location of the prison where the survey was conducted.
61. Ting, 2004.
62. Formal interviews with drug enforcers were conducted in the following border

towns of China: Ruili, Yingjiang, Lianghe, Longchuan, Luxi (also known as Mangshi), Lincang, Kenma, Yongde, and Nansan. An interviewer who was a teacher in a training school in Beijing was hired to conduct the interviews for us. Because of her affiliation with a powerful institution in Beijing that provides training to high-level party cadres, the interviewer was able to receive full cooperation from her subjects and their superiors. The authors also conducted informal or group interviews with drug enforcers in Beijing, Kunming, Chengdu, Chongqing, Guizhou, and Nanning.

63. Luo and Liang, 1999; Ting, 2004.
64. Chin, 2009; Takano, 2002.
65. Chin, 1996.
66. Chin, 2003.
67. Chin, 1999; Zhang, 2008; Zhang and Chin, 2002.
68. Chin and Finckenauer, 2012.

NOTES TO CHAPTER 2

1. Maung Maung, 1999; Steinberg, 2001; Thant Myint-U, 2001, 2006.
2. Shirk, 2008.
3. Ministry of Information, 2002.
4. Hla Min, 2000.
5. Thant Myint-U, 2001.
6. Elliott, 1999.
7. Callahan, 2003.
8. Lintner, 1990.
9. M. Smith, 1999.
10. Thant Myint-U, 2006.
11. Collignon, 2001, pp. 87–88.
12. Marshall, 2002.
13. Fink, 2001.
14. Steinberg, 2001.
15. Fink, 2001.
16. Taylor, 2001.
17. Charney, 2009; Mydans, 2007.
18. Choe, 2007; Fuller, 2007.
19. Most of the figures in American dollars have been converted from Burmese kyats or Chinese yuan (*renminbi*), and because of the fluctuation in exchange rates, the U.S. dollar amounts we present had to be ballpark estimates.
20. Fink, 2001.
21. Callahan, 2003; Sleth, 2001.
22. Zin, 2012.
23. Transnational Institute, 2012, p. 1.
24. Spence, 1991.
25. Ibid.

26. Fairbank, 1987.
27. Spence, 1991.
28. MacFarquhar and Schoenhals, 2006.
29. Kristof and WuDunn, 1995; Shirk, 2008.
30. van Kemenade, 1997.
31. Enright, Scott, and Chang, 2005.
32. Gittings, 2005.
33. Shirk, 2008.
34. Gittings, 2005.
35. Shirk, 2008.
36. Cardenal and Araujo, 2013.
37. Lo, 2009.
38. Steinberg and Fan, 2013.
39. Fan, 2012a.
40. Thant Myint-U, 2011.
41. Cowell, 2005.
42. Fan, 2012b.
43. Fan, 2012a.
44. Fan, 2012b.
45. Ibid.
46. Maung Maung, 1999.
47. Thant Myint-U, 2011.
48. Chachavalpongpun, 2012, p. 105.
49. Sun, 2012b.
50. Sun, 2012a, p. 75.
51. Ibid., p. 80.
52. Narayanan, 2010, p. 260.
53. Zin, 2012, p. 115.
54. Sun, 2012b.
55. Sun, 2012a.
56. Sun, 2012b, p. 51.
57. Ibid., p. 64.
58. Narayanan, 2010, p. 253.
59. Thant Myint-U, 2011.
60. United Nations Office on Drugs and Crime, 2005.
61. Lintner, 1998.
62. United Nations Office on Drugs and Crime, 2005, p. 3.
63. Office of Narcotics Control Board, 2002.
64. Thant Myint-U, 2001.
65. Thant Myint-U, 2011.
66. Chalk, 2000; Lintner, 1994; Ma, 1994.
67. Chen, 2006.
68. Jagan, 2009.

69. Myanmar Information Committee, 2005.
70. Yang, 2005.
71. The most common unit of measurement and package for opium traders and heroin producers in the Golden Triangle region. One *joi* or viss equals 10 *kang*, 100 *qie*, 3.3 *jin*, 3.5 pounds, or 1.6 kilograms.
72. Zhu, 2004.
73. Milsom, 2005; United Nations Office on Drugs and Crime, 2005.
74. Chin, 2009.
75. Kramer, 2007; Milsom, 2005.
76. Luo, 1995.
77. Kramer, 2007.
78. Chin, 2009.
79. Evans, 2000.
80. Yang, 2005.
81. Swanstrom and He, 2006, p. 10.
82. UNODC, 2009, p. 13.
83. Tanner, 2011, p. 1.
84. National Narcotics Control Commission, 2012.
85. Chin, 2009.
86. Paoli et al., 2009.
87. Ibid.
88. Lintner and Black, 2009.

NOTES TO CHAPTER 3

1. Pearson and Hobbs, 2001.
2. Gao, 2011.
3. Ma, 1999.
4. Ting, 2004.
5. Maung Pho Shoke, 1999.
6. Luoping (population 560,000) is located east of Kunming, near Guangxi and Guizhou Province. The major highway that links Kunming to Nanning (the capital of Guangxi) and Guiyang (the capital of Guizhou) and subsequently to Guangzhou (the capital of Guangdon Province), goes through Luoping.
7. Hu and Li, 2005.
8. Ting, 2004, p. 80.
9. Ibid., p. 79.
10. Chen, 2006.
11. Hu and Li, 2005.
12. Ting, 2004.
13. Gao, 2011.
14. In most urban centers of China, many settlement districts or areas are still called "village" or "city village." At one point, landowners in these villages were allowed to build as many so-called renting apartments as they wanted; the congregation of

large numbers of migrants from all over China in these poorly constructed and maintained apartments has created numerous problems for the local authorities. Many brothels are located there, and many criminals, drug users, and prostitutes are attracted to these apartments for their low rents and tolerance of dubious activities.

15. Chinese authorities describe the most advanced criminal organizations in China as "organizations with underworld characteristics" (or mafia-like gangs). The Standing Committee of the National People's Congress in 2002 stated that an organization with underworld characteristics would possess the following characteristics: (1) the formation of a relatively stable organization, with a large number of gang members and clearly identified organizers, leaders, and a reliable core group; (2) the pursuit of economic gains through organized crime or other illegal means, with sufficient economic strength to support its activities; (3) the repeated commission of organized crimes through violence, threat or other means, such as riding roughshod over people's rights, or cruelly injuring or killing them; and (4) by committing illegal or criminal activities, or by being harbored [protected] by government officials, it dominates people in a given area, or has illegal control or imposes a major influence in a certain region or trade, which seriously disrupts both the economic order and people's daily activities (Chin and Godson, 2006). Chinese authorities estimated that there were thousands of mafia-like gangs operating in China (Xia, 2006).
16. Varese, 2011. According to Chen Cunyi, a prominent drug enforcement official in China, Guangdong Province is now home to the largest number of drug users in China.
17. The identification card that all mainland Chinese carry reveals the specific region where the card carrier comes from. Police arrest statistics routinely indicate the suspect's region of residence.
18. One of our key informants echoed this subject's point by talking about how heroin dealers in Kunming rarely go to the border areas to buy heroin: "Big-time drug dealers in Kunming would not go to the Wa and the Kokang to buy drugs themselves. These dealers are very localized—they are big shots in Kunming, but they don't have much in the way of connections and influence once they leave Kunming. There is another bunch of people who are responsible for the trafficking of heroin into Kunming."
19. Ma and Ren, 1999.
20. In 1983, confronted by a sharp upsurge in crimes across China, the Communist government, through its Ministry of Public Security, launched a nationwide campaign, called *yanda* (or strike hard), to crack down on street crimes and punish serious and chronic offenders with long prison sentences (Wang, 2004). In a nationwide effort to purge criminal elements from the urban centers, thousands upon thousands of convicted and/or repeat offenders from coastal and interior provinces were exiled to labor camps deep in the Gobi Desert in Xinjiang Province, in the far northwest corner of China.

21. China's Supreme Court normally does not review death penalties unless there are constitutional issues or extraordinary circumstances, such as when foreign nationals are involved. Death penalties of Chinese citizens mostly only reach the provincial High Court.
22. H. Campbell, 2009, p. 23.
23. Hu and Li, 2005, p. 57.
24. June 26 is the International Day against Drug Abuse and Illicit Trafficking. Established by the United Nations General Assembly in 1987, this day serves as a reminder of the goals agreed to by member states of creating an international society free of drug abuse. The Chinese government normally will step up its efforts to crack down on drug use and drug trafficking right before June 26 and publicly sentence imprisoned drug traffickers to death and execute them promptly on that day.
25. Bunck and Fowler, 2012; Clawson and Lee III, 1998; Tuckman, 2012.
26. Desroches, 2003, p. 243.
27. Ibid., p. 239.
28. Dorn, Murji, and South, 1992.
29. Adler, 1985; Reuter and Haaga, 1989.
30. Bunck and Fowler, 2012; Grayson and Logan, 2012.
31. H. Campbell, 2009, p. 27.
32. Tuckman, 2012.
33. Bunck and Fowler, 2012, p. 43.
34. Chepesiuk, 2003.
35. H. Campbell, 2009; Grayson and Logan, 2012; Tuckman, 2012.
36. Bunck and Fowler, 2012.
37. Alves and Evanson, 2011; Arias, 2006.
38. Jacobs, 1999.
39. Decker and Chapman, 2008, p. 74.
40. Pearson and Hobbs, 2001, p. ix.
41. Desroches, 2003, p. 250.
42. Chepesiuk, 2003.
43. Desroches, 2003, p. 253.
44. Adler, 1985; Dorn et al., 1992; Reuter and Haaga, 1989.
45. Paoli et al., 2009.
46. Ibid., p. 213.

NOTES TO CHAPTER 4

1. "Ants-moving-house" is a terminology used in China by law enforcement agencies and policy makers alike to describe the common practice of drug traffickers using "mules" (or couriers) to move drugs in small quantities, resembling ants moving from one location to another, each carrying only a small parcel of their belongings.
2. Chin, 2009.

3. Bunck and Fowler, 2012.
4. Zhang, Chin, and Miller, 2007.
5. H. Campbell, 2009.
6. In China, there are five practical levels of local government: the province, prefecture, county, township, and village. China administers 33 province-level regions, 333 prefecture-level regions, 2,862 county-level regions, 41,636 township-level regions, and even more village-level regions.
7. A prefecture-level city is generally composed of an urban center and surrounding rural areas much larger than the urban core, and thus is not "city" but municipal in the strict sense of the term.
8. Guizhou Police College, 2004.
9. Liu, 1999; Sun, 2000.
10. Chin and Finckenauer, 2012.
11. Chin, 2009.
12. Lintner and Black, 2009.
13. Chen, 2006; Hu and Li, 2005; Ting, 2004.
14. Decker and Chapman, 2008.
15. Chen, 2006, p. 36.
16. Reuter and Haaga, 1989, p. xii.
17. Because the vast majority of our subjects (95%) were arrested for heroin trafficking, transportation, or sale, we will exclude other subjects who were charged with the trafficking, transportation, or sale of ATS, opium, or morphine from this analysis because the significance of the same unit of measurement for the various drugs is not the same.

NOTES TO CHAPTER 5

1. McIllwain, 2003.
2. D. Smith, 1975, 1978, 1980.
3. Hill, 2003; Kaplan and Dubro, 2003.
4. Reuter, 1983.
5. Zhang and Chin, 2002.
6. Curtis et al., 2003; Hurst, 2005; Mahlmann, 1999; Sullivan, 1996.
7. Huang et al., 2010, p. 150.
8. Zhang and Chin, 2003.
9. U.S. Department of State, 2006.
10. Varese, 2011, p. 176.
11. Chin, 2009.
12. Adler, 1985, p. 2.
13. Decker and Chapman, 2008, p. 13.
14. Ibid., p. 12.
15. He, 2002.
16. Chin and Godson, 2006; Xia, 2008.
17. The case was widely reported in China in 2007. A collection of news reports (in

Chinese) can be found at: http://yj2971520.blog.163.com/blog/static/5588249200711 5111832231/.

18. News reports of the death sentence can be found at: http://news.sina.com.cn/c/p/2010-12-24/004621696855.shtml.
19. Varese, 2011.
20. Gambetta, 1993.
21. Chin, 1999, 2009; Chin and Finckenauer, 2012; Finckenauer and Chin, 2006; Zhang, 2008, 2011.
22. Zhang and Chin, 2002.
23. As a common anti-theft measure, supermarkets in China typically do not allow customers to enter with hand bags, backpacks, or other sizeable containers. Instead, coin-operated lockers are set up at the entrance of these stores so that customers can safekeep their bags. After inserting coins, the locker spits out a paper slip containing a password, which the shopper can use to retrieve his or her belongings.
24. Chin, 1996.
25. Zhang and Chin, 2003.
26. Adler, 1985; Benson and Decker, 2010; Reuter and Haaga, 1989.
27. Dorn, Levi, and King, 2005.
28. Desroches, 2003, 2005.
29. Zaitch, 2002c.
30. Bunck and Fowler, 2012.
31. Ibid., p. 42.
32. Benson and Decker, 2010, p. 136.

NOTES TO CHAPTER 6

1. Ting, 2004.
2. Gao, 2011.
3. Ibid.
4. Weishan (population 300,000) is located in Dali, a Yi autonomous prefecture located west of Kunming and between Chuxiong and Baoshan. Weishan is an autonomous county of Yi and Hui minorities. Within the county there is a Hui township called Yongjian; it is one of the best known drug trafficking hot spots in China.
5. Xundian is a Hui and Yi autonomous county located northeast of Kuming. With a population of a half million, it is only about an hour's drive from Kunming.
6. Johnson et al. (1985) conducted a study on the heroin users in New York City, and according to them, "the public stereotype of a drug seller—someone who sells drugs that he does not use or seldom uses—is rarely found among research subjects. Most research shows that persons tend to sell drugs they use quite frequently and that the earnings from such dealings are generally used to support their drug consumption." Our findings support Johnson and his colleagues. Also,

punishment for drug offenses is significantly different in China. Offenders who are engaged in multi-kilos' or multi-hundred-grams' cross-border drug trafficking, long-distance transportation within China, and wholesale distribution mainly to make money are punished much more severely than drug addicts who are selling a few grams to support their drug use. Unlike the subjects we discussed in chapter 4 who were serving life or long prison terms for heroin trafficking, transportation, or distribution, the heroin retailers we interviewed had rarely been incarcerated for long for street-level drug sale.

7. Williams, 1989.
8. Bourgois, 1996; Jacobs, 1999.
9. Johnson et al., 1985.
10. Gao, 2011.
11. Heroin is translated into *hailuoyin* in Chinese. Heroin users in China use a variety of names when they refer to heroin, just to protect themselves from the law enforcement authorities. Among these terms is *haichan* (seafood), because the first word *hai* is the same as the first word of *hailuoyin*. Often, heroin is simply called *dongxi*, the "thing."
12. Zhaotong City (population 5.6 million) is located northeast of Kunming and it borders two provinces adjacent to Yunnan—Sichuan and Guizhou. There are many people from Zhaotong City living in Kunming, and these people have a reputation for being tough.
13. Kaiyuan (population 290,000) is the largest city in Honghe, a Hani and Yi autonomous prefecture located south of Kunming and bordering Vietnam. Like Pingyuan, Kaiyuan is a major drug and gun distribution center.
14. Tian, 2001.
15. Johnson et al., 1985, pp. 62–65.
16. Xiaguan (population 200,000) is a Hui-dominated town located between Dali City and Yongjian Township.
17. Gao, 2011.
18. Johnson et al., 1985.
19. Williams, 1989.
20. Bourgois, 1996.
21. Rengert, 1996.
22. Jacobs, 1999.
23. Curtis and Wendel, 2000.
24. H. Campbell, 2009.
25. Hagedorn, 1998; Jankowski, 1991; Venkatesh, 2008.
26. Goldstein, 1985, pp. 145–149.
27. Coomber, 2006, p. 142.

NOTES TO CHAPTER 7

1. Siebert, 1996.
2. Dino, 1998.

3. Resendiz, 2001.
4. Zhang, Chin, and Miller, 2002.
5. Siebert, 1996.
6. Zhang and Chin, 2003.
7. Block and Chambliss, 1981.
8. Jamieson, 2000.
9. Block and Chambliss, 1981.
10. Acker, 1990; Reskin, 2000.
11. Britton, 2000.
12. Maher, 1997; Steffensmeier, 1983.
13. Schur, 1984; Swart, 1991.
14. A. Campbell, 1993; Joe and Chesney-Lind, 1995; Steffensmeier and Allan, 1996.
15. Maher, 1997; Mullins and Wright, 2003.
16. Steffensmeier, 1983, p. 1010.
17. Maher, 1997.
18. Mullins and Wright, 2003.
19. Resendiz, 2001; Steffensmeier and Terry, 1986.
20. Miller, 1998.
21. Chin, 1996; Miller, 2001.
22. Siebert, 1996.
23. Lauderback, Hansen, and Waldorf, 1992; Miller, 1998.
24. Maher and Daly, 1996.
25. Shu, 2004, p. 311.
26. Shu, 2004; Tsui and Rich, 2002; Zhou et al., 2004.
27. Zuo and Bian, 2001.
28. Entwistle and Henderson, 2000.
29. Zuo, 2003.
30. Zhou and Logan, 1989, p. 818.
31. Mullins and Wright, 2003.
32. Maher and Daly, 1996; Maher, 1997.
33. Maher, 1997; Miller, 2001; Steffensmeier, 1983.
34. Chin, 1996.
35. Reskin, McBrier, and Kmec, 1999.
36. Maher, 1997; Mullins and Wright, 2003.
37. Shu, 2004; Tsui and Rich, 2002; Zhou et al., 2004; Zuo 2003.
38. Wright and Ellis, 2000.
39. Steffensmeier, 1983.

NOTES TO CHAPTER 8

1. Guo, 1997; Meyer and Parssinen, 1998.
2. Ouyang and He, 1993; Zhang and Chen, 1998.
3. Gao, 2011.
4. National Narcotics Control Commission, 2000.

5. National Narcotics Control Commission, 2011.
6. Ministry of Public Security, 2011.
7. Xinhua, 2012a.
8. National Narcotics Control Commission, 2002.
9. National Narcotics Control Commission, 2006, 2011.
10. Hao et al., 2002.
11. Guo, 1997; Liu et al., 2002; Zhou and Li, 1999.
12. Hao et al., 2002; Liu et al., 2000.
13. Huang, Zhang, and Liu, 2011.
14. Substance Abuse and Mental Health Services Administration, 2010.
15. Ibid.
16. Gao, 2011; Guo, 1997; Ouyang and He, 1993; Xue and Zhang, 2000.
17. Ouyang and He, 1993; Xue and Zhang, 2000.
18. Chin 2009; National Narcotics Control Commission 2003.
19. Xu and Li, 2000.
20. Kuah, 2000.
21. Cui, 1998.
22. Bazant, 2001.
23. McKenzie, 2002.
24. Qian and Wong, 2000.
25. Chu, 2001; Xu and Li, 2000; Zhang, 2002.
26. Oster, 2001.
27. National Drug Control Commission, 2010.
28. Oster, 2001.
29. Li, 2004.
30. Chu, 2001.
31. Merton, 1968.
32. Chu, 2001; Xu and Li, 2000; Xue and Zhang, 2000.
33. Cui, 1998.
34. Chin, 2009; Gao, 2011.
35. National Narcotics Control Commission, 2003.
36. Gao, 2011.
37. National Narcotics Control Commission, 2010, 2011.
38. National Narcotics Control Commission, 2002.
39. Ministry of Health, 2006.
40. National Narcotics Control Commission, 2011.
41. Gao et al., 2011.
42. Gao et al., 2011; Li et al., 2011.
43. Li et al., 2011.
44. Li et al., 2010; Liu, Lian, and Zhao, 2006.
45. Li et al., 2011.
46. McCoy et al., 1997; Wu et al., 2002; Yang et al., 1998.
47. McCoy et al., 1997.

48. Li et al., 2011.
49. Zane and Yeh, 2002.
50. Lee and Mock, 2005.
51. Wong, 1988; Zhang, 2002.
52. Ja and Aoki, 1993; Zhang, 2002.
53. Link, 1987.
54. Latkin et al., 1999; Link et al., 1989.
55. Gorski, 1990; Havassy, Hall, and Wasserman, 1991; Weisner et al., 2003.

NOTES TO CHAPTER 9

1. Ting, 2004.
2. National Narcotics Control Commission, 2012.
3. Ibid.
4. Xinhua, 2012a.
5. Ibid.
6. National Narcotics Control Commission, 2012.
7. Watts, 2009.
8. Ibid.
9. Xinhua, 2012b.
10. Watts, 2009.
11. Cui, 2012.
12. National Narcotics Control Commission, 2012.
13. Xinhua, 2012a.
14. People's Daily, 2002.
15. Xinhua, 2012c.
16. Chin, 2009.
17. Zhang and Musto, 2012.
18. People's Daily, 2003.
19. U.S. Department of Justice, 2003.
20. U.S. Department of State, 2005, 2006.
21. U.S. Department of State, 2006.
22. Ibid.
23. Ibid.
24. Ibid.
25. Ting, 2004.
26. Dikotter, Laamann, and Xun, 2004.

NOTES TO CHAPTER 10

1. Xinhua, 2012d.
2. UNODC, 2011.
3. Xinhua, 2012d.
4. Xinhua, 2012a.
5. Powell, 2007.

6. Ahmad, 2003; Netherlands Police Agency, 2005.
7. Bunck and Fowler, 2012; Geffray, 2001; Thoumi, 2002.
8. Chepesiuk, 2003; Godson and Olson, 1995.
9. Padgett, 2011.
10. Castaneda, 2011.
11. Zaitch, 2002a.
12. Kenney, 1999.
13. Zaitch, 2002b.
14. Paoli et al., 2009.

REFERENCES

Acker, Joan. 1990. "Hierarchies, Jobs, Bodies: A Theory of Gendered Organizations." *Gender & Society* 4: 139–158.

Adler, Patricia. 1985. *Wheeling and Dealing: An Ethnography of an Upper-Level Drug Dealing and Smuggling Community*. New York: Columbia University Press.

Ahmad, Khabir. 2003. "Asia Grapples with Spreading Amphetamine Abuse." *Lancet* 361 (9372): 1878–1879.

Albor, Teresa. 1992. "Myanmar's Heroin Trade Picks Up Despite US Isolation Policy." *Christian Science Monitor*, July 29, 6.

Alves, Maria Helena Moreira, and Philip Evanson. 2011. *Living in the Crossfire: Favela Residents, Drug Dealers, and Police Violence in Rio de Janeiro*. Philadelphia: Temple University Press.

Amnesty International. 2009. "Death Sentences and Executions in 2008." London: Amnesty International.

Arias, Enrique Desmond. 2006. *Drugs & Democracy in Rio de Janeiro: Trafficking, Social Networks, & Public Security*. Chapel Hill: University of North Carolina Press.

Bazant, Wayne. 2001. "Drugs and HIV: Shared Vulnerability of Mobile Populations." United Nations International Drug Control Program, Regional Center for East Asia and the Pacific. Bangkok, Thailand.

Belanger, Francis. 1989. *Drugs, the U.S., and Khun Sa*. Bangkok: Editions Duang Kamol.

Benson, Jana, and Scott Decker. 2010. "The Organizational Structure of International Drug Smuggling." *Journal of Criminal Justice* 38: 130–138.

Black, David. 1992. *Triad Takeover: A Terrifying Account of the Spread of Triad Crime in the West*. London: Sidgwick and Jackson.

Block, Alan, and William Chambliss. 1981. *Organized Crime*. New York: Elsevier.

Block, Alan, and Frank Scarpitti. 1986. "Casinos and Banking: Organized Crime in the Bahamas." *Deviant Behavior* 7: 301–312.

Booth, Martin. 1997. *Opium: A History*. London: Pocket Books.

———. 1999. *The Dragon Syndicates: The Global Phenomenon of the Triads*. New York: Carroll & Graf.

Bourgois, Phillipe. 1996. *In Search of Respect: Selling Crack in El Barrio*. New York: Cambridge University Press.

Britton, Dana. 2000. "The Epistemology of the Gendered Organization." *Gender & Society* 14: 418–434.

Bruinsma, Gerben, and Wim Bernasco. 2004. "Criminal Groups and Transnational

Illegal Markets: A More Detailed Examination on the Basis of Social Network Theory." *Crime, Law and Social Change* 41: 79–94.

Bunck, Julie, and Michael Fowler. 2012. *Bribes, Bullets, and Intimidation: Drug Trafficking and the Law in Central America*. University Park: Pennsylvania State University Press.

Burt, Ronald. 1992. *Structural Holes: The Social Structure of Competition*. Cambridge: Harvard University Press.

———. 2005. *Brokerage and Closure: An Introduction to Social Capital*. Oxford: Oxford University Press.

Callahan, Mary. 2003. *Making Enemies: War and State Building in Burma*. Ithaca: Cornell University Press.

Campana, Paolo, and Federico Varese. 2012. "Listening to the Wire: Criteria and Techniques for the Quantitative Analysis of Phone Intercepts." *Trends in Organized Crime* 15: 13–30.

Campbell, Anne. 1993. *Men, Women and Aggression*. New York: Basic Books.

Campbell, Howard. 2009. *Drug War Zone: Frontline Dispatches from the Streets of El Paso and Juarez*. Austin: University of Texas Press.

Cardenal, Juan Pablo, and Heriberto Araujo. 2013. *China's Silent Army*. New York: Crown.

Castaneda, Jorge. 2011. "The Way Forward—the U.S. Won't Change Its Nature but Could Change Its Policies." *Time*, July 11, p. 31.

Central Committee for Drug Abuse Control. 1999. *The War on Drugs: Myanmar's Efforts for the Eradication of Narcotic Drugs*. Yangon, Myanmar.

Chachavalpongpun, Pavin. 2012. "The Vexing Strategic Tug-of-War over Naypyidaw: ASEAN's View of the Sino-Burmese Ties." *Journal of Current Southeast Asian Affairs* 31: 97–114.

Chalk, Peter. 2000. "Southeast Asia and the Golden Triangle's Heroin Trade: Threat and Response." *Studies in Conflict & Terrorism* 23: 89–106.

Charney, Michael. 2009. *A History of Modern Burma*. New York: Cambridge University Press.

Chepesiuk, Ron. 2003. *The Bullet or the Bribe: Taking Down Colombia's Cali Drug Cartel*. Westport, CT: Praeger.

Chin, Ko-lin. 1996. *Chinatown Gangs*. New York: Oxford University Press.

———. 1999. *Smuggled Chinese: Clandestine Immigration to the United States*. Philadelphia: Temple University Press.

———. 2003. *Heijin: Organized Crime, Business, and Politics in Taiwan*. Armonk, NY: M. E. Sharpe.

———. 2009. *The Golden Triangle: Inside Southeast Asia's Drug Trade*. Ithaca: Cornell University Press.

Chin, Ko-lin, and James Finckenauer. 2012. *Selling Sex Overseas: Chinese Women and the Realities of Prostitution and Sex Trafficking*. New York: NYU Press.

Chin, Ko-lin, and Roy Godson. 2006. "Organized Crime and the Political-Criminal Nexus in China." *Trends in Organized Crime* 9: 5–44.

Choe, Sang-hun. 2007. "On Quiet Streets of Myanmar Fear Is a Constant Companion." *New York Times*, October 21, A1.

Chouvy, Pierre-Arnaud. 2010. *Opium: Uncovering the Politics of Poppy*. Cambridge: Harvard University Press.

Chouvy, Pierre-Arnaud, and Joel Meissonnier. 2004. *Yaa Baa: Production, Traffic and Consumption of Methamphetamine in Mainland Southeast Asia*. Singapore: Singapore University Press.

Chu, Yiu-kong. 2000. *Triads as Business*. London: Routledge.

Clawson, Patrick, and Rensselaer Lee III. 1998. *The Andean Cocaine Industry*. New York: St. Martin's Griffin.

Collignon, Stefan. 2001. "Human Rights and the Economy in Burma." Pp. 70–108 in *Burma: Political Economy under Military Rule*, edited by Robert Taylor. New York: Palgrave.

Coomber, Ross. 2006. *Pusher Myths: Re-situating the Drug Dealer*. London: Free Association Books.

Cornish, Derek, and Ronald Clarke, eds. 1986.*The Reasoning Criminal: Rational Choice Perspectives on Offending*. New York: Springer-Verlag.

Cowell, Adrian. 2005. "Opium Anarchy in the Shan State of Burma." Pp. 1–21 in *Trouble in the Triangle: Opium and Conflict in Burma*, edited by Martin Jelsma, Tom Kramer, and Pietje Vervest. Chiang Mai, Thailand: Silkworm Books.

Cressey, Donald. 1969. *Theft of the Nation*. New York: Harper & Row.

Curtis, Glenn, Seth Elan, Rexford Hudson, and Nina Kollars. 2003. *Transnational Activities of Chinese Crime Organizations*. Washington, DC: Federal Research Division, Library of Congress.

Curtis, Ric, and Travis Wendel. 2000. "Toward the Development of a Typology of Illegal Drug Markets." Pp. 121–152 in *Illegal Drug Markets: From Research to Prevention Policy*, edited by Mangai Natarajan and Mike Hough. Monsey, NY: Criminal Justice Press.

Decker, Scott, and Margaret Townsend Chapman. 2008. *Drug Smugglers on Drug Smuggling: Lessons from the Inside*. Philadelphia: Temple University Press.

Desroches, Frederick. 2003. "Drug Trafficking and Organized Crime in Canada." Pp. 237–255 in *Critical Reflections on Transnational Organized Crime, Money Laundering, and Corruption*, edited by Margaret Beare. Toronto: University of Toronto Press.

———. 2005. *The Crime That Pays: Drug Trafficking and Organized Crime in Canada*. Toronto: Canadian Scholars' Press.

———. 2007. "Research on Upper Level Drug Trafficking: A Review." *Journal of Drug Issues* 37: 827–844.

Dikotter, Frank, Lars Laamann, and Zhou Xun. 2004. *Narcotic Culture: A History of Drugs in China*. Chicago: University of Chicago Press.

Dino, Alessandra. 1998. "Women, Mafia and Ways of Communication." *Rassegna Italiana di Sociologia* 39: 477–512. In Italian.

Dobinson, Ian. 1993. "Pinning a Tail on the Dragon: The Chinese and the International Heroin Trade." *Crime & Delinquency* 39: 373–384.

Dorn, Nicholas, Michael Levi, and Leslie King. 2005. *Literature Review on Upper Level Drug Trafficking*. London: Home Office Online Report 22/05.

Dorn, Nicholas, Karim Murji, and Nigel South. 1992. *Traffickers: Drug Markets and Law Enforcement*. London: Routledge.

Elliott, Patricia. 1999. *The White Umbrella*. Bangkok: Post Books.

Enright, Michael, Edith Scott, and Ka-mun Chang. 2005. *Regional Power House: The Greater Pearl River Delta and the Rise of China*. New York: John Wiley & Sons.

Entwisle, Barbara, and Gail Henderson, eds. 2000. *Redrawing Boundaries: Gender, Households, and Work in China*. Berkeley: University of California Press.

Evans, Grant. 2000. Transformation of Jinghong, Xishuangbanna, PRC. Pp. 162–182 in *Where China Meets Southeast Asia: Social and Cultural Change in the Border Regions*, edited by Grant Evans, Christopher Hutton, and Kuah Khun Eng. New York: St. Martin's.

Fairbank, John King. 1987. *The Great Chinese Revolution 1800–1985*. New York: Harper & Row.

Fan, Hongwei. 2012a. "China-Burma Geopolitical Relations in the Cold War." *Journal of Current Southeast Asian Affairs* 31: 7–27.

———. 2012b. "The 1967 Anti-Chinese Riots in Burma and Sino-Burmese Relations." *Journal of Southeast Asian Studies* 43: 234–256.

Fijnaut, Cyrille, and Letizia Paoli, eds. 2004. *Organized Crime in Europe: Concepts, Patterns and Control Policies in the European Union and Beyond*. Dordrecht, The Netherlands: Springer.

Finckenauer, James, and Ko-lin Chin. 2006. "Asian Transnational Organized Crime and Its Impact on the United States." *Trends in Organized Crime* 10: 18–107.

Finckenauer, James, and Elin Waring. 1998. *Russian Mafia in America*. Boston: Northeastern University Press.

Fink, Christina. 2001. *Living Silence: Burma under Military Rule*. London: Zed Books.

Fuller, Thomas. 2007. "For Myanmar's Neighbors, Mutual Needs Trump Qualms." *New York Times*, October 2, A8.

Gambetta, Diego. 1993. *The Sicilian Mafia: The Business of Private Protection*. Cambridge: Harvard University Press.

Gao, F., Y. S. Zhu, S. G. Wei, S. B. Li, and J. H. Lai. 2011. "Polymorphism G861C of 5-HT Receptor Subtype 1B is Associated with Heroin Dependence in Han Chinese." *Biochemical and Biophysical Research Communications* 412: 450–453.

Gao, Huan. 2011. *Women and Heroin Addiction in China's Changing Society*. New York: Routledge.

Gaylord, Mark. 1997. "City of Secrets: Drugs, Money and the Law in Hong Kong." *Crime, Law & Social Change* 28: 91–110.

Geffray, Christian. 2001. "Introduction: Drug Trafficking and the State." *International Social Science Journal* 53: 421–426.

Gittings, John. 2005. *The Changing Face of China: From Mao to Market*. New York: Oxford University Press.

Godson, Roy, and William Olson. 1995. "International Organized Crime." *Society* 32: 18–30.

Goldstein, Paul. 1985. "The Drug/Violence Nexus: A Tripartite Conceptual Framework." *Journal of Drug Issues* 39: 143–174.

Gorski, Terence. 1990. "The Cenaps Model of Relapse Prevention: Basic Principles and Procedures." *Journal of Psychoactive Drugs* 22: 125–133.

Gottschalk, Peter. 2008. "How Criminal Organizations Work: Some Theoretical Perspectives." *Police Journal* 81: 46–61.

———. 2010. "Theories of Financial Crime." *Journal of Financial Crime* 17: 21–222.

Grayson, George, and Samuel Logan. 2012. *The Executioner's Men: Los Zetas, Rogue Soldiers, Criminal Entrepreneurs, and the Shadow State They Created*. New Brunswick, NJ: Transaction.

Hagedorn, John. 1998. *People and Folks: Gangs, Crime, and the Underclass in a Rustbelt City*. 2nd ed. Chicago: Lake View.

Hao, Wei, Shuiyuan Xiao, Teiqiao Liu, Derson Young, Shanmei Chen, Diran Zhang, Chao Li, Jianguo Shi, Guoqiang Chen, and Kun Yang. 2002. "The Second National Epidemiological Survey on Illicit Drug Use at Six High-Prevalence Areas in China: Prevalence Rates and Use Patterns." *Addiction* 97: 1305–1315.

Havassy, Barbara, Sharon Hall, and David Wasserman. 1991. "Social Support and Relapse: Commonalities among Alcoholics, Opiate Users, and Cigarette Smokers." *Addictive Behaviors* 16: 235–246.

Hill, Peter. 2003. *The Japanese Mafia: Yakuza, Law, and the State*. New York: Oxford University Press.

Hla Min. 2000. *Political Situation of Myanmar and its Role in the Region*. Yangon, Myanmar: Ministry of Defense.

Huang, Kaicheng, Jianhong Liu, Ruohui Zhao, and Paul Friday. 2010. "Chinese Narcotics Trafficking: A Preliminary Report." *International Journal of Offender Therapy and Comparative Criminology* 56: 134–152.

Huang, Kaicheng, Lening Zhang, and Jianhong Liu. 2011. "Drug Problems in Contemporary China: A Profile of Chinese Drug Users in a Metropolitan Area." *International Journal of Drug Policy* 22: 128–132.

Hurst, Cindy A. 2005. "North Korea: Government-Sponsored Drug Trafficking." *Military Review* 85: 35–37.

Ja, Davis, and Bart Aoki. 1993. "Substance Abuse Treatment: Cultural Barriers in the Asian-American Community." *Journal of Psychoactive Drugs* 25: 61–71.

Jacobs, Bruce. 1999. *Dealing Crack: The Social World of Streetcorner Selling*. Boston: Northeastern University Press.

Jagan, Larry. 2009. "The Yunnan Connection." *Irrawady Magazine* September, 17.

Jamieson, Alison. 2000. "Mafiosi and Terrorists: Italian Women in Violent Organizations." *SAIS Review* 20: 51–64.

Jankowski, Marin Sanchez. 1991. *Islands in the Street: Gangs and American Urban Society*. Berkeley: University of California Press.

Jelsma, Martin, Tom Kramer, and Pietje Vervest, eds. 2005. *Trouble in the Triangle: Opium and Conflict in Burma*. Chiang Mai, Thailand: Silkworm Books.

Jennings, Andrew. 1993. "From Marx to the Mafia." *New Statesman and Society* 6: 18–20.

Joe, Karen, and Meda Chesney-Lind. 1995. "Just Every Mother's Angel: An Analysis of Gender and Ethnic Variations in Youth Gang Membership." *Gender & Society* 9: 408–430.

Johnson, Bruce, Paul Goldstein, Edward Preble, James Schmeidler, Douglas Lipton, Barry Spunt, and Thomas Miller. 1985. *Taking Care of Business: The Economics of Crime by Heroin Users*. Lexington, MA: Lexington Books.

Kaplan, David, and Alec Dubro. 2003. *Yakuza: Japan's Criminal Underworld*. Expanded Edition. Berkeley: University of California Press.

Kenney, Michael. 1999. "When Criminals Out-Smart the State: Understanding the Learning Capacity of Colombian Drug Trafficking Organizations." *Transnational Organized Crime* 5: 97–119.

Kramer, Tom. 2007. *The United Wa State Party: Narco-Army or Ethnic Nationalist Party?* Washington, DC: East-West Center Washington.

Kristof, Nicholas, and Sheryl WuDunn. 1995. *China Wakes: The Struggle for the Soul of a Rising Power*. New York: Vintage Books.

Kuah, Khun Eng. 2000. "Negotiating Central, Provincial, and County Policies: Border Trading in South China." Pp. 72–97 in *Where China Meets Southeast Asia: Social and Cultural Change in the Border Regions*, edited by Grant Evans, Christopher Hutton, and Kuah Khun Eng. New York: St. Martin's.

Latkin, Carl, Amy Knowlton, Donald Hoover, and Wallace Mandell. 1999. "Drug Network Characteristics as a Predictor of Cessation of Drug Use among Adult Injection Drug Users: A Prospective Study." *American Journal of Drug and Alcohol Abuse* 25: 463–473.

Lauderback, David, Joy Hansen, and Dan Waldorf. 1992. "Sisters Are Doin' It for Themselves: A Black Female Gang in San Francisco." *Gang Journal* 1: 57–70.

Lee, Evelyn, and Matthew R. Mock. 2005. "Chinese Families." Pp. 302–318 in *Ethnicity and Family Therapy*, edited by Monica McGoldrick, Joe Giordano, and Nydia Garcia-Preto. New York: Guilford.

Li, Lei, Rassamee Sangthong, Virasakdi Chongsuvivatwong, Edward McNeil, and Jianhua Li. 2010. "Lifetime Multiple Substance Use Pattern among Heroin Users before Entering Methadone Maintenance Treatment Clinic in Yunnan, China." *Drug and Alcohol Review* 29: 420–425.

Li, Lei, Rassamee Sangthong, Edward McNeil, and Jianhua Li. 2011. "Multiple Substance Use among Heroin-Dependent Patients before and during Attendance at Methadone Maintenance Treatment Program, Yunnan, China." *Drug and Alcohol Dependence* 116: 246–249.

Link, Bruce. 1987. "Understanding Labeling Effects in the Area of Mental Disorders: An Assessment of the Effects of Expectations of Rejection." *American Sociological Review* 52: 96–112.

Link, Bruce, Francis Cullen, Elmer Struening, Patrick Shrout, and Bruce Dohrenwend. 1989. "A Modified Labeling Theory Approach to Mental Disorders: An Empirical Assessment." *American Sociological Review* 54: 400–423.

Lintner, Bertil. 1990. *The Rise and Fall of the Communist Party of Myanmar*. Ithaca: Cornell University Press.

———. 1991. *Cross-Border Drug Trade in the Golden Triangle (S.E. Asia)*. Durham, UK: Boundaries Research Press.

———. 1994. *Burma in Revolt: Opium and Insurgency since 1948*. Boulder, CO: Westview.

———. 1998. "Drugs and Economic Growth: Ethnicity and Exports." Pp. 165–183 in *Myanmar: Prospects for a Democratic Future*, edited by Robert Rotberg. Washington, DC: Brookings Institution Press.

Lintner, Bertil and Michael Black. 2009. *Merchants of Madness: The Methamphetamine Explosion in the Golden Triangle*. Bangkok: Silkworm Books.

Liu, Zhimin, Zhi Lian, and Chengzheng Zhao. 2006. "Drug Use and HIV/AIDS in China." *Drug and Alcohol Review* 25: 173–175.

Lo, Sonny Shiu-hing. 2009. *The Politics of Cross-Border Crime in Greater China*. Armonk, NY: M. E. Sharpe.

MacFarquhar, Roderick, and Michael Schoenhals. 2006. *Mao's Last Revolution*. Cambridge: Harvard University Press.

McCoy, Alfred. 1972. *The Politics of Heroin in Southeast Asia*. New York: Harper & Row.

———. 1992. "Heroin as a Global Commodity: A History of Southeast Asia's Opium Trade." Pp. 237–279 in *War on Drugs: Studies in the Failure of U.S. Narcotics* Policy, edited by Alfred McCoy and Alan Block. Boulder, CO: Westview.

———. 1999. "Requiem for a Drug Lord: State and Commodity in the Career of Khun Sa." Pp. 129–167 in *States and Illegal Practices*, edited by Josiah Heyman. Oxford, UK: Berg.

McCoy, Clyde, Shenghan Lai, Lisa Metsch, Xue-ren Wang, Cong Li, Ming Yang, and Yulong Li. 1997. "No Pain No Gain, Establishing the Kunming, China, Drug Rehabilitation Center." *Journal of Drug Issues* 27: 73–85.

McIllwain, Jeffrey. 2003. *Organizing Crime in Chinatown: Race and Racketeering in New York, 1890–1910*. Jefferson, NC: McFarland.

Mckenzie, Peter. 2002. "Strangers in the City: The *Hukou* and Urban Citizenship in China." *Journal of International Affairs* 56: 305–320.

Maher, Lisa. 1997. *Sexed Work: Gender, Race, and Resistance in a Brooklyn Drug Market*. Oxford, UK: Clarendon.

Maher, Lisa, and Kathleen Daly. 1996. "Women in the Street-Level Drug Economy: Continuity or Change?" *Criminology* 34: 465–491.

Mahlmann, Ning-Ning. 1999. "Asian Criminal Enterprise Program Overview: A Study of Current FBI Asian Criminal Enterprise Investigations in the United States." Criminal Investigative Division, Federal Bureau of Investigation.

Malm, Aili, and Gisela Bichler. 2011. "Networks of Collaborating Criminals: Assessing the Structural Vulnerability of Drug Markets." *Journal of Research in Crime and Delinquency* 48: 271–297.

Mansfield, Stephen. 2001. *China Yunnan Province: The Bradt Travel Guide*. Guilford, CT: Globe Pequot.

Marotta, Gemma. 1997. "The Anti-Mafia Inquiries in the VIII and IX Legislatures." *Sociologia* 31: 163–210.

Marshall, Andrew. 2002. *The Trouser People: A Story of Burma in the Shadow of the Empire*. Washington, DC: Counterpoint.

Maung Maung. 1999. *The 1988 Uprising in Burma*. New Haven: Yale University Southeast Asia Studies.

Maung Pho Shoke. 1999. *Why Did U Khun Sa MTA Exchange Arms for Peace?* Yangon, Myanmar: U Aung Zaw.

Merton, Robert. 1968. *Social Theory and Social Structure*. New York: Free Press.

Meyer, Kathryn and Terry Parssinen. 1998. *Webs of Smoke: Smugglers, Warlords, Spies, and the History of the International Drug Trade*. Lanham, MD: Rowman & Littlefield.

Miller, Jody. 1998. "Up It Up: Gender and the Accomplishment of Street Robbery." *Criminology* 36: 37–66.

———. 2001. *One of the Guys: Girls, Gangs and Gender*. New York: Oxford University Press.

Milsom, Jeremy. 2005. "The Long Hard Road Out of Drugs: The Case of the Wa." Pp. 61–93 in *Trouble in the Triangle: Opium and Conflict in Burma*, edited by Martin Jelsma, Tom Kramer, and Pietje Vervest. Bangkok: Silkworm Books.

Ministry of Information, Union of Myanmar. 2002. *Myanmar: Facts and Figures, 2002*. Yangon, Myanmar: Printing and Publishing Enterprise.

Morselli, Carlo. 2005. *Contacts, Opportunities, and Criminal Enterprise*. Toronto: University of Toronto Press.

Morselli, Carlo, and Julie Roy. 2008. "Brokerage Qualifications in Ringing Operations." *Criminology* 46: 71–98.

Mullins, Christopher, and Richard Wright. 2003. "Gender, Social Networks, and Residential Burglary." *Criminology* 41: 813–840.

Myanmar Information Committee (Yangon). 2005. "Information Sheet."

Mydans, Seth. 2007. "More Deaths in Myanmar, and Defiance." *New York Times*, September 27, A1.

Myers, Willard. 1996. "The Emerging Threat of Transnational Organized Crime from the East." *Crime, Law & Social Change* 24: 181–222.

Narayanan, Raviprasa. 2010. "China and Myanmar: Alternating Between 'Brothers' and 'Cousins.'" *China Report* 46: 253–265.

Netherlands Police Agency. 2005. "Crime Pattern Analysis: Synthetic Drugs 2002–2004." Driebergen, The Netherlands.

Nikiforov, Alexander. 1993. "Organized Crime in the West and in the Former USSR: An Attempted Comparison." *International Journal of Offender Therapy and Comparative Criminology* 37: 5–15.

Office of Narcotics Control Board. 2002. "Thailand Narcotics Annual Report 2001." Bangkok: Office of the Prime Minister.

Oster, Shai. 2001. "China: All the Rave in China: Police Are Struggling to Control Ecstasy, the Fast-Spreading Club Drug." *San Francisco Chronicle*, June 5.

Padgett, Tim. 2011. "The War Next Door—Why Mexico's Drug Violence Is America's Problem Too." *Time*, July 11, 24–30.

Paoli, Letizia, Victoria Greenfield, and Peter Reuter. 2009. *The World Heroin Market: Can Supply Be Cut?* New York: Oxford University Press.

Passas, Nikos, and David Nelken. 1993. "The Thin Line between Legitimate and Criminal Enterprises: Subsidy Frauds in the European Community." *Crime, Law and Social Change* 19: 223–243.

Pearson, Geoffrey, and Dick Hobbs. 2001. *Middle Market Drug Distribution*. London: Home Office Research.

People's Daily. 2002. "Chinese Police Capture Drug Boss in Joint Effort with Thailand." September 9.

———. 2003. "US Slandering China as Narcotics Producer Is Groundless." September 24.

Phongpaichit, Pasuk, Sungsidh Piriyarangsan, and Nualnoi Teerat. 1998. *Guns, Girls, Gambling, and Ganja: Thailand's Illegal Economy and Public Policy*. Bangkok: Silkworm Books.

Posner, Gerald. 1988. *Warlords of Crime*. New York: McGraw-Hill.

Potter, Gary. 1994. *Criminal Organizations—Vice, Racketeering, and Politics in an American City*. Prospect Heights, IL: Waveland.

Powell, Bill. 2007. "The Strange Case of Haji Bashar Noorzai." *Time*, February 19, 28–37.

Qian, Zhihong, and Tai-Chee Wong. 2000. "The Rising Urban Poverty: A Dilemma of Market Reforms in China." *Journal of Contemporary China* 19: 113–126.

Renard, Ronald. 1996. *The Burmese Connection: Illegal Drugs and the Making of the Golden Triangle*. Boulder, CO: Lynne Rienner.

Rengert, George. 1996. *The Geography of Illegal Drugs*. Boulder, CO: Westview.

Resendiz, Rosalva. 2001. "Taking Risks within the Constraints of Gender: Mexican-American Women as Professional Auto Thieves." *Social Science Journal* 38: 475–481.

Reskin, Barbara. 2000. "Getting It Right: Sex and Race Inequality in Work Organizations." *Annual Review of Sociology* 26: 707–709.

Reskin, Barbara, Debra McBrier, and Julie Kmec. 1999. "The Determinants and Consequences of Workplace Sex and Race Composition." *Annual Review of Sociology* 25: 335–361.

Reuter, Peter. 1983. *Disorganized Crime*. Cambridge: MIT Press.

———. 2010. "Systemic Violence in Drug Markets." *Crime, Law, and Social Change* 52: 275–289.

Reuter, Peter, and John Haaga. 1989. *The Organization of High-Level Drug Markets: An Exploratory Study*. Santa Monica, CA: Rand.

Sanders, Jimmy, and Victor Nee. 1987. "Limits of Ethnic Solidarity in the Enclave Economy." *American Sociological Review* 52: 745–767.

Savona, Ernesto. 1990. "A Neglected Sector: The Economic Analysis of Criminality, Penal Law and the Criminal Justice System." *Sociologia-del-Diritto* 17: 255–277.

Schur, Edwin. 1984. *Labeling Women Deviant: Gender, Stigma, and Social Control*. New York: Random House.

Shirk, Susan. 2008. *China: Fragile Superpower*. New York: Oxford University Press.

Shu, Xiaoling. 2004. "Education and Gender Egalitarianism: The Case of China." *Sociology of Education* 77: 311–336.

Siebert, Renate. 1996. *Secrets of Life and Death: Women and the Mafia*. Translated by Liz Heron. New York: Verso.

Sleth, Andrew. 2001. *Burma's Armed Forces: Power Without Glory*. Norwalk, CT: EastBridge.

Smith, Dwight. 1975. *The Mafia Mystique*. New York: Basic Books.

———. 1978. "Organized Crime and Entrepreneurship." *International Journal of Criminology and Penology* 6: 161–177.

———. 1980. "Paragons, Pariahs, and Pirates: A Spectrum-Based Theory of Enterprise." *Crime and Delinquency* 26: 358–386.

———. 1994. "Illicit Enterprise: An Organized Crime Paradigm for the Nineties." Pp. 121–150 in *Handbook of Organized Crime in the United States*, edited by Robert Kelly, Ko-lin Chin, and Rufus Schatzberg. Westport, CT: Greenwood.

Smith, Martin. 1999. *Myanmar: Insurgency and the Politics of Ethnicity* (revised and updated edition). London: Zed Books.

Southeast Asian Information Network. 1998. *Out of Control 2: The HIV/Aids Epidemic in Myanmar*.

Spence, Jonathan. 1991. *The Search for Modern China*. New York: Norton.

Steffensmeier, Darrell. 1983. "Organization Properties and Sex-Segregation in the Underworld: Building a Sociological Theory of Sex Differences in Crime." *Social Forces* 61: 63–101.

Steffensmeier, Darrell, and Emilie Allan. 1996. "Gender and Crime: Toward a Gendered Paradigm of Female Offending." *Annual Review of Sociology* 22: 459–487.

Steffensmeier, Darrell, and Robert Terry. 1986. "Institutional Sexism in the Underworld: A View from the Inside." *Sociological Inquiry* 56: 304–323.

Steinberg, David. 2001. *Myanmar: The State of Myanmar*. Washington, DC: Georgetown University Press.

Steinberg, David, and Hongwei Fan. 2012. *Modern China-Myanmar Relations: Dilemmas of Mutual Dependence*. Copenhagen: Nordic Institute of Asian Studies.

Substance Abuse and Mental Health Services Administration (SAMHSA). 2010. *Results from the 2009 National Survey on Drug Use and Health: Volume I. Summary of National Findings*. Rockville, MD: Office of Applied Studies, SAMHSA.

Sullivan, Brian. 1996. *International Organized Crime: A Growing National Security Threat*. Institute for National Strategic Studies, National Defense University.

Sun, Yun. 2012a. "China's Strategic Misjudgement on Myanmar." *Journal of Current Southeast Asian Affairs* 31: 73–96.

———. 2012b. "China and the Changing Myanmar." *Journal of Current Southeast Asian Affairs* 31: 51–77.

Swanstrom, Niklas, and Yin He. 2006. "China's War on Narcotics: Two Perspectives." Silk Road Paper. Washington, DC: Central Asia-Caucasus Institute.

Swart, William. 1991. "Female Gang Delinquency: A Search for 'Acceptably Deviant Behavior.'" *Mid-American Review of Sociology* 15: 43–52.

Takano, Hideyuki. 2002. *The Shore Beyond Good and Evil: A Report from Inside Myanmar's Opium Kingdom*. Reno, NV: Kotan.

Tanner, Murray Scot. 2011. "China Confronts Afghan Drugs: Law Enforcement Views of 'The Golden Crescent.'" Alexandria, VA.: Center for Naval Analyses (CNA).

Taylor, Robert, ed. 2001. *Burma: Political Economy under Military Rule*. New York: Palgrave.

Thant Myint-U. 2001. *The Making of Modern Burma*. Cambridge: Cambridge University Press.

———. 2006. *The River of Lost Footsteps: Histories of Burma*. New York: Farrar, Straus, and Giroux.

———. 2011. *Where China Meets India: Burma and the New Crossroads of Asia*. New York: Farrar, Straus, and Giroux.

Thoumi, Francisco. 2002. "Illegal Drugs in Colombia: From Illegal Economic Boom to Social Crisis." *Annals of the American Academy of Political & Social Science* 582: 102–116.

Ting, Chang. 2004. *China Always Says "No" to Narcotics*. Beijing: Foreign Languages Press.

Transnational Institute-Burma Centrum Nederland (TNI-BCN). 2012. "Burma at the Crossroads: Maintaining the Momentum for Reform." Burma Policy Briefing No. 9, June.

Tsui, Ming, and Lynne Rich. 2002. "The Only Child and Educational Opportunities for Girls in Urban China." *Gender & Society* 16: 74–92.

Tuckman, Jo. 2012. *Mexico: Democracy Interrupted*. New Haven: Yale University Press.

United Nations International Drug Control Program. 1997. *World Drug Report*. New York: Oxford University Press.

United Nations Office on Drugs and Crime (UNODC). 2005. *Myanmar Opium Survey 2005*.

———. 2009. *Addiction, Crime, and Insurgency: The Transnational Threat of Afghan Opium*.

———. 2010. *Myanmar: Situation Assessment on Amphetamine-Type Stimulants*. Vienna: Global SMART Programme.

———. 2011. *The Global Afghan Opium Trade: A Threat Assessment*. Vienna: UNODC.

———. 2012. *The World Drug Report*. Vienna: UNODC.

U.S. Department of Justice. 2003. "United States, China Announcing Historic Cooperation in Dismantling of International Heroin-Smuggling Ring." New York: U.S. Attorney's Office Southern District, May 16.

U.S. Department of State. 2003. *International Narcotics Control Strategy Report 2002*. Washington, DC: Bureau for International Narcotics and Enforcement Affairs.

———. 2005. *International Narcotics Control Strategy Report (INCSR)–2005*. March 1.

———. 2006. *International Narcotics Control Strategy Report–2006*. March 1.

Van-Duyne, Petrus C. 1997. "Organized Crime, Corruption and Power." *Crime, Law and Social Change* 26: 201–238.

van Kemenade, Willem. 1997. *China, Hong Kong, Taiwan, Inc.* New York: Knopf.

Varese, Federico. 2011. *Mafias on the Move: How Organized Crime Conquers New Territories*. Princeton: Princeton University Press.

Venkatesh, Sudhir. 2008. *Gang Leader for a Day*. New York: Penguin.

Watts, Jonathan. 2009. "Akmal Shaikh's Final Hours: Convicted Drug Smuggler Was First European to be Executed in China in More than Half a Century." *Guardian*, December 29.

Weisner, Constance, Thomas Ray, Jennifer Mertens, Derek Satre, and Charles Moore. 2003. "Short-Term Alcohol and Drug Treatment Outcomes Predict Long-Term Outcome." *Drug and Alcohol Dependence* 71: 281–294.

Williams, Terry. 1989. *The Cocaine Kids: The Inside Story of a Teenage Drug Ring*. Reading, MA: Addison-Wesley.

Wong, Morrison. 1988. "The Chinese American Family." Pp. 284–301 in *Ethnic Families in America: Patterns and Variations*, edited by Charles Mindel, Robert Habenstein, and Roosevelt Wright. Englewood Cliffs, NJ: Prentice Hall.

Wright, Richard, and Mark Ellis. 2000. "The Ethnic and Gender Division of Labor Compared among Immigrants to Los Angeles." *International Journal of Urban and Regional Research* 24: 583–600.

Wu, Zunyou, Roger Detels, Jiapeng Zhang, Virginia Li, and Jianhua Li. 2002. "Community-Based Trial to Prevent Drug Use among Youths in Yunnan, China." *American Journal of Public Health* 92: 1952–1956.

Xia, Ming. 2006. "Assessing and Explaining the Resurgence of China's Criminal Underworld." *Global Crime* 7: 151–175.

———. 2008. "Organizational Formations of Organized Crime in China: Perspectives from the State, Markets, and Networks." *Journal of Contemporary China* 17: 1–23.

Xinhua. 2012a. "China Focus: China Faces Drug Control Challenge." News release, June 26, 16:56:57.

———. 2012b. "Drug Traffickers Sentenced in China." News release, June 26, 17:03:48.

———. 2012c. "China Warns of Severe Battle against Cross-Border Drug Trafficking." News release, June 6, 21:59:09.

———. 2012d. "China Warns of Severe Battle against Cross-border Drug Trafficking." News release, June 5, 21:59:09.

Yawnghwe, Chao-Tzang. 1993. "The Political Economy of the Opium Trade: Implications for Shan State." *Journal of Contemporary Asia* 23: 306–326.

Zaitch, Damian. 2002a. "Bosses, Brokers and Helpers: Labour and Business Relations amongst Colombian Cocaine Traffickers." *Amsterdam Sociologisch Tijdschrift* 29: 502–529.

———. 2002b. "From Cali to Rotterdam: Perceptions of Colombian Cocaine Traffickers on the Dutch Port." *Crime, Law & Social Change* 38: 239–266.

———. 2002c. *Trafficking Cocaine: Colombian Drug Entrepreneurs in the Netherlands.* The Hague: Kluwer Law International.

Zane, Nolan, and May Yeh. 2002. "The Use of Culturally Based Variables in Assessment: Studies on Loss of Face." Pp. 123–138 in *Asian American Mental Health: Assessment Methods and Theories*, edited by Karen Kurasaki, Sumie Okazaki, and Stanley Sue. New York: Springer.

Zhang, Sheldon. 2002. "Family, Culture, and Control of the Delinquent Chinese Boy in America." Pp. 239–259 in *From Gold Mountain to the New Millennium: Chinese American Studies to the 21st Century*, edited by S. Lan Cassel. Walnut Creek, CA: AltaMira.

———. 2008. *Chinese Human Smuggling Organizations: Families, Social Networks, and Cultural Imperatives.* Stanford: Stanford University Press.

———. 2011. Sex Trafficking in a Border Community: A Field Study of Sex Trafficking in Tijuana, Mexico. Final report submitted to the National Institute of Justice.

Zhang, Sheldon, and Ko-lin Chin. 2002. "Enter the Dragon: Inside Chinese Human Smuggling Organizations." *Criminology* 40: 737–768.

———. 2003. "The Declining Significance of Triad Societies in Transnational Illegal Activities." *British Journal of Criminology* 43: 463–482.

Zhang, Sheldon, Ko-lin Chin, and Jody Miller. 2007. "Women's Participation in Chinese Transnational Human Smuggling: A Gendered Market Perspective." *Criminology* 45: 699–733.

Zhang, Yong-an, and David Musto. 2012. "Asia, International Drug Trafficking, and U.S.-China Counternarcotics Cooperation." Washington, DC: Brookings Institution, Center for Northeast Asian Policy Studies.

Zhou, Ling-Yi, Michelle Dawson, Candace Herr, and Sarah Stukas. 2004. "American and Chinese College Students' Predictions of People's Occupations, Housework Responsibilities, and Hobbies as a Function of Cultural and Gender Influences." *Sex Roles* 50: 547–563.

Zhou, Min, and John Logan. 1989. "Returns on Human Capital in Ethnic Enclaves: New York City's Chinatown." *American Sociological Review* 54: 809–820.

Zin, Min. 2012. "Burmese Attitude toward Chinese: Portrayal of the Chinese in Contemporary Cultural and Media Works." *Journal of Current Southeast Asian Affairs* 31: 115–131.

Zuo, Jiping. 2003. "From Revolutionary Comrades to Gendered Partners: Marital Construction of Breadwinning in Post-Mao Urban China." *Journal of Family Issues* 24: 314–337.

Zuo, Jiping, and Yanjie Bian. 2001. "Gendered Resources, Division of Housework, and Perceived Fairness: A Case in Urban China." *Journal of Marriage and Family* 63: 1122–1134.

Works in Chinese

Chen, Beidi. 2006. *Investigating Drug Abuse in China*. Beijing: Xinhua.

Chu, Chen-ge. 2001. "The Present Situation and Development Tracks of Drugs Crimes in Shangxi Province." *Journal of Fujian Public Security College* 15: 59–69.

Cui, Muyang. 1998. "Predicting Drug Related Crimes in the Next 13 Years in China." *University of Public Security* 1: 35–39.

———. 2012. "Drug Enforcement Police and Their Sacrifices." *Beijing News*, May 14, A06.

Guizhou Police College. 2004. *Drug Prohibition Strategy in Guizhou*. Research report supported by the 2002 Guizhou Province Philosophy and Social Sciences Planned Research.

Guo, Xiang. 1997. "Drug Abuse and Control in China." *Journal of Research in Juvenile Delinquency* 1: 7–10.

He, Bingsong. 2002. *Organized Crime in China*. Beijing: China Legal.

Hu, Yue, and Xianhui Li. 2005. *Face-to-Face between a Female Journalist and Drug Kingpin Liu Zhaohua*. Beijing: China Youth Publisher.

Li, Shuangqi. 2004. "On the Causes of Drug Abuse: A Survey of 240 Drug Addicts." *Research on Criminal Offending and Corrections* 2: 6–13.

Liu, Shuwei. 1999. "An Analysis of Drug Trafficking Groups in Ningxia." *Journal of Delinquency Study* 8–9: 61–64.

Liu, Xuanlue, and Cheng Yuan. 1999. "Exploring and Thinking about the Uniqueness of Drug Suppression in China." Pp. 21–34 in *Essays on the Suppression of Drugs in Yunnan*, edited by Bingsen Luo and Jinyun Liang. Beijing: Qunzhogn.

Liu, Zhimin, Xianxiang Lu, Yue Mu, Zhi Lian, Weihua Zhou and Jiazuo Cao. 2002. "Epidemiological Survey for Drug Abusers in China." *Chinese Journal of Drug Abuse Prevention and Treatment* 5: 27–30.

Liu, Zhimin, Weihua Zhou, Zhi Lian, Yue Mu, Jiaqi Cao, Zhiji Cai, Zheng Yang, Senlin Song, Wenlin Gong, Xiaoping Wang, Yingqun Teng, Dayong Cai, and Guanrong Zhu. 2000. "Epidemiological Survey on Poly-Drug Abuse among Drug Addicts." *Chinese Journal of Clinical Pharmacology* 16: 272–276.

Luo, Bingsen, and Jinyun Liang. 1999. *Essays on the Suppression of Drugs in Yunnan*. Beijing: Qunzhong.

Luo, Zhiji. 1995. *The History and Culture of Wa Society*. Beijing: Central Ethnology University Press.

Ma, Minai. 1999. "New Trends in Drug Trafficking in China." Pp. 58–66 in *Essays on the Suppression of Drugs in Yunnan*, edited by Bingsen Luo and Jinyun Liang. Beijing: Qunzhong.

Ma, Mojen. 1994. *Drugs in China*. Taipei: Kenin.

Ma, Wenyuan, and Kejin Ren. 1999. *The Drug Problem in Guangzhou*. Beijing: Police Education Publication.

Ministry of Health (China). 2006. "Working Plan for Community-Based Methadone Maintenance Program for Opioid Drug Addicts."

Ministry of Public Security (China). 2011. The National Narcotics Control Commission Issues Its 2011 Annual Report of Chinese Narcotics Control. *Press Release* May 31.

National Narcotics Control Commission. 1999. "1998 Annual Report on Drug Control in China." Beijing: Office of the National Narcotics Control Commission.

———. 2000. "Annual Report on Drug Control in China–2000."

———. 2002. "Annual Report on Drug Control in China–2002."

———. 2003. "Annual Report on Drug Control in China–2002."

———. 2006. "Annual Report on Drug Control in China–2006."

———. 2009. "Annual Report on Drug Control in China–2009."

———. 2010. "Annual Report on Drug Control in China–2010."

———. 2011. "Annual Report on Drug Control in China–2011."

———. 2012. "Annual Report on Drug Control in China–2012."

Ouyang, T., and L. He. 1993. "Drug Addiction and Sales: A Current Analysis." *Sociological Research* 3: 62–68.

Sun, Dahong. 2000. "The Crackdown on Drug Crime in Weishan Yongjian: Actual Practice and Lessons Learned." *Journal of Yunnan Public Security College* 33: 20–24.

Tian, Hongjie. 2001. "A Study of the Crime of Sheltering or Pampering Mafia-Like Groups." *Journal of Hunan Public Security College* 13: 11–19.

Wang, Mingliang. 2004. *A Rational Evaluation of the Strike Hard Campaign*. Beijing: Peking University Press.

Wang, Yi, and Liang Jinyun. 1999. "The Drug Problem in Lincang and Its Drug Control Strategies." Pp. 102–112 in *Essays on the Suppression of Drug in Yunnan*, edited by Luo Bingsen and Liang Jinyun. Beijing: Qunzhong.

Xu, Jiwu, and Li Zhuchong. 2000. "The Characteristics of Drug Retail in Kunming and Law Enforcement Strategy Against It." *Journal of Yunnan Public Security College* 32: 56–58.

Xue, Shuanliang, and Xiaomei Zhang. 2000. "Our Country's Drug Related Crimes, Characteristics, and Consequent Social Problems." *Journal of Gansu College of Political Science and Law Institute* 53: 104–107.

Yang, Jiafu. 2005. *Gambling Prohibition: China Declares War on Gambling in the Border Areas*. Beijing: Chaohua.

Yang, Raoxia, Jun Wang, and Wei Hao. 1998. "One-year Follow-up of Heroin Addicts after a Detoxification Treatment." *Chinese Journal of Clinical Psychology* 6: 53–54.

Zhang, C., and Y. Chen. 1998. *China's Battle against Narcotics*. Beijing: New Star.

Zhao, Shilung, and Ke Suya. 2003. *Golden Triangle: A Future without Heroin?* Beijing: Economic Daily.

Zhou, Yong, and Xiaoming Li. 1999. "Demographic Characteristics and Illegal Drug Use Patterns among Attendees of Drug Cessation Programs in China." *Substance Use & Misuse* 34: 907–920.

Zhu, Mingshan. 2004. *Drug Crimes Involving the Trafficking, Sale, Transportation, and Manufacturing of Illicit Drugs*. Beijing: China Legal.

INDEX

Page numbers in italics refer to tables and figures.

ABOUT THE AUTHORS

Ko-lin Chin is Distinguished Professor at the School of Criminal Justice at Rutgers University–Newark. He is the co-author of the award-winning *Selling Sex Overseas: Chinese Women and the Realities of Prostitution and Global Sex Trafficking* (NYU Press).

Sheldon X. Zhang is Professor of Sociology at San Diego State University. He is the author of *Chinese Human Smuggling Organizations—Families, Social Networks, and Cultural Imperatives*, and *Smuggling and Trafficking in Human Beings: All Roads Lead to America.*